ANOMALOUS STATES

IRISH WRITING AND
THE POST-COLONIAL MOMENT

DAVID LLOYD

THE LILLIPUT PRESS

First published in 1993 by
THE LILLIPUT PRESS LTD
4 Rosemount Terrace, Arbour Hill,
Dublin 7, Ireland.

A CIP record for this
title is available from
The British Library.

ISBN 0 946640 91 2 cloth
ISBN 1 874675 00 7 paper

Jacket & cover design by Howard Noyes
Set in 10 on 12 Goudy with Frutiger display titles by
m e r m a i d
t u r b u l e n c e
Printed in Dublin by
Colour Books Ltd of Baldoyle

ANOMALOUS STATES

WITHDRAWN

for Leo Lowenthal

CONTENTS

ACKNOWLEDGMENTS

The first three essays of this book were originally published in *Boundary 2, Modern Fiction Studies* and *Qui Parle?*, and I am grateful to the editors for their permission to reprint them here, as well as for their substantial suggestions for revisions. Apart from the first, all of these essays have had their origin in lectures or seminars, and consequently it would be impossible to acknowledge fully all those whose comments and remarks, perhaps even unwittingly at times, have gone into the making of this book. Instead, may this serve as a register of the pleasure and stimulation that so many such occasions have given me. But *Anomalous States* has also grown out of more sustained conversations and, especially over the last year or so, I have been challenged and aided to an extraordinary degree by Luke Gibbons and Kevin Whelan. Without their generous input this would have been a more inaccurate and far less attentive work, even if as a result I have occasionally felt drawn to take up issues that I have been unable fully to address. Others also, through their work and their conversation, have helped me over and over again. I am especially grateful to Liz Butler-Cullingford, for the insights she has occasioned, and also for her generosity as the Director of the Yeats International Summer School in twice allowing me the opportunity for various and unexpected encounters. Clair Wills, Angela Bourke, Kevin Barry, Declan Kiberd, Bill Mc Cormack and Pat Sheeran have all, in most disparate ways, been unfailing and invaluable inter-locutors. To Carol Coulter I am especially grateful for drawing my attention to issues beyond my habitual sphere and to the contempor-ary relevance of historical work. Norma Alarcón, Alfred Arteaga, Zita Nunes, Camillo Penna and Julio Ramos have kept me alert to the possibilities of exchange and connection between differing geographical and historical sites, possibilities which have been vital to the perspective of these essays. This book is equally the record of, and reflection on, continuing and very diverse conversations with Homi Bhabha, Dipesh Chakrabarty, Abdul JanMohamed and Lisa Lowe on the subject of post-colonialism: they may recognize in it echoes and influences of which I may no longer be aware. At a crucial point in the first research for 'Violence and the Constitution of the Novel', Nellie Haddad and Evaristo Bocanegra gave me indispensable and spirited assistance. Pam Stafford gave me invalu-

ACKNOWLEDGMENTS

able help at the last minute. And without the intellectual insight and practical help of Nasser Hussain this book would have been impossible for me to complete. I am, of course, solely responsible for any errors or misconceptions which may have slipped through so many attentive and critical readers. My thanks are due also to my present editors, Antony Farrell, Ken Wissoker and especially Angela Rohan, for all their assistance and forbearance. The possibility of any book lies not merely in intellectual exchange, and I hope that this may also be for Nora, Sam and Talia, a tribute to their patience and a record of where I've been from time to time: a postcard from the homeland.

INTRODUCTION

This book has taken shape over several years and under the very different intellectual pressures of two quite distinct locations, Ireland and the United States. And having been shaped by dialogues, both private and public, which have been inflected by those locations, this book maps out in retrospect a shifting but consistent trajectory. It addresses a set of recurrent concerns in Irish and post-colonial culture but does so from a gradually unfolding and altering set of perspectives. Its concerns and its perspectives are almost everywhere twofold. On the one hand they involve the matter of Ireland and the theoretical and political terms by which historically it has been understood. In that respect they have always been principally directed at debates about politics and culture which have been in process in Ireland over the past ten years or so, and have been conceived as interventions in those debates. On the other hand, if only as the inevitable result of my having worked for most of the time in the United States, I have written them also in the context of, and in engagement with, continuing theoretical and cultural debates in the Anglo-American academy.

If the essays reveal the traces of their double context, however, it will not be simply a matter of an Irish context for which they were written and an American one from which they are addressed. As I have tried to indicate by the expression 'Anglo-American', Irish intellectual life is, for better or worse, profoundly marked by metropolitan circuits of theory, and in particular by English and American influences, as we apprehend our own productions refracted through international prisms. In a fashion not unfamiliar in other post-colonial locations, Irish culture is marked by a self-estrangement which can take forms ranging from simple commodification to an almost formalist defamiliarization, from the begrudger's suspicion to radical irony, and which is the site of a profoundly contradictory and intensely political ambivalence.] In the Irish context, that percep-

1

tion of self-estrangement, of being perceived and perceiving through alien media, has been expressed frequently and variously, from Joyce's famous 'cracked lookingglass of a servant' to the radical (and less radical) reformulations of the question of identity in process over the last fifteen years or so, north and south of the border. These essays explore different forms of that self-estrangement, one encouraged as much by official nationalism as by colonial powers, and attempt to trace an alternative cultural politics in the resources of recalcitrance.

It does not therefore seem inappropriate to have engaged throughout with theoretical apparatuses which, though not that often invoked in Irish cultural studies, have in the United States been not simply tools for analysis but more importantly the sites themselves of intense debates around ideology and cultural politics. At the same time, though it is a self-evident function of international power relations that Irish concerns have had little or no reciprocal influence on American intellectual work, I have increasingly had to confront in the writing of these essays the extent to which attention to the specific historical determinants of cultural forms more often than not calls for radical rethinking of theoretical paradigms developed for other, usually dominant, traditions. This has, for instance, been especially the case in my attempts to use terms derived from Mikhail Bakhtin, the Russian theorist of the novel, in order to understand the Irish tradition, or in rethinking Benedict Anderson's now celebrated account of the origins of nationalism in relation to Ireland. But, by the same token, I have also become increasingly aware of the value of another theoretical circuit, that emanating from other postcolonial locations in all their disjunctions and analogies with one another, to find ways in which to comprehend the apparent peculiarities of Irish cultural history. Of particular importance here have been the historical work of Indian 'subaltern' historians and the cultural struggles of American minorities.

In writing this book, I have not tried to erase the traces of this multiple location or to integrate too neatly the quite varied communities to which they were addressed. Rather, I have preferred to let that uncertainty of location stand as an allegory of a more fundamental dislocation quite familiar in a culture which is geographically of Western Europe though marginal to it and historically of the decolonizing world, increasingly assimilated to that Europe, while in part still subject to a dissimulated colonialism, and which continues to lose up to 30,000 people annually to emigration. With peculiar intensity, Irish culture plays out the anomalous states of a population whose most typical experience may be that of occupying multiple locations, literally and figuratively.

Doubtless only a culture similarly deracinated could pose the question of identity with such insistence as it has been posed historically in Ireland. The first essays in this volume are more concerned with the manner of its posing than with any resolutions. Accordingly, I recur several times to what I take to be the founding moments of Irish cultural politics, those within which the aspirations of Irish identity and nationality are framed again and again with striking consistency: Young Ireland, the Irish Literary Revival, the immediate post-colonial period, and, most recently, the continuing anti-colonial struggle in Northern Ireland. What is at stake here is the gradual transformation of a counter-hegemonic concept within an oppositional nationalism into a hegemonic concept within a new nation state, a transformation which is, as I have elsewhere argued, written already into the precepts of bourgeois nationalism. The problem is not the questioning of identity, a process which can, on the contrary, be imbued with quite radical consequences, but rather the way in which the theme of identity saturates the discursive field, drowning out other social and cultural possibilities. The hegemonic force of identity thinking stems in large part from the logic of a structure which is replicated in disparate domains of social practice – aesthetic, political, ethical/legal – endowing the forms of each with an apparently incontrovertible and mutually reinforcing self-evidence. This characteristic has been peculiarly evident in the recent resurgence of notions of identity, in attempts to contain and interpret the Northern Irish conflict outside of colonial and class paradigms. No longer oppositional in any very critical sense, such attempts have been too oriented towards seeking reconciling resolutions to engage with the more radical, if less predictable, political and cultural possibilities emerging in Ireland. The result has been an aestheticization of politics, in the strictest sense, all the more mystified by its resolute detachment from the militant nationalism of which, in fact, it is the wan heir.

It was the structure and implications of a resurgent politics of identity that I sought to critique in "'Pap for the dispossessed'", written at the moment when Seamus Heaney was clearly attaining a canonical status nationally and internationally which gave sanction to the 'tribalist' interpretation of the Anglo-Irish conflict, if in the sophisticated form of viewing it as the atavistic residue of pre-modern and irrational social formations. At that point, it seemed important to dismantle the discourse of identity by drawing out the logical and historically determined contradictions that it disavows. To judge by Heaney's undiminished status and his subsequent work, which, perhaps predictably, continues to play out an uneasy oscillation between local piety and universalist cultural claims, the need for such ideological critique remains. Though it addressed only the poetry up to *Field Work*, I have not felt it necessary to update the essay since the central arguments have retained their validity.

The counterpart to '"Pap for the dispossessed"', 'Writing in the Shit', could be said to move concerns from the orality of identity to the dissolution of the anal. There can scarcely be a writer more devoted than Beckett to the thorough and elegant elaboration of the insurmountable contradictions of identity. Yet despite the fact that the effect of his work is to unsettle the very grounds of political subjectivity, Beckett has rarely been addressed in terms of the political implications of his work or even in relation to his historical moment. I have tried here to situate the significance of his writing in relation to Ireland's post-colonial moment and to read his anti-nationalism as a critical political intervention. This involves relocating Beckett in relation to other post-colonial contexts, which cuts against the grain of his habitual reception as a European post-modernist even as it posits a certain questioning of identity as an indispensable element of the decolonizing project.

The rationale for this position lies in the implicit violence of identity formation, not so much in the sense that identity seems to provoke and legitimate a sectarian antagonism towards the different, as in the far more fundamental sense in which the formation of identity requires the negation of other possible forms of existing. That negation can take many forms, ranging from openly violent suppression to the liberal narrative of development which relegates incompatible modes of life to 'pre-modern' or underdeveloped stages of humanity. To the monopoly of violence claimed by the state, then, corresponds the monopoly of representation claimed by dominant culture. The final three essays of this book are concerned less with the question of identity *per se* than in the conjunction between identity formation and the emergence of the state. Pivotal here is my analysis of Yeats's later poetry in 'The Poetics of Politics' as constituting in its very extremities a profound interrogation of the process of foundation by which states come into being, a process predicated on a performative violence which his own poetry dramatically appropriates. Though Yeats seems mostly unable in his own writing to move beyond performative violence, he does constantly, if a little perplexedly, invoke those moments of disintegration which open the space for another history and another sexuality. The following essays, 'Adulteration and the Nation' and 'Violence and the Constitution of the Novel', are sketches towards an elaboration of that space.

From the slightly different perspective of these essays, the question of identity has to be rethought not in terms of any ontological or ethnic determination, responding to the question 'Who or what are we?', but in terms of the function of this insistently *unanswerable* question in the assimilation of subjects as citizens for the state. For the constitution and reconstitution of the terms of Irish identity has principally been aimed at the integration of a highly differentiated population into the modern nation state, a project which has always sought to transcend antagonisms, contradictions and social differences for the sake of a unified conception of political subjectivity. This has meant that, despite the invaluable work of cultural retrieval undertaken by successive nationalist movements, one principal and consistent dynamic of identity formation has been the negation of recalcitrant or inassimilable elements in Irish society. In the writings of nationalism we can observe, as it were, the anxieties of canon formation, since negation largely takes place through the judgment that a given cultural form is either too marginal to be representative or, in terms that recapitulate those of imperialism itself, a primitive manifestation in need of development or cultivation. Both judgments relegate their objects to the domain of low rather than high culture.

In the last two essays, then, I have made some attempt not simply to revalue marginal elements of Irish culture, but to reinsert them in the dynamic of identity formation and to restore to them some of the critical force for which in the first place they had to be expunged as 'unrepresentative'. In 'Adulteration and the Nation', Irish street ballads and folk-songs are read, against nationalist refinements of them, as being vital representations of the hybridity of a colonial culture. That these songs, while stylistically and tonally inassimilable to nationalist representations, were nonetheless sites of resistance and possibly even means of popular instruction, illuminates the politics of style of *Ulysses* in relation to a popular rather than aesthetic consciousness. Both *Ulysses* and this popular tradition are recalcitrant to the emergent nationalist as to the imperial state formation precisely in refusing the homogeneity of 'style' required for national citizenship.

What is at issue here is effectively a matter of *verisimilitude*: which narrative of 'Irishness' comes to seem self-evident, normative, truthful. Control of narratives is a crucial function of the state apparatus since its political and legal frameworks can only gain consent and legitimacy if the tale they tell monopolizes the field of probabilities. The state does not simply legislate and police against particular infringements, it determines the forms within which representation can take place. Access to representation is accordingly as much a question of aesthetics as of power or numbers, and not to be represented often as intrinsically a function of formal as of material causes. The crisis of representation which seems to have afflicted the early-nineteenth-century novel is thus of peculiar interest and I have tried in the last essay to read in it the symptoms of a more profound struggle over modes of narrative and of political organization and identity than that given by standard histories of the novel. In the insurrectionary rural movements of the period I have traced not so much an expression of 'endemic Irish violence' or archaic peasant values as the record of forms of social organization and resistance inassimilable to either the legality of the British state or the political desire of nationalism which is for the state. Though these movements have been occluded to an extent that, despite the excellent historical work of the last decade, they remain virtually unreadable to us now, it is still possible to decipher in their residual forms the elements of a recurrent and still emergent counter-hegemony.

Paradoxically, then, the trajectory of these essays has enacted what Frank O'Connor once called a 'backward look'. Their counter-chronological ordering, which was in fact their order of composition, reflects the need I have felt to move beyond the critique of identity politics into two mutually reinforcing projects. One of these engages in an archaeology of Irish culture devoted to the reconstitution or rereading of subordinated or occluded cultural forms. In distinction from a Foucaultian archaeology, however, the focus of such work is less on the genealogy of *institutional discourses* and more on cultural practices which have appeared discontinuous, submerged, from the perspective of such discourses. The other is an analysis of the developing state apparatus in Ireland which is at one and the same time the analysis of the hegemonic role of culture in the formation of citizen-subjects. The understanding of the latter process, however, depends increasingly on the attempt to recover subterranean or marginalized practices which have been understood variously as aberrant, pre-modern and residual, or incoherent. Without the recovery and interpretation of such occluded practices as an expansion of the field of possibilities for radical democracy, the critique of representative national democracy and the state formation remains more or less formalist. This is, at least, how I have come to understand Walter Benjamin's vivid formulation of the task of the materialist historian as 'brushing history against the grain'.

But the movement of these essays has not been informed simply by the contemplation of Irish cultural history, and I would hope that inasmuch as my understanding of Irish matter has been inflected by work on other domains, these essays will in their turn open out onto discussions for which the Irish instance is no more than one often anomalous example. For the theory and practice of decolonization, however, Ireland is, to a sometimes distressing extent, more exemplary than anomalous. One of the earliest post-colonial nations, Ireland has largely conformed to the model of bourgeois nationalism that Frantz Fanon analysed – presciently for other newly independent nations – in *The Wretched of the Earth*. The adoption, virtually wholesale, of the state institutions of the colonizing power, and conformity to its models of representative democracy, poses what Fanon terms the 'sterile formalism' of bourgeois politics against the popular movements its institutions are designed to contain. The state, which represents the point of intersection of the nation with the unilaterally defined universality of the world economic order, becomes an effective brake on the decolonizing process culturally as well as economically. The larger movement of Fanon's own work, from the critique of the identity politics of the negritude movement in *Black Skin, White Masks* to the critique of the national state in *The Wretched of the Earth*, has been increasingly important in the writing of these essays. What I have tried to indicate in the final essays, however, is that what Fanon characterizes as the 'occult instability' of popular movements in fact has its own intricate history which is

7

occluded only because it cannot be represented within the terms of dominant institutions.[2] Precisely in the inassimilability of those movements and tendencies to a statist nationalism lie the signs of another social formation within which alone they could find voice.

The movement from a politics of identity to one which seeks to understand the complex dynamic of the interaction between subaltern groups and the state formation is not without relevance to the contemporary cultural and political struggles of minority groups within the United States. Even at the empirical level, such connections are more than analogical: there have, for example, been continual transactions between American minority writers and their Irish counterparts, while, as is well known, the Northern Irish Civil Rights Movement of the 1960s took much of its style as well as its politics from the American Civil Rights campaigns. Yet I have learnt in other ways also from the very different situation of minorities, a situation which precisely in lacking territorial solutions highlights the partiality of the state formation. At the same time, a nationalist politics of ethnic identity finds its limits as soon as it must be articulated within the discourse of civil rights or wherever it confronts the inevitable hybridity of internally colonized cultures. The contradictions of the American state formation and of its oppositional movements have illuminated for me characteristics of Irish cultural politics which are often obscured by the historical achievement of *territorial* nationhood.[3]

Throughout these essays, then, I have been constantly aware of the points of contact between historically very different cultural situations and have at moments attempted to address these explicitly. A paradoxical thesis that derives from this exploration is that by and large the more specific the cultural analysis, the more useful is the articulation of different histories with one another. It may seem improbable, for example, that three such canonical writers as Yeats, Joyce and Beckett could be read in relation to minority cultures in the United States or even to writers of more recently decolonizing states. This is, however, to forget that canonization is itself a process of appropriation, abstracting works from their dialogical relation to traditions which the canon cannot accommodate. My aim in these essays has been to restore to such writers their function in relation to cultural dynamics that are invisible to the metropolis and in doing so to analyse the engagement of literature as a specific cultural practice in the differential processes of social formation and transformation.

This is not, of course, to attempt the relegation of these writers to some form of localism, but rather to understand their peculiar modes of dislocation in relation to the no less radical dislocations undergone by a colonized culture in every sphere.[4] In such a differential analysis of cultural forms I would trace the possibility of articulating the very disparate histories of colonized peoples without succumbing to the universalizing drive of 'comparative' studies.

For this reason I have found in Antonio Gramsci a constant point of theoretical reference throughout these essays. It is not simply that Gramsci's work provides the basis for any theorization of cultural hegemony, a concept indispensable for the analysis of modes of domination within the democratic state, but that it also stands as a paradigmatic instance of the transformation of theoretical concepts in their elaboration through specific national situations. Suspicion of much contemporary 'post-colonial theory' has been justly grounded in the criticism of its easy transferability which, like metaphor itself, risks discovering identity at the expense of significant difference. Gramsci, on the contrary, offers a model in which a given conceptual apparatus gains in complexity according to the levels of specificity with which it is applied. At the same time, he recognizes in what he terms the 'ethical state' the expression of the finally universal claims of hegemonic institutions within which conflicting and contradictory interests are negotiated. But whereas Gramsci suggests that the conflict between hegemonic and counter-hegemonic blocks in any given society has as its object of contention the domination of state institutions, it takes only a slight modification of his terms to propose that the counter-hegemonic is precisely that which is resistant to the unifying drive of the ethical state.[5]

I have tried to enact such a modification of Gramsci's thinking in 'Adulteration and the Nation', arguing that the state formation is itself the locus of 'Western' universalism even in decolonizing states. Formations which resist incorporation within the state are not simply residues of pre-colonial cultures to be celebrated by nativists, but strictly speaking the 'unrepresentable' of the state. Recent postcolonial theories, fascinated by the apparent collapse of representation in narratives of subalternity, have been especially exercised by what are effectively problems of agency resulting from that collapse. In other words, where subaltern historians like Ranajit Guha have been largely concerned with the problem of the *consciousness* of subaltern groups, with the historian's attempt to reconstruct their own understanding of their actions, post-colonial cultural studies have been more concerned with how the unrepresentable can be said to have subjectivity and, by logical extension, agency at all.[6] Such a question can in fact only be posed from within the perspective of a state formation for which neither political subjectivity nor agency are conceivable outside the framework of representative narratives. The ultimate argument of this book is that any radical cultural studies, and particularly one which seeks to articulate the potential of residual *and* emergent formations, will have to engage explicitly with the critique of the state for which those formations are its unrecognizable.[7] To do so is simultaneously to give back to those formations their insistent contemporaneity, their dialogical relation to institutions whose dominance is always in process of construction. But that is equally to recognize the constitutive paradox of what have become known as 'post-colonial studies', namely, the paradox that though they name a moment historically 'after colonialism', their insistent object has been less the Utopian project of decolonization than the spaces and processes of colonized cultures that were always already outside of, or marginal to, dominant representations. This paradox is not, however, a fault, but rather the implicit acknowledgment that the 'post-colonial' is only a moment, and one that takes place in a specific space, that of the state, and within a specific history, that of a modernity that would relegate incompatible cultural forms to its own pre-history. The punctual 'foundation of the state' that so exercised Yeats in a newly independent Ireland is traversed by other histories whose continuities, unlikely though it may seem, move to a different time.

'We Irish' have often enough been accused of indulging an obsession with the past. The accusation is usually made in the name of a modernity defined not so much by the erasure of the past as by the discrimination of those elements of the past which can be incorporated in a progressive narrative from those which must be relegated to the meaningless detritus of history. But, as Benjamin well understood, such 'historicism' entails a drastic reduction of the field of possibilities for the sake of a singular verisimilitude called 'progress' and 'development'.[8] To capitulate to such historicism, rather than continually opening the historical narrative to undeveloped possibilities, is to accept the reductive logic of domination. If this 'obsession with the past' is indeed Ireland's anomaly, and not the logical condition of any decolonizing nation whose history is yet to be made, it is nonetheless an anomaly which, against all probability, suspends the laws of verisimilitude and disperses the post-colonial moment among the episodes and fragments of a history still in process.

NOTES

1. For different versions of that sense of 'self-estrangement' or ambivalence, see for example, and apart from the classic studies by Albert Memmi and Frantz Fanon cited throughout this work, Nicanor Tiongson et al., 'Ideology and Culture of the New Society', in Lilia Quindoza Santiago (ed.), Synthesis, Before and Beyond February 1986 (The Edgar M. Jopson Memorial Lectures, Manila: Interdisciplinary Forum of the University of Philippines 1986), pp. 49–65; Ngugi Wa Thiong'o, Decolonizing the Mind: The Politics of Language in African Literature (London 1986), pp. 90–4; and Homi K. Bhabha, 'Introduction: Narrating the Nation' in Homi K. Bhabha (ed.), Nation and Narration (London 1990), pp. 1–2.

2. On this 'zone of occult instability where the people dwell', see Homi Bhabha's 'Dissemination; Time, Narrative and the Margins of the Modern Nation', Nation and Narration, p. 303. Though I have learnt much from this rich essay, it will be clear throughout that I would differ from the implications in Bhabha, and perhaps therefore in Fanon, that this zone lacks a history. My contention is rather that popular movements have their histories and forms of history that are unreadable to and occluded by canonical historiography.

3. On some of these issues, see my essay 'Ethnic Cultures, Minority Discourse and the State', forthcoming in Peter Hulme and Francis Barker (eds), Colonial Discourse/Post-colonial Theory (Manchester 1993).

4. I write this in part as a response to Franco Moretti's rhetorical and theoretically groundless question in 'The Long Goodbye: Ulysses and the End of Liberal Capitalism', in Signs Taken for Wonders: Essays in the Sociology of Literary Forms, Susan Fischer, David Forgacs and David Miller (trans.) (London 1983), p. 190: 'Cultural phenomena cannot be explained in the light of their genesis (whatever has emerged from the studies that interpreted Joyce on the basis of Ireland?); what counts is their objective function.' Such high-handedness with the dynamics of colonized cultures is not, of course, confined to metropolitan Marxists, but structures, if only less explicitly, the academic industries that have clustered around 'major' Irish writers. (On the British Left's current disregard of the Irish situation, see W.J. Mc Cormack, The Battle of the Books: Two Decades of Irish Cultural Debate [Mullingar 1986], pp. 78–9.)

5. On the notion of the national situation and of the ethical state, see Antonio Gramsci, Selections from the Prison Notebooks, Quintin Hoare and Geoffrey Nowell Smith (ed. and trans.) (New York 1971), pp. 240–1 and 258–9, 261–3 respectively. For excellent discussions of Gramsci's relevance in contemporary cultural studies, see, for example, Stuart Hall, 'Gramsci's Relevance for the Study of Race and Ethnicity' in Journal of Communication Inquiry, 10 (1986), pp. 5–25, and 'Cultural Studies: Two Paradigms', Media, Culture and Society, 2 (1980), pp. 57–72; and Lisa Lowe, Critical Terrains: British and French Orientalisms (Ithaca 1991), pp. 10–21.

6. For seminal reflections on this topic, see Gayatri Chakravorty Spivak, 'Can the Subaltern Speak?' in Cary Nelson and Lawrence Grossberg (eds), *Marxism and the Interpretation of Culture* (Urbana/Chicago 1988), pp. 271–313.

7. On the 'residual' and the 'emergent' elements of cultural formations, see Raymond Williams, *Marxism and Literature* (Oxford 1977), pp. 121–7.

8. For this and his remark on 'the grain of history' above, see Walter Benjamin, 'Theses on the Philosophy of History', in *Illuminations*, Hannah Arendt (ed.), Harry Zohn (trans.) (London 1973), pp. 260–2, 259 respectively.

'PAP FOR THE DISPOSSESSED':[1]
SEAMUS HEANEY AND THE POETICS OF IDENTITY

I

I believe they are afflicted with a sense of history that was once the peculiar affliction of the poets of other nations who were not themselves natives of England but who spoke the English language ... A desire to preserve indigenous traditions, to keep open the imagination's supply lines to the past ... to perceive in these a continuity of communal ways, and a confirmation of an identity which is threatened – all this is signified by their language.

Seamus Heaney, 'Englands of the Mind', Preoccupations, p. 150

The centrality of the question of identity to Irish writing and critical discussion of it since the nineteenth century is not due simply to the contingent influence of political preoccupations. Rather, it indicates the crucial function performed by literature in the articulation of those preoccupations, inasmuch as literary culture is conceived as offering not merely a path towards the resolution, but the resolution itself of the problems of subjective and political identity. At present, the Irish poet whose work has most evidently gained such authority is Seamus Heaney, the dust-jackets of whose volumes of poetry since *Field Work* carry such banal assertions as 'Everyone knows by now that Heaney is a major poet ... '[2] Heaney's quasi-institutional acceptance on both sides of the Atlantic as a major poet and bearer of the tradition coincides with a tendency to regard his work as articulating important intuitions of Irish identity, and as uttering and reclaiming that identity beyond the divisive label, 'Anglo-Irishness'. Therefore, it is not untimely to interrogate these assumptions in the context of an historical elaboration of the principal concepts which founded and still dominate literary and political formulations of Irish identity.

An isomorphism can be traced not only between Heaney's formulations of his poetic and the poetic theories current at the inception of Irish nationalism, but furthermore, between his poetic and the aesthetic politics whose 'atavisms' and 'archetypes' it pretends to sound. This is not to suggest, with some, the uncanny 'Orphic' potential of this poet to 'lead us through that psychic hinterland which we will have to chart before we can emerge from the northern crisis', or even to substantiate the interpretative validity of his 'unwavering pursuit of a myth through which we might understand Northern Ireland today'.[3] Rather, it is to address a crucial insufficiency in the poetic itself, one which permits Heaney to pose delusory moral conflicts whose real form can better be understood as a contradiction between the ethical and the aesthetic elements of bourgeois ideology. Heaney's inability to address such contradictions stringently stems from the chosen basis of his poetic in the concept of identity. Since this concept subtends the ethical and aesthetic assumptions that his poetry registers as being in conflict, and yet thoroughly informs his work, he is unable ever to address the relation between politics and writing more than superficially, in terms of thematic concerns, or superstitiously, in terms of a vision of the poet as a diviner of the hypothetical pre-political consciousness of his race.

It is within the matrix of British Romanticism that the question of Irish identity is posed, with the result that the critique of imperialism is caught up within reflected forms of imperialist ideology. This is already apparent in the initial formulations on literature and identity of Young Ireland's ideologists in the 1840s, which in fact present the predicament they would pretend to be resolving. The nationalist critic D.F. MacCarthy provides a representative instance. Insisting that any knowledge of a people's genius is incomplete 'unless it be based upon the revelations they themselves have made, or the confessions they have uttered', MacCarthy argues that full knowledge of the ballad poetry of Ireland would furnish not only an aid to an archaeology of the Irish genius, but the very foundation on which an Irish literature might construct a distinctive identity:

that we can be thoroughly Irish in our feelings without ceasing to be English in our speech; that we can be faithful to the land of our birth, without being ungrateful to that literature which has been 'the nursing mother of our minds'; that we can develop the intellectual resources of our country, and establish for ourselves a distinct and separate existence in the world of letters without depriving ourselves of the advantages of the widely-diffused and genius-consecrated language of England, are facts that I conceive cannot be too widely disseminated.[4]

Beneath the affirmation of MacCarthy's text persists the disturbance in which it originates, an apprehension of the real state of Ireland, its identifications split between the 'real' and the 'nursing' mother.

This passage, and its implicit resolution, is representative of Irish nationalist thinking in the nineteenth century: rather than oppose their apprehension of a real incoherence against the imperial call to union and identity, the Irish nationalists chose to seek an alternative principle of unity on which to base their opposition. Hence it is for the writer to seek beyond the evidence of disintegration for counter-evidence of the continuity of an Irish spirit in his writings. What allows him privileged access to that spirit – and here the argument is resolutely circular – is his total integration with it, 'saturated with Irish feeling ... sympathising in every beat of an Irish peasant's pulse', as an anonymous contributor in the Young Ireland journal of the 1840s, the *Nation*, phrases it.[5]

The writer, like the analogous figure of the martyr, attains 'saturation' with meaning, and hence representativeness, for nationalism by partaking of that which he represents, the spirit of the nation. Both represent the ideal resolution of the problem faced by the ideologists of the bourgeois nation state which comes into existence by deposing 'arbitrary' power: how, that is, 'to reconcile individual liberty with association'.[6] The resolution is primarily ethical, since it locates the nature and form of human liberty in identification with the spirit or *Geist* of the people. The identity of the individual, his integrity, is expressed by the degree to which that individual identifies himself with and integrates his differences in a national consciousness. This identification becomes in Ireland, as across the whole spectrum of European nationalisms, a precondition to politics rather than a political option.[7] But while the martyr provides the high points or, as the 1916 nationalist leader Patrick Pearse was later to express it, the 'burning symbols', through which the call to identity achieves its moments of intensity, it is the function of the writer to mediate the continuity of the national spirit. The distinctively Irish literature intended by nationalist theorists was to have uncovered a common ground beneath political conflicts, whether between peasant and landlord, Catholic and Protestant, or class and class, which could then be seen as mere surface phenomena of Irish society. In such a way, Irish literature was to become a 'central institution or idea', forming a 'social bond' to replace the historically evolved constitution that was thought to override and integrate social differences in England. Twenty years before Arnold's famous formulations, Irish culture is envisaged as performing the work of integration, uniting simultaneously class with class and the primitive with the evolved.[8]

Writing is accordingly endowed with the function of grounding, a term which serves to conduct the uneasy shifts between organic metaphors of the spirit and growth of the nation and architectural metaphors of the construction of an institution. The slogan of the *Nation* succinctly expresses the ramifications of the nationalist project: 'To foster public opinion and make it racy of the soil.' The act of fostering, by which a people 'separated from their forefathers' are to be given back an alternative yet equally arbitrary and fictive paternity, is renaturalized through the metaphor of grounding: through its rootedness in the primary soil of Ireland, the mind of Ireland will regain its distinctive savour. The 'root' meaning of culture is implicit here, and certainly, insofar as a literary culture is envisaged as the prime agent and ground of unification, it is literary taste which is subjected to the most rigorous 'reterritorialization'. In an essay entitled 'Our National Language' Thomas Davis diagnosed the consequences of imposing a foreign language on a native population as a primary deterritorialization, a decoding of the primitive relation of the Irish to their territory, 'tearing their identity from all places'.[9] That deterritorialization is seen by Davis as occurring in three main forms: in the relation of identity to territory, in the relation of placename to territory, in the relation of the people to their history, envisaged as the continuity of a patrimony. Language mediates each of these relations. The reterritorialization of language as the literary language of culture is accordingly threefold. The identification of the writer with that spirit of the nation which his researches reveal supplies his relation to the 'entail of feeling' which links him to his patrimony; that identification similarly ensures the revitalization of the relation of his language to native place or ground, despite the fact that that language will, as MacCarthy was only too aware, be English; and thirdly, the revitalized relation of write to place sutures that writer's formerly ruptured identity, ensuring, as if to complete the topology, his relation to the paternal spirit or genius of the nation. Since nationalism offers a theory of the integration of the individual subject with the destiny of the race, it is not surprising that the dynamic sketched above resembles that of the 'family romance' by which, supposedly, the victory of the race over the individual is achieved.[10] As in the family, so in the nation, as nationalist ideologists have so often stressed. Within the triangle of his family romance, the writer mediates between his motherland and a symbolic fatherland. He elevates his imaginary relation with the land of his birth to an identification with a spiritual nation which is that of his forefathers in the double sense of *their* possession and *his* inheritance. His identity is thus assured in assuring the quasi-procreative relationship between land and culture.

The recourse to the 'racial archetype', in the ever more commodified and familiar images of Irish nationalism, and the manipulation of the relation of Irishness to Irish ground, linked as these are through Kathleen Ni Houlihan, the motherland, together produce the forms in which the aestheticization of Irish politics is masked. Aesthetics, understood here to be ultimately the concept of man as producer and as producer of himself through his products, posits an original identity which precedes difference and conflict and which is to be reproduced in the ultimate unity that aesthetic works both prefigure and prepare. The naturalization of identity effected by an aesthetic ideology serves to foreclose historical process and to veil the constitution of subjects and issues in continuing conflict, while deflecting both politics and ethics into a hypothetical domain of free play.[11] This is, *par excellence*, the domain of culture, envisaged by Arnold as the end of historical process and as the timeless zone within time where one may cultivate one's 'best self' beyond or outside historical conflict. Aesthetic politics in turn represents images of origin and unity to convey an ethical demand for the political coherence which will override whatever differences impede a unification in continuity with original identity.

It would be generally true to say that the history of Ireland in the last seventy years – to regress no further – exemplifies both the efficacy and the disabling contradictions of the politics of identity. The peculiar and largely anomalous position of Ireland as an ex-colonial state in a Western European context has led to political and social developments which are untypical of, but by no means entirely alien to, the general political frame of recent European history. Nationalism, and the concomitant concern with racial and cultural identity, are, as has been suggested, political phenomena, oriented towards the production of a sense of popular unity and conceived within a generally oppositional framework. Under normal circumstances, the efficacy of the appeal to racial identity as a unifying principle would wither away once political victory has been achieved and consolidated in the nation state. Other modes of political organization tend to displace nationalism in the politically stabilized nation state, although it is clear enough that at moments of crisis

17

appeal to some form of nationalist ideology is a constant resource of both governments and their oppositions.[12]

The anomalous character of recent Irish history derives from the fact that, unlike most other Western European states, the moment of nationalist victory did not constitute a moment of apparent national unification, but rather institutionalized certain racial and sectarian divisions. The Treaty of 1922, which, after prolonged guerilla warfare, established the Irish Free State, did so only at the expense of also establishing the Northern Irish state, a self-governing enclave with a deliberately and artificially constructed majority of Protestant citizens. But although the Treaty appears thus to have instituted simply another divisive factor in Irish politics, within the two states themselves its effect was to perpetuate forms of nationalist ideology as dominant and hypothetically unifying forces.

In the Republic, it has not been hardline nationalists alone who have appealed to partition as the major block to the attainment of a full Irish identity. The doctrine of the territorial and political integrity of Ireland was enshrined in the Irish constitution and has been conceived, if only formally, as a primary political objective of any Irish government. Moreover, and more importantly, the perpetuation of partition has allowed the persistence of what is effectively a two-party system, dominated by parties whose origins lie in the initial rejection of the Treaty's provisions by one group of nationalists. Since the parties – Fine Gael and Fianna Fáil – serve urban and rural bourgeois interests respectively, the instant articulation of Irish politics in relation to the questions of the border and of Irish identity has historically been detrimental to the development of the smaller Labour party. The politics of identity, precisely by locating division and difference at the border of the Irish state, has tended to obscure another internal political reality: class difference.[13] The contradiction is, of course, that although in the short term such policies have served bourgeois interests, and even drawn working-class support for what would seem objectively unlikely policies, it has in the longer term helped to retard the development of capitalism in Ireland by dividing bourgeois interests. Ireland remains accordingly in a classical post-colonial situation in which economic underdevelopment continually undermines attempts to forge political cohesion.

In Northern Ireland, on the other hand, the figment of Protestant identity, with all its racial overtones, immediately masked certain internal differences of sect and geographical origin as well as of economic interest. More importantly, 'Protestantism' acted for bourgeois politicians as a means to divide Protestant and Catholic workers along sectarian lines. In a manner reminiscent of the ideological function of the English constitution as a barrier against Jacobinism in the late eighteenth century, the border played a crucial role in externalizing the threat of difference, placing it outside the Protestant community and the ideally Protestant state, and permitting the definition of the Catholic population as alien.[14] Through the crises of recent years, those internal differences have returned with manifest political effects in the splitting of the Unionist Party and in the increasing militance of working-class loyalists. The effects of sectarian and political differences between Protestants and Catholics, unionists and republicans within Northern Ireland needs little emphasis.

What may need emphasis, however, is the role which a politics of identity has played in producing the form of the current civil war in Ireland. The combined effect of political thinking on each side of the border has been to perpetuate not only nationalist ideologies, but their articulation along sectarian and, effectively, racial grounds. The real basis of the present struggle in the economic and social conditions of a post-colonial state, and the peculiar twist given to class differences by such conditions, has consequently been systematically obscured. This obscurantism has further permitted, both within and without Ireland, a subtle knotting in popular liberal and conservative interpretations of Irish history: vociferous mystification as to the apparently insistent repetitiveness of Irish history joins with a persuasive insinuation that the reasons for repetition lie in the nature of Irish identity. It is the argument of this essay that such mystifications are inherent in the cultural and aesthetic thinking which dominates both the Irish and the English traditions, and that the apparent freedom of the aesthetic realm from politics is in itself a crucially political conception. The political function of aesthetics and culture is not only to suggest the possibility of transcending conflict, but to do so by excluding (or integrating) difference, whether historically produced or metaphysically conceived, insofar as it represents a threat to an image of unity whose role is finally hegemonic.[15] The poetics of identity is intimately involved in both the efficacy and the contradictions of aesthetic politics and political aesthetics.

II

And when we look for the history of our sensibilities I am convinced, as Professor J.C.
Beckett was convinced about the history of Ireland generally, that it is to what he
called the stable element, the land itself, that we must look for continuity.

Heaney, 'The Sense of Place'

Since his earliest volumes, Seamus Heaney's writings have rehearsed
all the figures of the family romance of identity, doubled, more often
than not, by an explicit affirmation of a sexual structure in the
worker's or the writer's relation to a land or place already given as
feminine. A certain sexual knowingness accounts in part for the win-
some quality of such poems as 'Digging', 'Rite of Spring', or 'Undine'
in the early volumes.[16] The winsomeness and the knowingness are
compounded by the neatness with which the slight *frissons* produced
by the raised spectres of patricide, rape or seduction are stilled by
dénouements which stress the felicities of analogy or cure the implied
violence of labour and sexuality with a warm and humanizing morality. That such knowledge should be so easily borne and contained
makes it merely thematic, and renders suspect the strenuousness of
that 'agon' which Harold Bloom seems to identify in Heaney's work
as the effort to evade 'his central trope, the vowel of the earth'.[17]
Bloom here correctly identifies a crucial theme in Heaney's work,
and one which indeed organizes his preoccupation with the establishment of poetic identity. The relevant questions, however, is
whether that 'agon' ever proceeds beyond thematic concerns, and,
further, whether it could do so without rupturing the whole edifice
within which the identity of the poet, his voice, is installed.

To be sure, Heaney makes much play, both in his poems and in
his prose writings, with the deterritorialization inflicted both on a
national consciousness by the effects of colonialization, and on the
individual subject by acculturation. But in Heaney's writing such
perceptions initiate no firm holding to and exploration of the quality
of dispossession; rather, his work relocates an individual and racial
identity through the reterritorialization of language and culture.
Heaney's rhetoric of compensation – 'You had to come back/To learn
how to lose yourself,/To be pilot and stray' (*Door into the Dark*, p. 50)
– uncritically replays the Romantic schema of a return to origins
which restores continuity through fuller self-possession, and accordingly rehearses the compensations conducted by Irish Romantic nationalism. But his poetic offers constantly a premature compensation,
enacted through linguistic and metaphorical usages which promise a

healing of division simply by returning the subject to place, in an innocent yet possessive relation to his objects. 'Digging', an instance still cited sometimes with the authority of an *ars poetica*, finds its satisfactions in a merely aesthetic resolution, which, indeed, sets the pattern for most of the subsequent work:

> Between my finger and my thumb
> The squat pen rests; snug as a gun.
>
> Under my window, a clean rasping sound
> When the spade sinks into gravelly ground:
> My father, digging. I look down
>
> Till his straining rump along the flowerbeds
> Bends low, comes up twenty years away
> Stooping in rhythm through potato drills
> Where he was digging.

That which is posed as problematic, the irreducible difference between physical and cultural labour, and consequently the relation of the writer to his subjective history, is neatly resolved merely by reducing physical labour to a metaphor for cultural labour, while displacing the more intractable question of subjective history beyond the frame of the poem as the project of that labour. At the same time, the intimation of violence, of a will to power, carried in the opening lines already with more fashionable swagger than engagement – 'snug as a gun' – is suppressed at the end by suppressing the metaphorical vehicle:

> Between my finger and my thumb
> The squat pen rests.
> I'll dig with it.

With that suppression the writer can forget or annul the knowledge of writing's power both for dispossession and subjection – 'I look down' – and represent it instead as the metaphorical continuation of a work which has already been taken as a metaphor for writing. What assures that continuity, both across generations and across the twenty-year span of the writer's own history, is the symbolic position of the father in possession of and working the land. Standing initially as a figure for the writer's exclusion from identity with land and past, the father, by way of his own father, slides across into the position of a figure for continuity:

> By God, the old man could handle a spade.
> Just like his old man.

My grandfather cut more turf in a day
Than any other man on Toner's bog.
Once I carried him milk in a bottle
Corked sloppily with paper. He straightened up
To drink it, then fell to right away
Nicking and slicing neatly, heaving sods
Over his shoulder, going down and down
For the good turf. Digging.

The cold smell of potato mould, the squelch and slap
Of soggy peat, the curt cuts of an edge
Through living roots awaken in my head.
But I've no spade to follow men like them.

'Digging' holds out the prospect of a return to origins and the consolatory myth of a knowledge which is innocent and without disruptive effect. The gesture is almost entirely formal, much as the ideology of nineteenth-century nationalists – whose concerns Heaney largely shares – was formal or aesthetic, composing the identity of the subject in the knowing of objects the very knowing of which is an act of self-production. This description holds for the writer's relation to the communal past as well as to his subjective past: in the final analysis, the two are given as identical. Knowledge can never truly be the knowledge of difference: instead, returned to that from which the subject was separated by knowledge, the subject poses his objects (perceived or produced) as synecdoches of continuity:

poetry as divination, poetry as revelation of the self to the self, as restoration of the culture to itself; poems as elements of continuity, with the aura and authenticity of archaeological finds, where the buried shard has an importance that is not diminished by the importance of the buried city; poetry as a dig, a dig for finds that end up being plants.[18]

Poetry as divination, poetry as dig: in both these formulations Heaney resorts to metaphors which seek to bypass on several fronts the problematic relation of writing to identity. Firstly, the objectification of the subject that writing enacts is redeemed either through the fiction of immediate self-presence, or in the form of the significant moment as synecdoche for the whole temporal sequence, in which is composed the identity of the subject as a seamless continuum. Secondly, the predicament of a literary culture as a specialized mode of labour is that it is set over against non-cultural labour, yet Heaney's writing continually rests in the untested assumption that a return is possible through writing back to the 'illiterate' culture from which it stems and with which, most importantly, it remains at all times continuous. The actual, persisting relation between the literate and the non-literate, at times antagonistic, at times symbiotic, disappears along with such attendant problems as class or ethnic stratification in a temporal metaphor of unbroken development.[19] No irreparable break appears in the subject's relation to his history by accession to culture, nor is culture itself anything but a refined expression of an ideal community of which the writer is a part. Thirdly, given that the 'touchstone' in this context is Wordsworth, the specific relation of an 'Irish identity' to the English literary – and political – establishment provides not only the language, but the very terms within which the question of identity is posed and resolved, the terms for which it is *the* question to be posed and resolved. For it is not simply the verse form, the melody, or whatnot, that the poet takes over;[20] it is the aesthetic, and the ethical and political formulations it subsumes, that the Romantic and imperial tradition supplies.

To this cultural tradition, it is true, Heaney seeks to give an Irish 'bend', grafting it on to roots which are identified as rural, Catholic, and, more remotely, Gaelic. That grafting is enabled by the return to place, a reterritorialization in a literal sense initially, which symbolically restores the interrupted continuity of identity and ground. An implicit theory of language operates here, for which the name is naturally integrated with place, the sign identified with the signified, the subject with the object. The putative sameness of place supplies an image of the continuity underlying the ruptures so apparent in the history of language usage in Ireland. If identity slips between belonging in and owning the land, between object and subject, between nature and culture, in unrelenting displacement, the land as 'preoccupation' furnishes the purely formal ground, the matrix of continuity, in which identity ultimately reposes. The signs of difference that compose the language are underwritten by a language of containment and synthesis, that is, 'the living speech of the landscape', which is in turn identified with the poem itself, the single, adequate vocable: a word 'with reference to form rather than meaning'.[21] In all its functions, language performs the rituals of synthesis and identity, from the mysterious identification of the guttural and the vowel with Irishness, the consonantal with Englishness, to the symbolic function of metaphor which produces those recurrent stylistic traits of Heaney's metaphors of identity born by the genitive, the copula or the compound: 'the hammered shod of a bay'; 'the tight vise of a stack'; 'the challenger's intelligence/is a spur of light,/a blue prong'; 'My body was braille'; 'Earth-pantry, bone-vault,/sun-bank'.

Place, identity and language mesh in Heaney, as in the tradition of cultural nationalism, since language is seen primarily as naming, and because naming performs a cultural reterritorialization by replacing the contingent continuities of an historical community with an ideal register of continuity in which the name (of place or of object) operates symbolically as the commonplace communicating between actual and ideal continua. The name always serves likeness, never difference. Hence poems on the names of places must of their nature be rendered as gifts, involving no labour on the part of the poet, who would, by enacting division, disrupt the immediacy of the relation of culture to pre-culture:

I had a great sense of release as they were being written, a joy and a devil-may-careness, and that convinced me that one could be faithful to the nature of the English language – for in some sense these poems are erotic mouth-music by and out of the anglo-saxon [sic] tongue – and, at the same time, be faithful to one's own non-English origin, for me that is County Derry.

The formulation renovates the concerns, even the rhetoric, of early nationalist critics.

Thus the name 'Anahorish' resides as a metonym for the ancient Gaelic culture that is to be tapped, leading 'past the literary mists of a Celtic twilight into that civilization whose demise was effected by soldiers and administrators like Spenser and Davies' (*Preoccupations*, p. 36). 'Anahorish', 'place of clear water', is at once a place-name and the name of a place-name poem in *Wintering Out*. The name as title already assures both continuity between subject and predicate and the continuity of the poet's identity, since titular possession of this original place which is itself a source guarantees the continuity of the writing subject with his displaced former identity:

Anahorish

My 'place of clear water',
the first hill in the world
where springs washed into
the shiny grass ...

The writer's subjective origin doubles the Edenic and absolute origin, the untroubled clarity of his medium allowing immediacy of access to the place and moment of original creation, which its own act of creation would seem to repeat and symbolize, knowledge cleansed and redeemed to graceful polish. The poem itself becomes the adequate vocable in which the rift between the Gaelic word and its English equivalent is sealed in smooth, unbroken ground, speech of the land-scape:

> Anahorish, soft gradient
> of consonant, vowel-meadow.

The rhetoric of identity is compacted not only in these metaphors, representative again of Heaney's metaphors of identity, but in the two sentences that compose the first and most substantial part of the poem, where no main verbs fracture the illusion of identity and pres-ence. The name itself asserts the continuity of presence as an 'after-image of lamps', while in the last sentence, those lamps appear to illuminate genii of the place – 'those mound dwellers' – a qualifica-tion which expels history, leaving only the timelessness of repeated, fundamental acts. Their movement unites the visible with the invisible, while the exceptional moment of fracturing is regained as a metaphor for access to the source and the prospect of renewed growth:

> With pails and barrows
>
> those mound-dwellers
> go waist-deep in mist
> to break the light ice
> at wells and dunghills.

What is dissembled in such writing is that the apparent innocence, the ahistoricity, of the subject's relation to place is in fact preceded by an act of appropriation or repossession. 'Anahorish' provides an image of the transcendental unity of the subject, and correspond-ingly of history, exactly insofar as it is represented – far from innocently – as a property of the subject. The lush and somewhat indulgent sentiment of the poems of place in *Wintering Out* ('Anahorish', 'Toome', 'Broagh', and 'A New Song') can be ascribed to that foreclosed surety of the subject's relation to place, mediated as it is by a language which seeks to naturalize its appropriative func-tion.

'Erotic mouth-music': it is indeed the seduction of these poems to open what would in the terms of its aesthetic be a regressive path through orality beyond the institution of difference in history and in writing. Hence perception of difference, through the poet's sense of his own difference, which is in fact fundamental to their logic of identity, has finally to be suppressed. Difference is of course registered throughout Heaney's work, at all those points of division and dispossession previously observed. Those divisions are, furthermore, embraced within sexual difference, which comes to provide for political, national and cultural difference a matrix of the most elementary, dualistic kind: 'I suppose the feminine element for me involves the matter of Ireland, and the masculine strain is drawn from the involvement with English literature' (*Preoccupations*, p. 34). This difference, however, is posed as the context for a resolution beyond conflict, in the poem as in relation to the land, which is at once pre-existent and integrating:

I have always listened for poems, they come sometimes like bodies come out of a bog, almost complete, seeming to have been laid down a long time ago, surfacing with a touch of mystery. They certainly involve craft and determination, but chance and instinct have a role in the thing too. I think the process is a kind of somnambulist encounter between masculine will and intelligence and feminine clusters of image and emotion (p. 34) ... It is this feeling, assenting, equable marriage between the geographical country and the country of the mind, whether that country of the mind takes its tone unconsciously from a shared oral inherited culture, or from a consciously savoured literary culture, or from both, it is this marriage that constitutes the sense of place in its richest possible manifestation. (*Preoccupations*, p. 132)

For all their rigid, dualistic schematization, which is only the more rigid for its pretension to be instinctual and unsystematic, and for all the inanity of the content of that dualism – oral, feminine, unconscious image and emotion versus cultured, masculine, conscious will and intelligence – such formulations acutely register the form of integration which is projected. Non-differentiation lies in the matter which precedes all difference and is regained in the product which is the end of difference, the aesthetic object, the poem. Culture repeats primary cultivation, its savour is oral, racy of the soil. Masculine and feminine marry likewise in the moment the poem is forged out of their difference, reproducing a unity of word and flesh always assumed to pre-exist that difference. In the insistent formalization of this rigidly gendered representation of difference, Heaney elides the complex and often contradictory heterogeneity of Irish social formations and their histories, recapitulating his similar dualization of the oral and literate elsewhere.[22]

Only when special and explanatory status is pleaded for this consolatory myth do contradiction and difference return, to use a Heaneyish notion, with a vengeance, as in the series of bog poems which commences with 'The Tollund Man' in *Wintering Out*, and is extended through *North*. The origin of these poems in P.V. Glob's *The Bog People* is doubtless familiar, but it is as well to reproduce Heaney's own account:

It [Glob's book] was chiefly concerned with preserved bodies of men and women found in the bogs of Jutland, naked, strangled or with their throats cut, disposed under the peat since early Iron Age times. The author, P.V. Glob, argues convincingly that a number of these, and in particular the Tollund Man, whose head is now preserved near Aarhus in the museum at Silkeburg, were ritual sacrifices to the Mother Goddess, the goddess of the ground who needed new bridegrooms each winter to bed with her in her sacred place, in the bog, to ensure the renewal and fertility of the territory in the spring. Taken in relation to the tradition of Irish political martyrdom for that cause whose icon is Kathleen Ni Houlihan, this is more than an archaic barbarous rite: it is an archetypal pattern. And the unforgettable photographs of these victims blended in my mind with photographs of atrocities, past and present, in the long rites of Irish political and religious struggles. (*Preoccupations*, pp. 57–8)

Heaney here posits a psychic continuity between the sacrificial practices of an Iron Age people and the 'psychology of the Irishmen and Ulstermen who do the killing' (*Preoccupations*, p. 57). This is effectively to reduce history to myth, furnishing an aesthetic resolution to conflicts constituted in quite specific historical junctures by rendering disparate events as symbolic moments expressive of an underlying continuity of identity. Not surprisingly, it is the aesthetic politics of nationalism which finds its most intense symbolism in martyrdom.

As with the question of identity, so the question as to whether archetypes and archetypal patterns exist is less significant than the formal role their invocation plays. Something of that role emerges in 'The Tollund Man' (*Wintering Out*), apparently the first of the bog poems to have been written:

> Some day I will go to Aarhus
> To see his peat-brown head,
> The mild pods of his eye-lids,
> His pointed skin cap.
>
> In the flat country nearby
> Where they dug him out,
> His last gruel of winter seeds
> Caked in his stomach,
>
> Naked except for
> The cap, noose and girdle,
> I will stand a long time.
> Bridegroom to the goddess,

> She tightened her torc on him
> And opened her fen,
> Those dark juices working
> Him to a saint's kept body ...

The distance of the historical observer rapidly contracts in this first section into an imaginary immediate relation to the corpse, and ultimately to the putative goddess as, in a singularly deft piece of composition, the appositions 'Naked except for/The cap, noose and girdle,' and 'Bridegroom to the goddess' slip between the poet and the victim. The immediacy of that relation, brought thus to the very brink of identification, facilitates the elimination of human agency, which is distilled to thematically equivalent operations of sacrifice (by which the corpse is worked 'to a saint's kept body') and poetic rememoration which reverses, by analogy with exhumation, the direction of sacrifice without invalidating it. The subordination of human agency to aesthetic form is reinforced in the second section as the two atrocities there described are contained within the faintly redeeming notion of their possible germination, their flesh scattered like seed:

> I could risk blasphemy,
> Consecrate the cauldron bog
> Our holy ground and pray
> Him to make germinate
>
> The scattered, ambushed
> Flesh of labourers,
> Stockinged corpses
> Laid out in the farmyards,
>
> Tell-tale skin and teeth
> Flecking the sleepers
> Of four young brothers, trailed
> For miles along the lines.

The matter of the form in which they will germinate, as Cadmus's warriors, perhaps, or as 'The Right Rose Tree', is carefully hedged.[23] In so purely aesthetic a performance, which evades the logic even of its own mythologies, the 'risk' of 'blasphemy' is easily carried. In the third section, the poet is confirmed as the stable centre of this tableau of identifications:

> Something of his sad freedom
> As he rode the tumbril
> Should come to me, driving,
> Saying the names

> Tollund, Grabaulle, Nebelgard,
> Watching the pointing hands
> Of country people,
> Not knowing their tongue.
>
> Out there in Jutland
> In the old man-killing parishes
> I will feel lost,
> Unhappy and at home.

What is the 'sad freedom' that the poet as tourist or pilgrim in Jutland will take over from the Tollund man other than that derived from the aesthetic rehearsal of rites whose continuity with the present is preassured by the unquestioned metaphoric frame of the writing, a writing whose dangers have been defused into pathos by their subordination to that same metaphoric function? Thus the repetition of place-names ('Tollund, Grabaulle, Nebelgard'), abstracted from context and serving a cultural purpose as synecdoches of continuity, overrides the actual alienation of one 'Not knowing their tongue', only to issue in the 'at home-ness' always available to those whose culture is a question of reterritorialization. The bodies of Jutland are, one recalls, 'disposed under the peat' for the poet-archaeologist's appropriation.

Metaphorical foreclosure of issues, by which the proposed matter of the poem acts simultaneously as the metaphor justifying the mode of its treatment, has been a constant feature of Heaney's writing since such early poems as 'Digging', perfectly sustaining its drive towards cultural reterritorialization and the suturing of identity, because the concepts of culture and individuation thus appear as the formal repetition of the primary ground to which they are thereby returned. The racial and psychological archetype, like the reified human nature of bourgeois ideology from which it stems, subserves this circularity. The archetype allows the process of individuation and the specific forms taken on by any given culture to be envisaged as retaining a continuity with an homogeneous, undifferentiated ground, such as indeed the symbol is supposed to retain with that which it represents and, crucially, of which it partakes. The regressive nature of this model is significant less in the evident psychoanalytical sense, which doubles Heaney's own temporal schema, than in the neatness with which the location of that archetypal or indifferent ground can be pushed back as far as required – from oral culture and territory to the abstract form of the land, for example. This regression, nevertheless, does not affect the essential structure by which the immediacy of a primary relation to origins and ground can be replaced by a cultural medium, though in sublimated form and with the gain of pathos, as in Heaney's myth of Antaeus:

> a blue prong graiping him
> out of his element
> into a dream of loss
>
> and origins – the cradling dark,
> the river-veins, the secret gullies
> of his strength,
> the hatching grounds
>
> of cave and souterrain,
> he has bequeathed it all
> to elegists.
> (North)

That which is foregone is the most efficient myth of integration, supplying the lost object by which the work of mourning is transformed into the work of identification, specifically, here, identification with an inheritance.

Contradiction returns where the myth that has most effectively furthered the goal of integration by obviating the state's need for overt coercion clashes with those 'civilized values' that it underwrites. For both unionists and nationalists in Ireland, in ways which agree in form but differ in specific content, concepts of racial identity asserted since the nineteenth century have performed such an integrative function in the service of domination, at the cost of institutionalizing certain differences. That the interests promoted by these myths should have come into conflict at various periods, of which the current 'troubles' are only the latest instance, does not affect the correspondence that subsists between those ideologies. Even insurgent or anti-colonial violence, generally speaking directed against the state apparatus, can become in the strict sense 'terrorist' where it seeks by symbolic rather than tactical acts to forge integration or identity within the discursive boundaries already established and maintained by dominant hegemony. A socialist or feminist critique of such tendencies has to be located not in a generalized criticism of 'men of violence', but in the analysis of the totalizing effect of an identity thinking that discretely links terrorism to the state in whose name it is condemned. For what is at stake is not so much the practice of violence – which has long been institutionalized in the bourgeois state – as its aestheticization in the name of a freedom expressed in terms of national or racial integration. This aesthetic frame deflects attention from the interests of domination which the national state expresses both as idea and as entity.

The aestheticization of violence is underwritten in Heaney's recourse to racial archetypes as a means 'to grant the religious intensity of the violence its deplorable authenticity and complexity' (*Preoccupations*, pp. 56–7). In locating the source of violence beyond even sectarian division, Heaney renders it symbolic of a fundamental identity of the Irish race, as 'authentic'. Interrogation of the nature and function of acts of violence in the specific context of the current 'troubles' is thus foreclosed, and history foreshortened into the eternal resurgence of the same Celtic genius. The conflict of this thinking with 'the perspectives of a humane reason' (*Preoccupations*, p. 56) is, within the poetry that results, only an apparent contradiction, insofar as the function of reason is given over to the establishment of myths. The unpleasantness of such poetry lies in the manner in which the contradictions between the ethical and aesthetic elements in the writing are easily resolved by the subjugation of the former to the latter in order to produce the 'well-made poem'. Contempt for 'connivance in civilized outrage' is unexamined in the frequently cited 'Punishment' (*North*) where the 'artful voyeurism' of the poem is supposedly criticized as the safe stance of the remote and lustful 'civilized' observer, yet is smuggled back in as the unspoken and unacknowledged condition for the understanding of the 'exactness' of 'tribal, intimate revenge':

> I can feel the tug
> of the halter at the nape
> of her neck, the wind
> on her naked front.
>
> It blows her nipples
> to amber beads,
> it shakes the frail rigging
> of her ribs.
>
> I can see her drowned
> body in the bog,
> the weighing stone,
> the floating rods and boughs.
>
> Under which at first
> she was a barked sapling

that is dug up
oak-bone, brain-firkin ...

My poor scapegoat,

I almost love you
but would have cast, I know,
the stones of silence.
I am the artful voyeur

of your brain's exposed
and darkened combs,
your muscles' webbing
and all your numbered bones:

I who have stood dumb
when your betraying sisters,
cauled in tar,
wept by the railings,

who would connive
in civilized outrage
yet understand the exact
and tribal, intimate revenge.

The epithet 'tribal' cannot, in this context, be immanently questioned, since it at once is sustained by and reinforces the metaphor of
tribal rites which organizes the whole poem, and which is at once its
pretext and its subject-matter. Neither the justness of the identification of the metaphor – the execution of an adulteress by Glob's Iron
Age people – with the actual violence which it supposedly illuminates – the tarring and feathering of two Catholic 'betraying sisters' –
nor the immediacy of the observer's access to knowledge of his object
('I can feel ... I can see') is ever subjected to a scrutiny which would
imperil the quasi-syllogistic structure of the poem. Voyeurism is criticized merely as a pose, never for its function in purveying the intimate knowledge of violence by which it is judged. As so often in
Heaney's work, the sexual drive of knowing is challenged, acknowledged, and let pass without further interrogation, the stance condemned but the material it purveys nevertheless exploited. Thus a
pose of ethical self-query allows the condemnation of enlightened
response – reduced in any case to paralytic 'civilized outrage', as if
this were the only available alternative – while the supposedly
irrational is endowed as if by default with the features of enlightenment – exactitude, intimacy of knowledge – in order to compact an
understanding already presupposed in the selection and elaboration
of the metaphor. The terms of the dilemma are entirely false, but the

poem rehearses with striking fidelity the propensity of bourgeois thought to use 'reason' to represent irrationality as the emotional substratum of identifications which, given as at once natural and logical, are in fact themselves thoroughly 'irrational'.[24]

III

So much in Ireland still needs to be done ... the definition of the culture, and the redefinition of it. If you could open students into trust in their own personality, into some kind of freedom and cultivation, you could do a hell of a lot.[25]

In its play with atavisms, with the irrational substrata of its identifications, aesthetic ideology effectively excludes both violence and difference from the ideal image of its own internal structure. The irrational – all which eludes the governing principle of identity – is reduced to the originating matter which is repeatedly to be cultivated into unity. While it supplies the ground for culture, it is debarred from either real agency or representation, and figures thenceforth when 'active' as a 'disruption' of the supposedly natural ordering of cultivation. Thus its return merely bolsters up the rationale of an essentially exclusive culture, supplying at once the pretext and the matter upon which that culture's work is performed. The discourse of culture itself originates in the moment that the division of intellectual and physical labour has become such that 'culture' as a specialization is privileged yet entirely marginalized in relation to productive forces, and seeks to disguise, or convert, both privilege and marginalization in a sublimation which places it beyond division and into a position whence it can appear to perform the work of unification. Hence the importance not only of the image of the man of culture as a non-productive worker, but also the idea of a method which brings to an epistemology already analogous to industrial processes the privilege of unity retained even in transition, that of the 'science of origins' which reconciles where it first dissolves and finds differences.[26] The discourse of culture consistently seeks, by representing itself as withdrawn from implication in social divisions, as indifferent, to forge a domain in which divisions are overcome or made whole. The realization of human freedom is deferred into this transcendent domain, with the consequence that an ethical invocation is superadded to the exhortations of culture.

It is a cultural resolution of this order that Heaney proposes in *Field Work*, a generally acclaimed volume.[27] The sonnets composed in the 'hedge-school of Glanmore' pose as an apt centre-piece to the book, thematizing at once the notion of withdrawal and the agricultural root of that culture which is its goal: 'Vowels ploughed into other, opened ground,/Each verse returning like the plough turned round' (Glanmore Sonnets, II). Though this withdrawal is envisaged as a return and a grounding, it is still a ground whose otherness is carefully contained as a metaphor for the locus and source of poetic activity, and as such is resolutely cultivable. Secure in its protected, pastoral domain, the writing is full of unrealized resolve, governed primarily by a conditional mood which mimes the celebration of conditions for writing, yet is in actuality reduced to the almost contentless formal reiteration of the paradigms which sustain its complacencies. The small reminders that might threaten the benediction of that 'haven', the word with which Heaney obliquely encapsulates his relief at being harboured in a poetic which allows him the shelter of the English tradition and voice (Glanmore Sonnets, VII), are either framed carefully on the outside – 'Outside the kitchen window a black rat/Sways on the briar like infected fruit' (Glanmore Sonnets, IX) – or smothered in a rhetoric so portentous that it merely accentuates the bathos of its referents:

> This morning when a magpie with jerky steps
> Inspected a horse asleep beside the wood
> I thought of dew on armour and carrion.
> What would I meet, blood-boltered, on the road?
> How deep into the woodpile sat the toad?
> What welters through this dark hush on the crops?
> (Glanmore Sonnets, VIII)

It is difficult to credit the solemnly voiced pursuit of an 'apology for poetry' (Glanmore Sonnets, IX) in these sonnets with any real intellectual strenuousness, reduced as they are to such highly strung aestheticism. Whatever slight resonances they evoke are gained from political and ethical concerns which the knowledge of matters beyond their refined scope must supply.

The sonnets' implicit thesis that the preciousness of art – and the pathos of human being – may lie in the vulnerability of its fragile pieties to the 'ungovernable and dangerous' ('Elegy') is elsewhere delivered over to the test of more exacting conditions. The elegy 'Casualty' – which, of the three in the volume, most nearly confronts the supposed saving power of art with 'danger' – labours uneasily with the realization of the remoteness of this art from the pathos of the everyday which it celebrates elsewhere, and, as if in abreaction, asserts the more strongly the difference of art as the image of freedom posed against conformity to putative 'tribal' values. The assertion nevertheless regrounds itself through finding its paradigm in labour, in a labour, however, which is crucially predetermined as gratuitous, 'natural' and free, that of 'A dole-kept breadwinner/But a natural for work.' This image of the fisherman's labour as essentially free under-writes the concluding lines, which render fishing as a paradigm for art in its transcendence:

> I tasted freedom with him.
> To get out early, haul
> Steadily off the bottom,
> Dispraise the catch, and smile
> As you find a rhythm
> Working you, slow mile by mile,
> Into your proper haunt
> Somewhere, well out, beyond ...

At once natural and transcendent, freedom finds its image in gratuit-ous creative work, in a 'taste' which is shared beyond the divisions established by the 'incomprehensibility' of the poet's 'other life'. That such 'condescension' is always one-sided is debarred from con-sideration, as is the wider context of unfreedom which sustains that aesthetic once the idea of constraint has been reduced to the myth of the tribe.

The cautious limits which Heaney's poetry sets round any poten-tial for disruptive, immanent questioning may be the reason for the extraordinary inflation of his current reputation. If Heaney is held to be 'the most trusted poet of our [sic] islands',[28] by the same token he is the most institutionalized of recent poets. At the functional level of school and college teaching and examination, much of the prom-inence given to Heaney's writing may be attributed to its aptness for the still dominant discipline of practical criticism. Almost without exception, the poems respond compliantly to analysis based on assumptions about the nature of the well-made lyric poem: that it will crystallize specific emotions out of an experience; that the metaphorical structure in which the emotion is to be communicated will be internally coherent; that the sum of its ambiguities will be an integer, expressing eventually a unity of tone and feeling even where mediated by irony; that the unity will finally be the expression of a certain identity, a poetic 'voice' (Preoccupations, pp. 43–4). On the side of the writer, writing is envisaged as at once constitutive and expressive of an identity liberated from the incoherent unity of its ground. That act of self-production gives the writer his representativeness as human despite the specialization of his labour. For the reader, the act of reading appears also as a liberating act. To read, to criticize, is to exercise the right of private judgment and thereby to develop one's best self. The illusion of a free-market economy, where taste pretends to be an expression of the consumer's uncoerced judgment, thrives in the pedagogical method that furnishes the core of those literary institutions which in fact arbitrate cultural values.

In this period where the illusion of a free-market economy is disintegrating in crisis, it is appropriate that, within the increasingly marginalized domain of high culture, a pedagogy locating the autonomy of the individual subject in the private arbitration of value should become increasingly retrenched and all the more earnestly defended. It is perhaps only a small irony that the product of this pedagogy turns out to be such an unprecedented homogeneity of 'taste' that a reviewer can state, 'Everyone knows by now that Heaney is a major poet', and be confirmed not only by the accord of his peers, but by the remarkably high sales of the volumes concerned.[29] But that small irony – scarcely to be attributed to the benevolent dissemination of the sweetness and light of culture – is nonetheless symptomatic of a contradiction implicit in cultural discourse, and in some sense even recognized there, as if the terms of the discourse already resolved it. The contradiction, formally congruent with that produced by bourgeois ideology's attempts to 'reconcile individual liberty with association', lies in the fact that the cultivation of the individual's best self is to be conducted under the arbitration of an authority whose end is the constitution of a more integrated whole beyond divisions.[30] If that authority has tended to shift from the individual critic-teacher to institutions in which the existence of single tone-setting figures is much less apparent, this tendency belongs with a general shift from the concentration of power in the entrepreneur to its disposition through larger structures.[31] So much is implicit in common parlance when one speaks of one or other 'critical industry'.

The democratization of education that has stemmed in large part from nineteenth-century cultural discourse has followed the track of industrialization, and with similar effects in view. Where the net effect of increased technological efficiency has been to override the perception of difference with the homogenizing image of general prosperity, the end of literary education has been to override class and individual difference with the image of a common culture, both as something inherited and as something currently produced. The concept of a common culture can be seen to double that of the common land (whence, indeed, the concept of 'culture' has always derived its specific etymological and metaphorical resonances), and this conveniently underwrites the nominal decentralization of literary production. Pre-programmed as this development is, the resulting notion of the revitalization of the centres of culture through the influence of less deracinated, less cultivated regional sensibilities, continues to subserve the linked fictions of indigenous and subjective identity. Just as rhetoric about enterprise and the free market exploits the image of individualism while masking the actual diffusion of power through larger heterogeneous structures, so the celebration of regionalism dulls perception of the institutional and homogenizing culture which has sustained its apparent efflorescence at the very moment when the concept of locality, enclosed and self-nurturing, has become effectively archaic, and, indeed, functions as such. The pathos which the defenders of high culture and regional identity win from a stance offering to protect the vulnerable and vanishing against imponderable forces of technology and progress is gained in spite of the contradiction that the higher integration, which culture was to maintain beyond the class society, coincides perfectly with that being produced by technological development. The thematizing and defusing of these elements within Heaney's poetry provides the basis of the trust with which it is currently accepted, at every point confirming – as only such poetry can – the aesthetic and cultural expectations whence it stemmed and to which it promises an apparently authentic renovation. The seeming coherence between this scenario of the elevation of a minor Irish poet to a touchstone of contemporary taste and a discourse whose most canonical proponent argued for the Celtic literature as a means to the integration of Ireland with Anglo-Saxon industrial civilization is appropriate and pre-programmed.[32] It is, for all that, profoundly symptomatic of the continuing meshing of Irish cultural nationalism with the imperial ideology which frames it.

NOTES

1. Seamus Heaney, 'Hercules and Antaeus', *Wintering Out* (London 1972).
2. Seamus Heaney, *Field Work* (London 1979). The citation is from John Carey, 'Poetry for the World We Live In', review of Seamus Heaney, *Field Work*, and Craig Raine, *A Martian Sends a Postcard Home* (Oxford 1979), in *The Sunday Times*, 18 November 1979, p. 40.
3. Mark Patrick Hederman,'"The Crane Bag" and the North of Ireland', *The Crane Bag* (Dublin), 4, no. 2 (1980–1), p. 102, and Blake Morrison, *Seamus Heaney* (London 1982), p. 69.
4. Denis Florence MacCarthy (ed.), *The Book of Irish Ballads*, new edition (Dublin n.d.), pp. 15, 25–6.
5. 'Recent English Poets, No. 1 – Alfred Tennyson and E.B. Browning', *Nation*, 15 February 1845, p. 314.
6. Anonymous, 15 February 1845, 'Union Against the Union', *Nation*, 11 March 1848, p. 168. See also E. Kamenka (ed.), *Nationalism: The Nature and Evolution of an Idea* (London 1973), pp. 9–10. Marx's 'Critique of Hegel's Doctrine of the State' in *Early Writings*, Rodney Livingstone and Gregor Benton (trans.) (New York 1975), pp. 57–197, comprises an extensive critique of the state in terms of the split between the civil state of individualism and the political state of 'association'.
7. Elie Kedourie's *Nationalism* (London 1961) supplies the wider European context of nationalism, and emphasizes the ethical nature of its demands.
8. See the anonymous article, 'The Individuality of a Native Literature', *Nation*, 21 August 1847, p. 731.
9. In this particular context, I use the term 'reterritorialization' in a more literal sense than do Gilles Deleuze and Félix Guattari, from whose *Anti-Oedipus* (New York 1977) and *Kafka: pour une littérature mineure* (Paris 1975) it is derived. This, and related terms, are well analysed in Vincent Descombes, *Le Même et l'Autre: quarante-cinq ans de philosophie française, 1933–1978* (Paris 1979), pp. 205–6. Davis's essay was published in the *Nation*, 1 April 1843, p. 394.
10. Sigmund Freud, 'Some Psychical Consequences of the Anatomical Distinction between the Sexes', *The Complete Psychological Works* (London 1958–68), xix, p. 257.
11. I understand ideology, briefly, in relation to Gramsci's concept of hegemony, as consisting of the general shared structure of disseminating institutions and a set of discourses of analogous structure which operate not through coercion but through the 'naturalization' of certain forms of thought. See, for example, Antonio Gramsci, *Selections from the Prison Notebooks*, ed. and trans. Quintin Hoare and Geoffrey Nowell Smith (New York 1971), pp. 240–6. I have used the verb 'to double' throughout this essay to describe – by analogy with the word's musical sense – the way in which the structure of one discourse may appear congruent with that of another, giving rise to the 'knotting together' (see Gramsci, p. 240) of disparate hegemonic discourses into an apparently self-reinforcing, limiting structure of thought.
12. This is the general argument of John Breuily's persuasive study, *Nationalism and the State* (New York 1982), see especially chapters 2 and 3.
13. See George Boyce, *Nationalism in Ireland* (London 1982), p. 239, where he

remarks that 'one of the most important unifying themes of southern politics after the 1920s was *Hibernia Irredenta*'.

14. See Boyce, *Nationalism in Ireland*, pp. 364–5.

15. 'Difference' is employed throughout less in the Derridean sense than as the dialectical contrary to the concept of identity, i.e that which cannot be assimilated to the unity of identitarian thinking. Theodor Adorno argues this to be an inescapable contradiction within such thinking; see *Negative Dialectics*, E.B Ashton (trans.) (New York 1973), pp. 5–6.

16. Seamus Heaney, *Death of a Naturalist* (London 1966), pp. 13–14, and *Door into the Dark* (London 1969), pp. 25–6.

17. Harold Bloom, 'The Voice of Kinship', *TLS*, 8 (February 1980), pp. 137–8.

18. Seamus Heaney, 'Feeling into Words', *Preoccupations* (London 1980), p. 41.

19. On the continuing vital relation between literate and non-literate, high and low, see the last two essays in this volume.

20. Frank Kinahan, 'Artists on Art: An Interview with Seamus Heaney', *Critical Inquiry*, 8.3 (Spring 1982), p. 406; see also Seamus Heaney's lines in 'The Ministry of Fear', *North* (London 1975), p. 65: 'Ulster was British, but with no rights on/The English Lyric.'

21. See *Preoccupations*, pp. 36–7. I allude to the COED definition of 'vocable'.

22. For further discussion of gender issues in Heaney's writings that have appeared since this essay was first published, see Elizabeth Butler Cullingford, '"Thinking of Her ... as ... Ireland": Yeats, Pearse and Heaney', *Textual Practice*, 4.1 (Spring 1990), pp. 1–21, and Patricia Coughlan, '"Bog Queens": The Representation of Women in the Poetry of John Montague and Seamus Heaney' in Toni O'Brien Johnson and David Cairns (eds), *Gender in Irish Writing* (Milton Keynes 1991), pp. 88–111.

23. See Richard Kearney's comments on the intertwining of both aspects of this mythology in 'The IRA's Strategy of Failure', *The Crane Bag*, 4, no. 2 (1980–1), p. 62.

24. See Theodor Adorno's remarks on this subject, specifically in relation to the mobilizing of 'additional regressive memories of its archaic root' in the bourgeois nation state, in *Negative Dialectics*, p. 339.

25. See the interview with Seamus Heaney in John Haffenden, *Viewpoints* (London 1981), pp. 59–60.

26. See Coleridge, 'Essays on Method', *The Friend*, Barbara Rooke (ed.) (Princeton 1969), p. 476; Matthew Arnold, 'On the Study of Celtic Literature' in R.H Super (ed.), *Lectures and Essays in Criticism*, vol. III of *The Complete Prose Works* (Ann Arbor: Michigan 1962), p. 330. Adorno comments on the duplication of the mechanical reproductive process in Kant's *Critique of Pure Reason*. See *Negative Dialectics*, p. 387.

27. Reviews acclaiming *Field Work* range from Harold Bloom's in the *TLS* to one by Gerard Smyth in *The Irish Times* ('Change of Idiom', *IT*, 20 October 1979, p. 11). Reviewers are almost unanimous in regarding the volume as a steady advance on the previous body of work.

28. Christopher Ricks, 'The Mouth, the Meal, and the Book', review of *Field Work* in *The London Review of Books*, 8 November 1979, p. 4.

29. Neither Faber and Faber nor Farrar, Straus and Giroux have been willing to divulge detailed figures concerning sales of Heaney's works. I am, however,

obliged to Craig Raine of Faber and Faber for the following 'approximate figures', whose 'general lesson is sound and obvious enough': 'We would probably have printed 2000–3000 copies of his first book, whereas now we would print somewhere in the region of 20,000 copies' (letter, 12 October 1983).

30. See Matthew Arnold, 'The Function of Criticism in the Present Time', *Lectures and Essays*, pp. 265–6: '*Force till right is ready*; and till right is ready force, the existing order of things, is justified, is the legitimate ruler' (original emphasis).

31. John Kenneth Galbraith, *The New Industrial State*, 2nd ed. (Harmondsworth 1974), especially chapter 5, 'Capital and Power'. The analysis, if not the conclusion, of this study is valuable, and challenging to any materialist view of the current economy.

32. Arnold, 'On the Study of Celtic Literature', pp. 296–7.

WRITING IN THE SHIT: BECKETT, NATIONALISM AND THE COLONIAL SUBJECT

It was in this byre, littered with dry and hollow cowclaps subsiding with a sigh at the poke of my finger, that for the first time in my life, and I would not hesitate to say the last if I had not to husband my cyanide, I had to contend with a feeling which gradually assumed, to my dismay, the dread name of love. What constitutes the charm of our country, apart of course from its scant population, and this without the help of the meanest contraceptive, is that all is derelict, with the sole exception of history's ancient faeces. These are ardently sought after, stuffed and carried in procession. Wherever nauseated time has dropped a nice fat turd you will find our patriots, sniffing it up on all fours, their faces on fire. Elysium of the roofless. Hence my happiness at last. Lie down, all seems to say, lie down and stay down. I see no connection between these remarks. But that one exists, and even more than one, I have little doubt, for my part. But what? Which?

Samuel Beckett, *First Love*, pp. 30–1

The narrator of Beckett's *First Love* thus summons us disingenuously to address the questions he will himself displace in the name of love. Disingenuously, perhaps, but then only because the traces of an answer litter this dry and hollow text. The question is, what connects the apotheistic discourse of nationalism to that on love within the framework of an 'excremental vision'? To try to answer under the rubric suggested in my title, namely, in relation to colonialism, will doubtless seem perverse and strained, particularly where we are concerned with so notoriously 'apolitical' a writer. But such perversity is rightly out of place in the context of a writing as transgressive as this, while the supposition of an apolitical writing silently invokes an aesthetic which requires that the subject of discourse be consubstantial with the subject of writing. The query we turn back upon the text becomes twofold. Under what conditions does this writing emerge that so thoroughly sifts the grounds whereon Western metaphysics and a related ethics of subjectivity have rested, its forms implying a radical negation of the aesthetic which has been for a period a principal agent in the formation of ethical subjects? What has it to say concerning the question of the subject who is left in the post-colonial situation, that is, to the subjective aspect of a politics which is no less engaged in negating the objective hegemonic force of the Western ethos? The intent of this double interrogation is not to reactivate the jejune slogan 'the personal is the political', whose ideological serviceability becomes ever more apparent as it wears ever thinner. Rather it is to claim that the aesthetic domain occupies a privileged place in the legitimation of the bourgeois state during the period of expansive colonialism, and to derive that claim, as do the aestheticians, from the work's ethical capacity to mediate subject and object, to produce reconciliations between individual and totality.[1] Given that claim, a connection ('But what? Which?') may be discerned between the erosion of the aesthetic domain and the demise of colonialism itself, a connection which implies, it may be stressed, not the end of hegemony but possibly its migration to another, necessarily less discrete sphere.

I

'What goes by the name of love is banishment, with now and then a postcard from the homeland,' declares the narrator of *First Love*.[2] His remark scrupulously disdains a Western tradition for which, from the *Odyssey* to *Ulysses*, love is the figure simultaneously for homecoming and for truth. We are, of course, left in the dark as to whether banishment is the condition of love, or love that of banishment, nor are we offered the surety that through banishment home truths will lapse forever into love's oblivion: postcards maintain some kind of sporadic connection, if only a dim reminder of origins and dependence. Both aspects of this love are written into its original title: if *Premier Amour* speaks of a first love, it does so in the language of exile itself. The original language of first love is adoptive, not natural, and as such implies a provocative refusal of the naturalization and the nationalization of language as the ground of a proper subjectivity. The text, the first work which Beckett published in French, raises at the level of the most primary decision, the language of 'self-expression', the questions of exile and translation in their relation to the formation of the subject.

Both questions are the troublesome but constitutive matter of Irish nationalism wherever it touches on the crucial question of national culture. According to Daniel Corkery, writing on John Millington Synge less than a decade after the founding of the Irish Free State, the perpetual condition of 'expatriation' accepted by Irish writers has produced a virtually pathological absence of national culture in Ireland.[3] Though Corkery acknowledges that this expatriation is primarily due to 'the proximity of the English market' (p. 26), the acquiescence of the Irish writer in the economy of imperialism has its psychic effects. On the one hand, a writing directed towards an English market serves to perpetuate the alien stereotypes of the Irish: it is a 'colonial literature, written to explain the quaintness of the humankind of this land, especially the native human-kind, to another humankind that was not quaint, that was standard, normal' (pp. 7–8). On the other hand, and more significantly, it is not simply that their presentation as alien to an English market is a misrepresentation, but that in the dissymmetry of representation what is left in Ireland is not the true identity of the Irish, unmasked and intact, but rather its absence. Into the cultural vacuum left by the export trade in Irish writers rushes an English culture, which, being alien, deforms where it is intended to form harmonious subjects:

Everywhere in the mentality of Irish people are flux and uncertainty. Our national consciousness may be described, in a native phrase, as a quaking sod. It gives no footing. It is not English, nor Irish, nor Anglo-Irish; as will be understood if one think a while on the thwarting it undergoes in each individual child of the race as he grows into manhood ... His education, instead of buttressing and refining his emotional nature, teaches him the rather to despise it, inasmuch as it teaches him not to see the surroundings out of which he is sprung, as they are in themselves, but as compared with alien surroundings: his education provides him with an alien medium through which he is henceforth to look at his native land! (pp. 14–15)

The proper function of the Irish writer would accordingly be to represent the people, in every sense of that word. If at one level, this involves the demand to depict Irish people and their ways, it is intrinsic to Corkery's argument that proper depiction is a function of the representativeness of the writer as Irish. In a sense of the word quite strictly analogous to its usage in democratic political theory, the writer is the people's representative. Accordingly, the concept of representation in play here involves an implicit narrative of development: by representing in himself the common identity of the Irish people, by canalizing 'some share of Irish consciousness so that that consciousness would better know itself' (p. 6) the writer produces the national and subjective unity which is as yet only a latent potential.

Corkery thus insists upon a continuity between individual and national identity which is borne by literature, and insists, moreover,
that only a national literature can be considered literature at all,
since only such a literature is representative: 'Is the writer the
people's voice? has there ever been, can there be, a distinctive literature that is not a national literature?' (p. 2)

We will pass over momentarily the normalizing function which
national literature performs for Corkery – 'normal and national are
synonymous in literary criticism' (p. 3) – to address rather the
question which is critical but constantly displaced in this essay on
Anglo-Irish literature, namely the very presence of the prefix
'Anglo'. Though in later writings, Corkery vehemently espouses the
gaelicization of Irish culture, in *Synge and Anglo-Irish Literature* the
problem of the predominant anglicization of Irish culture is largely
elided.[4] What might seem at first a strange displacement is in fact
intrinsic to Corkery's essay and to the nationalist discourse to which
it belongs; indeed, his sketchy treatment of the matter is allowed by
those previous writings of Irish nationalists that seek to resolve the
founding contradiction of their political culture. For Irish nationalism emerges in consequence of a relatively rapid though uneven
modernization of parts of Irish society in the early nineteenth
century, which produced an expanding middle class along with the
technical and administrative apparatus capable of producing and
disseminating the concept of the nation as a whole.[5] By virtue, however, of the commercial and bureaucratic activities which produced
and occupied this class, all necessarily transacted primarily if not
exclusively in English, the political doctrines of nationalism are
conceived and propagated in English. Simultaneously, the emergence
of an increasingly politically conscious middle class coincides with
the critical decline of the Irish language as the medium of daily life
for the people, a decline that appeared to pass the 50 per cent mark
by the mid-1840s.[6] Irish nationalism thus emerges at the moment of
virtual eclipse of what would have been its 'natural' language, and
mainly among a class which was already, necessarily, estranged from
that language. The peculiar forms taken by Irish nationalism develop
from this vividly apprehended dislocation and from the consequent
absence of the political legitimation available to other European
nationalisms through the putatively a priori transcendent unity of a
national language.[7]

In his 1843 article on the Irish language, cited already in '"Pap for the dispossessed"', Thomas Davis gave vivid expression to the problem caused by the loss of a national language to a nationalism predicated on European models:

> To impose another language on such a people is to send their history adrift among the accidents of translation – 'tis to tear their identity from all places – 'tis to substitute arbitrary signs for picturesque and suggestive names – 'tis to cut off the entail of feeling, and separate the people from their forefathers by a deep gulf – 'tis to corrupt their very organs, and abridge their power of expression.[8]

To take on another language is already to live as an exile, to lose one's identity with one's paternity, to be condemned to translate. But we should note again that the paternity to which Davis lays claim is a family romance: his case, as with most of his Young Ireland collaborators, is absolutely not that of a Gaelic speaker forced to abandon the language of his literal father and to speak or write in English. On the contrary, Davis and the Young Irelanders were mostly raised and educated in English and were hence obliged to graft themselves back on to a Gaelic past in order to claim it as their proper heritage. This backward movement has double-edged consequences: on the one hand, the paternal language, like the paternal heritage which it represents, becomes a sublimated ideal; on the other, the actual Gaelic language, still current even if culturally embattled, is projected as a lost mother-tongue which is at once natural and in need of supplementation. Irish nationalist writings inaugurate a subtle but decisive shift from the recognition of the economic and political threat that Gaelic culture faced from British imperialism to the representation of that culture as lost, past, primitive, fragmented and, indeed, feminine. This shift is inseparable from the specific project of bourgeois nationalism in Ireland, namely, the forging of a sense of Irish identity that would transcend historically determined cultural and political differences and form the reconciliatory centre of national unity. This project is engaged at the level of the culture as a whole, through the various research and propaganda activities which nineteenth-century nationalists carried out and encouraged, and equally significantly at the level of the individual, whose ethical development was prerequisite to his integration with a still to be realized fatherland. The future-oriented project of Irish nationalism, devoted to the ethical formation of Irish subjects through powerful sublimated identifications, ironically supplants the Gaelic culture in whose name it speaks, furthering its transformation into a primitive or undeveloped substrate of nationalist culture.

In the field of language politics, it could be argued that the obsession with national identity, conceived as an ideal to be forged rather than an actual set of cultural and historical determinants, contributed to the decay of the Irish language. For the reconciliation which the Young Irelanders pursued, given that they regarded any attempt to promote a national linguistic revival as impractical, called for a work of translation, of translation redefined so that Davis's 'accidents' were replaced by principles. Since the Gaelic culture which was the sign of a separate political identity would have in any case to be mediated to an already anglicized people by translation, the theory of translation adopted proclaimed the possibility of transmitting entirely the generative spirit (the 'genius') of the Irish language into the English. This act could, however, be performed only by writers who were representative of, already integrated spiritually with, the racial spirit and who, accordingly, prefigured for the fragmentary actual population the unity which was to come. The gulf which separates us from our putative forefathers on the material level is sutured by a second-level identification with the paternal spirit of the nation, assuring the reproduction of an identity and unity of the people that supposedly pre-existed the shattering invasion of an alien power.

Paradoxically, in adopting such a model of cultural identification, whose complement is the development through literature of a feeling of nationality in the citizen, Irish nationalists reproduce in their very opposition to the Empire a narrative of universal development which is fundamental to the legitimation of imperialism. What we apprehend actually as difference and fragmentation is no more than the process of differentiation or individuation by which what was an original, unreflective unity progresses to an identity which sublates difference in self-conscious unity. This ethical metaphysic finds its practical realization in the gradual assimilation of subjected peoples into the more advanced civilization of the Empire, whose temporal position within the universal narrative guarantees its greater proximity to that normative humanity which is our collective goal. Within this schema, it is constantly the ethical function of the aesthetic work to furnish representative instances of this narrative, as it is the function of aesthetic history, the history of aesthetic forms, to demonstrate the congruity of aesthetic works of increasing self-reflexive complexity with the preordained stages of humankind's development. Crucial to this process are two notions developed in aesthetic thought: that the artwork arouses a contemplative desire that reconciles subject and object, and, complementarily, that the formal identity of humanity resides in the formative capacity of human beings in general.[9]

Hence, from Young Ireland through to Corkery, a normal literature is a national literature, and the function of a national literature is normalizing. Conceived in terms entirely consonant with the aesthetic and developmental theories current in the major European imperial states, the aesthetics of Irish nationalism similarly espouses a literature which will develop from its primitive, native incoherence to the status of a representative national institution and which will operate, at the individual as at the national level, to develop ethical identity.

II

The aesthetic domain emerges in the need to resolve contradictions which subsist both within the subject and in the relationship between each individual subject and the state, which, in Marx's terms, represents man's 'species-being'.[10] In the light of the foregoing analysis, it is perhaps one and the same thing to note this special function of the aesthetic domain, and that it is in the face of his dead father that the narrator of *First Love* glimpses a hint 'at some form of aesthetics relevant to man' (p. 26). For every moment of reconciliation retains the trace of the contradiction which generated it, as the identification with the father is predicated on his absence, on the splitting of the material from the spiritual form. And which then is the remainder? Thus even in their apotheosis, 'stuffed and carried in procession', the turds of the subject of history represent the condition of alienation: 'Elysium of the roofless.' Reconciliation is thus always projected into an indefinite future, as Robert Emmet forbade the writing of his epitaph until his nation should be free.[11] For the narrator of *First Love*, on the contrary, the proper epitaph is that which reminds us that death is recurrent in the structure of subjectivity, and life a continual dying, and a dying in every moment:

> Hereunder lies the above who up below
> So hourly died that he survived till now. (p. 12)

The epitaph is the model of, or merely another mode of, a writing whose subject is a perpetual oscillation between fading and return, the writing of *First Love*.

In saying this, however, we should not overlook the fact that the narrator of *First Love* is one before whose pursuit of identity even the most ardent of nationalists would pale:

> What mattered to me in my dispeopled kingdom, that in regard to which the disposition of my carcass was the merest and most futile of accidents, was supineness in the mind, the dulling of the self and of that residue of execrable frippery known as the non-self and even the world, for short. (p. 18)

It is the repeated logic of Beckett's writing that the pursuit itself produces its negation, 'reduc[ing] the dark where there might have been, mathematically at least, a door'.[12] In the case of *First Love*, that rigorous logic adopts two modes: there is the rigour of death, in which the ethical will of the absent father is played out, and the rigour of desire, inspired by the ever-present absence of a woman. I will deal with each by turn, though that is inevitably to separate elements which are, according to the logic of the text, as inseparable as are the aesthetics of nationalism from that which connects history's faeces to love's writing:

> I associate, rightly or wrongly, my marriage with the death of my father, in time. That other links exist, on other planes, between these two affairs, is not impossible. I have enough trouble as it is in trying to say what I think I know. (p. 11)

The text opens at one pole of these linked 'affairs', with the visit of the narrator to his father's grave, in the presence of his father's absence. The digressive motion of the text which this visit inaugurates is, in the tradition of ethical autobiography, a movement to rejoin the 'great disembodied wisdom' (p. 16) of the dead father. Its transgressiveness, particularly with respect to that tradition, is initiated by the narrator's expulsion from his room in his father's house in consequence of the latter's death. The condition of possib-ility for the son's expulsion by the family is given by the death of the father. The actual event is in turn permitted by another condition, the narrator's constipation – or is it diarrhoea? – which detains him in his motions long enough for his eviction to take place, as it must, in his absence. The narrator's expulsion is linked to his excretions, on some plane, and to the polarity of marriage and paternal death is added another term, excrement, which will mediate the motion between them: 'It's all a muddle in my head, graves and nuptials and the different varieties of motion' (p. 15).

The excremental logic of this text pursues one path in relation to the father. If we accept the depiction of an infantile symbolic logic

for which the faeces are the first gift and therewith the first realization of a potential self-alienation, ending a process of assimilation to
self and inaugurating an assimilation to others, we may read in the
fetishization of excrement the index of a negative dialectic of identity. One motion draws the narrator to be back in the shelter of the
room, flat on his back in that 'supineness in the mind' which is the
Beckettian simulation of self-identity. The contrary motion is the
project to regain the father's protection by identification with his
spirit, one which necessarily contradicts the first, since it involves
identification with another. That identification leaves a double residue across which the splitting of the subject is articulated as always a
motion and not just a moment, namely, the residue of the self-
identical self and the remains of the corporeal father left behind in
the projection of the father as spirit. These two remainders may be
integrated and the split subject sutured only in the moment of death.
That impossible demand nonetheless structures the ideological project of nationalism and imperialism alike through the logic of self-
sacrifice to the state, whose transcendental function is always 'to take
up the matter' and ensure that every subject gets his epitaph (p. 12).

But the father survives also in another form, that of money
which, left to the narrator in his father's will, he conserves in his
pocket, 'leaving it lie' against his old age (p. 19). But unspent and
unexchanged for determinate objects, this money signals all the
more purely towards another of the 'different varieties of motion'
which play through the text, namely, that of circulation. The
paradoxical logic of circulation is that it establishes the indifference
of the subject by virtue of his/her always becoming, taking the place
of another. Since, according to the logic of capitalist circulation in
the labour as in the commodity market, any thing can be exchanged
for any other, including humans, the very forces that unleash the
individual from traditional ties and impose the injunction to moral
and economic 'self-making' are those that assert the identity of all
subjects. Thus the logic of identity, which seeks the self-identity of
the subject in absolute differentiation from the 'non-self', is again
displaced by another logic, that of desire, which passes by way of
identification with another to initiate a second banishment:

But man is still today, at the age of twenty-five, at the mercy of an erection, physically
too, from time to time, it's the common lot, even I was not immune, if that may be
called an erection. It did not escape her naturally, women smell a rigid phallus ten
miles away and wonder, How on earth did he spot me from there? One is no longer

oneself, on such occasions, and it is painful to be no longer oneself, even more painful if possible than when one is. For when one is one knows what to do to be less so, whereas when one is not one is any old one irredeemably. What goes by the name of love is banishment, with now and then a postcard from the homeland, such is my considered opinion this evening. (p. 18)

It is the common lot: to become not oneself is to become 'any old one irredeemably'. To be in perpetual debt is the normative condition of the subject, since an identity gained by way of the other can never be autonomous; in other terms, one labours to produce oneself for others.

It is accordingly entirely appropriate that the woman in question should be a prostitute, and that she should moreover possess neither definite bodily form – 'it might have been anything or anyone, an old woman or a little girl' (pp. 24–5) – nor proper name, the latter changing at one juncture from the repetitive 'Lulu' to the chiastic 'Anna'.[13] For the prostitute embodies the anxiety of dispossession, perpetually self-alienated in exchange for money and in consequence chastised for manifesting what is otherwise the always discrete form of social relations. But in this instance, the literalization of that exchange collapses the discriminations which fence the prostitute outside the law and oppose her to paternal will. For Anna/Lulu is here not exchanged for money, but rather, by furnishing a room for the narrator, takes the place at once of the money the son will not spend and of the will of the father. Ironically, in making such provision, it is the prostitute who demonstrates the logic of identity that passes through the father to be one of exchangeability in which all apparent oppositions dissolve.

In the space of 'not being oneself' which is opened by desire, a writing takes place which is at once in and of the non-identical 'remains' of identity. Troubled by the insistence of his own desire in the form of Lulu/Anna, the narrator enacts his banishment from the bench of their trysts to seek refuge in a deserted cowshed, only to find himself 'tracing the letters of Lulu in an old heifer pat' (p. 22). A circuit of displacements occurs whose vertiginous motions can be difficult to grasp: shit becomes the medium and the trace of a writing whose purpose is naming but whose effect is the articulation of a desire which displaces the subject continually in the 'banishment' of love; but while the locus of writing migrates to the zone of anality, that zone is reconnected to the mouth which, liberated from any expressive demand, is restored to its prior oral function: 'Would I

50

have been inscribing her name in old cowshit if my love had been pure and disinterested? And with my devil's finger into the bargain, which I then sucked?' (p. 22) At this point also, the name 'Lulu' is exchanged for the name 'Anna', an exchange of phonetic repetition that is perhaps infantile for one of specularity that is perhaps narcissistic, imaginary, but nonetheless 'not more like her but no matter'. The written shit which thus substitutes for Lulu/Anna stands in relation to her as does the money to the father, describing the movement between identity and non-identity with the object of desire. But while this formal analogy dissolves the opposition between the sublimated father, the sphere of ethics and identity, and the prostitute, the site of desire and displacement, it would nonetheless be misleading, not to say hasty, to assert that the resultant work is one which in writing off identity manages to write non-identity. Rather, it draws us to the threshold of a writing of which we can now only theoretically conceive and which would perforce seem to us from here the babble of psychosis.

First Love circulates between the poles suggested by the woman's songs. On the one hand are those fragmentary, wordless airs which Kristeva identifies, in an only too rigorous opposition, with 'undifferentiated woman': 'All she had done was sing, sotto voce, as to herself and without words fortunately, some old folk songs, and so disjointedly, skipping from one to another and finishing none, that even I found it strange' (p. 17).[14] The archaic song appears to belong in the realm of primary identity, absolutely indifferent and interchangeable, and sung for herself alone. In this it is opposed to the song that she later sings at the narrator's request, which is self-identical and unique, and fixes the singer momentarily: 'I thought at first she was going to refuse, I mean simply not sing, but no, after a moment she began to sing and sang for some time, all the time the same song it seemed to me, without change of attitude' (p. 25). Kristeva suggests that the song probably remains 'in that unnamable domain of the father' (p. 153), but the narrator's remark that 'It had something to do with lemon trees, or orange trees, I forget' may take us further. Though 'neatness of identification'[15] is always made problematic by the very dynamic of Beckett's texts, those citrus fruits probably take us to Mignon's song in Goethe's *Wilhelm Meister's Apprenticeship*, which opens, 'Kennst du das Land, wo die Zitronen bluhn,/Im dunkeln Laub die Gold-Orangen gluhn'. The allusion is richly significant in its context, for Mignon's song, recorded by a hero who, unlike the narrator of *First Love*, is assuredly on the path to self-formation, is itself a translation of Mignon's fragmentary language and a reduction to uniformity of 'its broken phraseology' and 'its disjointed parts'. The specifically thematic significance of this song to the motions of *First Love* lies not only in the fact that the singer longs for a land of protected ease, but that the child will enter it only accompanied by the protecting father: the song concludes 'o Vater, laß uns ziehn!'[16] Lulu/Anna's song thus does not merely remain in the father's land, but gestures towards it just before she is to offer the narrator a room in her place, as she is herself to take the place of the father.

With this song the narrator first plays a game which might seem to play out the perpetual motions of the text itself. As he leaves her, the song grows faint, leaving him in doubt as to whether she has ceased or he has ceased to hear. As he returns the song seems to resume: 'First I didn't hear it, then I did, I must therefore have begun hearing it, at a certain point, but no, there was no beginning, the sound emerged so softly from the silence and so resembled it' (p. 26). The song, which describes the movement that connects prostitute and father, which is a child's song, seems to have no origin and captures the subject accordingly in a movement of rising and fading. On the uncertainty of the origins of any movement of this nature, *First Love* is predicated, and if the doubtful beginning of one song calls its presence in doubt and sets up a painful, almost 'somatic' oscillation in the subject, its opposite numbers are those archaic indifferent songs which have no stable identity by virtue of all being the same. This oscillation is inevitable, for both songs are always caught up in the movement of representation and assigned a place in the economy of identity formation, *Bildung*. The very fragmentariness of the archaic or 'undifferentiated' is, like the Irish 'mother-tongue', a backward projection, since for one already embarked on the project of *Bildung*, the primitive can appear only as lacking and in need of supplementation. On the other hand, within the same economy, the origin and authenticity of the formed song becomes equally problematic, since self-identity is precisely what is lost in the process of self-formation.

The question of origins calls identity in question and the logic of identity calls the origin in question. And if, according to a legal code dating back to Roman times, the identity of the father is as the nuptial ceremony declares, the legal fiction retains constantly the trace of that anxiety which inspired the arbitrariness of its namings. The uncertainty that attaches to the paternal origin, both biologically and 'morally', threatens always to undermine the integrity of the name, of the determination of paternal property and of identity itself.[17] But since the self-identity of the subject, to which indeed the father calls him, must always be established in opposition to the father, identity itself contradicts the appeal to originality which founds it. Hence the ambivalence that inheres in the concept of originality, and the anxiety which always afflicts the autobiographical text. Hence, also, the reason that any nationalism must police the desire of women, and, indeed, contain the mother within the matrix of a 'motherland' which is always to be possessed by the sons of the fathers as their rightful inheritance. Purity of race and patrimony demands control over reproduction.

But *First Love* concludes with a birth and a banishment as the narrator becomes in his turn the father in name of a child which, given the mother's profession, may or may not be his. As he departs at the moment of birth, the cries of the infant, the purely phonic prototype of all song and all speech, displace the unoriginal, residual song of the mother, only to have the same game played upon them by the banished father:

As long as I kept walking, I didn't hear them, because of the footsteps. But as soon as I halted I heard them again, a little fainter each time, admittedly, but what does it matter, faint or loud, cry is cry, all that matters is that it should cease. For years I thought they would cease. Now I don't think so any more. (p. 36)

The first cry displaces both mother and father, is the primary expression of their mutual banishment, and establishes equally the unending motions of love. Unending, because the moment of union towards which love's motions tend takes place in the absence of the subject, over his dead body.

Occurring at the very moment in which he believes he has returned to himself – 'Try and put me out now, I said' – the narrator's own act of union takes place in double inauthenticity, between the enigmatic smile of a Giaconda and the unspeakable silence of the phallus:

She was smiling. A little later she went away, taking the lamp with her ... I woke next morning, quite spent, my clothes in disorder, the blankets likewise, and Anna beside me, naked naturally. One shudders to think of her exertions ... I looked at my member. If only it could have spoken! Enough about that. It was my night of love. (p. 31)

If possession of the phallus is the index of authenticity, of control over identity, its operation as a sign of difference precludes it from ever speaking truth: authenticity is relegated to the domain of a perpetual 'if only!' The enigma of a smile is the enigma of duplicity to which meaning can be ascribed only by another, and then always only partially. It is the purest sign of inauthenticity, since to be inauthentic is to be made or read by another, to be given meaning.

III

Such inauthenticity is equally the perpetual condition of the colonized: dominated, interpreted, mediated by another. Against this othering, the ambivalent smile – of servility transforming constantly to contempt – is the repeated reserve of the colonized subject even as it becomes the locus of a stereotype. The project of nationalism, conversely, is to break down this reserve and to restore authenticity to the colonized subject on the basis of a return to principles. Within this project the paternal metaphor necessarily dominates as the expression of a desire to reoccupy and control one's origins, and of the drive to restore the continuity of descent, which will recompose those remains of national selfhood made derelict by the colonizer. But these origins are a fiction, and still the colonized subject is grasped as an object to be transformed quite inauthentically into subjectivity by way of an alien absent presence. Even in its oppositional stance, nationalism repeats the master narrative of imperialism, the narrative of development which is always applied with extreme rigour and priority to colonized peoples. As is made manifest by the continuity between European nationalism and European imperialism, the nationalist desire to develop the race into authenticity, borrowed already from a universalist ideology, produces the hegemonic conditions for the ultimate perpetuation of imperial domination even after independence is achieved. So much is evident in the naturalness which accrues to the rhetoric of economic development by way of its congruity with the schema of development in the subjective economy: where the individual subject, within a narrative which to function must be universally the same, is to be integrated first with the nation and then with 'humanity' (the family of nations), so each individual nation state must be developed into increasing integration in the global capitalist market.[18]

Nationalism remains suspended: paradoxically it cannot develop beyond a reterritorialization of the dislocated subjectivity of the colonized people since its ends are to forge the political union of a heterogeneous population in the service of political liberation. But since that unity is always necessarily the expression of the political consciousness of a dominant class within the subjected nation, produced and 'bourgeoisified' in the movement from dominant to hegemonic colonialism, its initial progressive tendency virtually inevitably decays into a reactionary false universality. The fetish-ization of national identity over and above the continuing reality of class difference within the new nation state is the index of what Fanon describes as the 'sterile formalism' in which the post-colonial bourgeoisie 'imprison national consciousness'.[19]

Clearly, the primary response to such conditions must entail a continuing struggle against domination at the material level. Nonetheless, in the dialectic of liberation it is unwise to neglect the subjective aspect within which the power of ideology is crucially effective. Where ideology perpetually takes the form of a natural-ization predicated upon a premature assertion of reconciliation, the project of an anti-identitarian thinking is of crucial importance in the critique of false immediacies. The perpetuation of difference against ideological identifications is carried through by a narrative mode which refuses any single model of integration (or even of oppositional positioning): no integration is called for by an aesthetic of non-identity. Such an aesthetic equally writes out the inauthenti-city enforced upon the colonized subject, and, we might now add, upon all those subjected to a globalized capitalism whose mechanism is a perpetual decoding and recoding of ideological identifications. Crucially, however, that writing out of inauthenticity refuses to substitute any authenticity in its place, constituting rather a critical refusal of integration at any level. If Fanon famously apprehends the inauthenticity of the colonized in the phrase 'black skin, white masks', it is of importance to stress with Octavio Paz that for a post-modern post-colonialism, that mask conceals no prior or defaced authenticity:

A truly modern art would be the one that would reveal the hollowness rather than mask it ... For the primitive, the function of the mask is to reveal and conceal a terrible, contradictory reality: the seed that is life and death, fall and resurrection in a fathomless *now*. Today the mask hides nothing. In our time it may well be impossible for the artist to invoke presence. But another way, cleared for him by Mallarmé, is still open to him: manifesting absence, incarnating emptiness.[20]

ANOMALOUS STATES

Samuel Beckett's work similarly reappropriates certain modernist
procedures from the marginal site of a post-colonial nation, commen-
cing quite programmatically in the 1930s with a rejection of the
already ossifying obsession of Irish writers with 'antiquarianism', the
recurrent reproduction of Celtic material as a thematic of identity.
His opposition is made in the name of a recognition of a 'new thing
that has happened', the breakdown of the object, or, by reverse, that
of the subject.[21] His working out of that new condition, by no means
complete even in *First Love*, approaches the threshold of another
possible language within which a post-colonial subjectivity might
begin to find articulation. That we cannot do so yet is a reminder of
the insistence of the objective conditions which inhere as a constraint and as a limit upon the efficacy of a purely critical thinking.
The last two essays in this book seek to elaborate the materials towards which Beckett's work, in its moment, can only formally if
critically gesture. Their premise is, in effect, that it is in whatever lies
in the gapped, disjointed songs of Anna/Lulu, in the unrepresentable
of the narratives of identity which Beckett's work so thoroughly
excoriates, that the project of decolonization finds its unpredictable
resources. In the meantime, Beckett's own œuvre, as inaugurated by
First Love/Premier Amour, stands as the most exhaustive dismantling
we have of the logic of identity that at every level structures and
maintains the post-colonial moment.

NOTES

1. I have elaborated the political function of aesthetic culture in relationship to
British imperialism in Ireland in 'Arnold, Ferguson, Schiller: Aesthetic Culture
and the Politics of Aesthetics', *Cultural Critique*, no. 2 (Winter 1985–6), pp.
137–69.
2. Samuel Beckett, *First Love and Other Stories* (New York 1974), p. 18. Page
references cited in the text hereafter.
3. Daniel Corkery, *Synge and Anglo-Irish Literature* (Cork 1931), pp. 2–4. Page
references cited in the text hereafter.
4. For a discussion of Corkery's shift in attitude, see Declan Kiberd, 'Writers in
Quarantine? The Case For Irish Studies', *The Crane Bag*, 3, no. 1 (1979), p. 348.
5. On the background to administrative modernization in nineteenth-century Ireland generally, see F.S.L. Lyons, *Ireland Since the Famine* (London 1971), chapter
3. Jacqueline Hill, 'The Intelligentsia and Irish Nationalism in the 1840s', *Studia
Hibernica*, 20 (1980), p. 94, argues for the impact of the British state in Ireland on
the integration of the population as well as on the centralization of its apparatuses. She also shows, *passim*, the primarily middle-class composition of the Young

Ireland movement.

6. See note 18 to 'Adulteration and the Nation' below for some sources for and reservations about these widely held assumptions. The main point here is that the belief in the virtually irrevocable decline of Irish speaking had a decisive effect on early Irish cultural nationalism.

7. The best general survey of the linguistic orientation of European nationalisms is still Elie Kedourie, *Nationalism* (London 1961).

8. Thomas Davis, 'Our National Language', *Nation*, 1 April 1843, p. 304.

9. On these two aspects of aesthetic culture and their relation to a quasi-political theory of representation, see my article 'Arnold, Ferguson, Schiller', pp. 163-9.

10. See Karl Marx, 'On the Jewish Question', in *Early Writings*, Rodney Livingstone and Gregor Benton (trans.) (New York 1975), p. 220.

11. James Joyce connects this famous oratorical moment to Bloom's mellifluous fart in *Ulysses* (New York 1986), pp. 238-9. See Colin MacCabe's discussion of this passage in *James Joyce and the Revolution of the Word* (London 1979), pp. 87-8.

12. Samuel Beckett, 'MacGreevy on Yeats', in Ruby Cohn (ed.), *Disjecta: Miscellaneous Writings and a Dramatic Fragment* (New York 1984), p. 97. This essay contains some caustic remarks on nationalist appropriations of Jack B. Yeats's painting.

13. The transformations of the prostitute's name here recall two equally celebrated prostitutes in literary history: Wedekind's Lulu and Thomas De Quincey's Ann. As is well known, the latter recurs throughout the *Confessions of an English Opium-Eater* as the dream figure of De Quincey's identity in flight.

14. Julia Kristeva, 'The Father, Love, and Banishment', in Leon S. Roudiez (ed.), *Desire in Language: A Semiotic Approach to Literature and Art*, Thomas Gora, Alice Jardine and Leon S. Roudiez (trans.) (New York 1980), p. 149. This gapped song recalls the 'great gaps in Irish song' that inspired Thomas Davis and the Young Ireland movement to recompose the Irish literary tradition by translation and invention. See Davis, 'Irish Songs', *Nation*, 4 January 1845, p. 202, and below, 'Adulteration and the Nation', for further discussion of the loaded representation of Irish oral culture as 'gapped' or disjointed.

15. See Beckett, 'Dante ... Bruno. Vico ... Joyce', *Disjecta*, p. 19.

16. See J.W. von Goethe, *Wilhelm Meisters Lehrjahre* in *Werke*, vol. 10: *Romane und Erzählungen II* (Berlin 1962), pp. 149-50, and, for English translation used here, Thomas Carlyle, *Wilhelm Meister's Apprenticeship and Travels. Translated from the German of Goethe*, 3 vols (London 1888), pp. 124-5. Space does not allow the fuller discussion of the disjunctive relation everywhere observable between Beckett's prose writings and the tradition of the *Bildungsroman*. Kristeva refers to this song as 'probably remaining in that unnamable domain of the father', but does not identify it further: 'The Father, Love, and Banishment', p. 153. It is perhaps opportune to mention here that, whereas it is the burden of Kristeva's argument to suggest that Beckett's writings lead one to the threshold of a properly feminine writing, my argument would be that a similar case could be argued for his relation to the writing of post-colonialism.

17. On this law, and the contradictions within monogamous marriage forms which it seeks to resolve, see Friedrich Engels, *The Origin of the Family, Private Property and the State*, Eleanor Burke Leacock (ed.) (New York 1972), pp. 130-1.

18. On the application to Ireland of 'dependency theory', originally produced to

account for structures of dependency in 'developing' Latin American nations, see Colm Regan, 'Latin American Dependency Theory and Its Relevance to Ireland', *The Crane Bag*, 6.2 (1982), pp. 15–20.

19. Frantz Fanon, *The Wretched of the Earth*, Constance Farrington (trans.) (New York 1968), p. 204.

20. Octavio Paz, 'Primitives and Barbarians', in *Alternating Currents*, Helen R. Lane (trans.) (New York 1973), p. 27.

21. Beckett, 'Recent Irish Poetry', *Disjecta*, p. 70.

THE POETICS OF POLITICS: YEATS
AND THE FOUNDING OF THE STATE

But not a single form of government is legitimate for all their eternal principles. You see *principle* means *origin*, you must always go back to a revolution, an act of violence, some transient event.

Gustave Flaubert, *Sentimental Education*[1]

The reading and rereading of Yeats's later poetry and prose with a view to comprehending the political implications of his post-nationalist writing might well bring to mind a remark of Bertolt Brecht's on Shakespeare's *Coriolanus*. When an actor was troubled by Shakespeare's representation of the plebeians, Brecht insisted on finding value in this awkwardness, 'Because it gives rise to discomfort.'[2] Certainly Yeats continues to cause discomfort, at least to any critic unwilling to separate the aesthetic too readily from the political. The difficulty lies most evidently, of course, in the fact that we must acknowledge, when all quibble and interpretation 'is done and said', the avowed authoritarianism, if not downright fascist sympathies, of his stated politics, while at the same time acknowledging the power of his writing to return and to haunt. I do not think that these terms, borrowed from a Yeatsian lexicon, are too strong: it is as if the very obsessiveness of Yeats's own later poetry, living and reliving its relatively sparse themes and symbols, speaks to a situation, at once 'psychic' and 'political', which we have yet to work through. For when Yeats broods late in life on the probability that that play of his 'sent out certain men the English shot', this is by no means an overweening assessment of the extraordinary part his writings played in the forging in Ireland of a mode of subjectivity apt to find its political and ethical realization in sacrifice to the nation yet to be.[3] If then, as I believe to be the case, the later Yeats dwells poetically on the consequences both for the political state and for individual subjects of the triumph of a nationalism whose militant expression absorbs and displaces his own cultural nationalism, we have good

59

reason to attend. This is all the more so when in the lines just alluded to, as so often, the meditation on the conditions for the foundation of the state intersects with a meditation on the conditions for writing poetry – on its founding 'themes'.

All this is to suggest neither that we abandon political judgment to aesthetic adoration nor that there is anything to be gained by simple ethical condemnation. Several critics have discussed at length the extent of Yeats's commitment to fascism and have disagreed in their conclusions.[4] There is no need to recapitulate their arguments here. For, though I hope to show that Yeats's authoritarian political predilections are as insistent as they are consistent with his aesthetic, that argument is of little avail when it comes to the attempt to comprehend the obsessive, haunting quality of his poetry. For whether we condemn the politics and proceed to address the poetry as if it were purged of its political implications or cast out the poetry with the politics, we must assume either the separability of the poetic and the political or the secondariness of the poetic to the political, its status as a translation of political interest, so to speak. In either case the constitutive role played by the aesthetic in the political sphere, as by the political in the aesthetic, is left unaddressed. Any judgment made in the absence of such a questioning is able to assume equally that the difficulties raised by the seeming inexorability with which the logic of Western European history and culture led to fascism are peripheral to the continuing work of aesthetic culture. In the era of what the Frankfurt School termed the 'administered society', we might be better to ask whether fascism, in all its specificities, represents an end or a beginning.[5] Insofar as the ends of any state are questioned in the questioning of its foundations, Yeats's insistent brooding on the issue of political and poetic foundation holds these questions open in a manner which continues to arrest our thinking.

I shall argue that the political questions raised by Yeats's later poetry are inseparable from aesthetic questions, just as, in his earlier writings, a symbolist aesthetic is inseparable from the politics of cultural nationalism. But where the earlier writings are devoted to the project of founding and forging a nation, the later writings, in the wake of the Irish Free State's foundation, subject all acts of foundation to the most rigorous examination within a set of aesthetic terms which are profoundly antithetical to any tradition of symbolism.[6]

I will commence then, not with a thematic discussion of Yeats's politics as revealed in his later poetry, for all the difficulty they may cause us, but, rather, with another kind of difficulty which the volume presents in the most intimate workings of its poetic language. Yeats is not a poet usually associated with semantic obscurity: the difficulties presented by his work are usually held to be resolvable through a proper, or fuller, understanding of his symbols or images, complex as these and their interrelationships may be. Nonetheless, a volume like *The Winding Stair* presents numerous instances of obscurities which are grounded in its rhetorical strategies and which precede any attempt to interpret its structures of imagery or argument. The kind of problem I have in mind is well exemplified at certain moments in 'Byzantium', a poem already notoriously obscure on account of the density of its imagery. The obscurity of the poem might well cause us a little amused perplexity, since Yeats composed it in part as a gloss for Sturge Moore of the earlier 'Sailing to Byzantium'.[7] That the poem should have the status of a gloss is not inappropriate to its theme. As we know from *A Vision*, Byzantium represented for Yeats a culture which had achieved 'Unity of Being':

I think that in early Byzantium, maybe never before or since in recorded history, religious, aesthetic and practical life were one, that architects and artificers – though not, it may be, poets, for language had become the instrument of controversy and must have grown abstract – spoke to the multitude and the few alike. The painter, the mosaic worker, the worker in gold and silver, the illuminator of sacred books, were almost impersonal, almost perhaps without the consciousness of individual design, absorbed in their subject-matter and that the vision of a whole people. (pp. 279–80)

Only the poets are excluded here – 'though not, it may be, poets' – from what is otherwise an image of changeless unity. The unity of Byzantium, however, is similarly troubled by theological dispute: clearly there is something in the use of language and in the process of gloss and interpretation which profoundly disturbs the achievement of unity in architectural, sculptural or visual arts. In its turn, the poem 'Byzantium', itself an interpretation, seems haunted by the trouble of a language which insistently invokes interpretation. Take, for example, its second stanza:

> Before me floats an image, man or shade,
> Shade more than man, more image than a shade;
> For Hades' bobbin wound in mummy-cloth

May unwind the winding path;
A mouth that has no moisture and no breath
Breathless mouths may summon;
I hail the superhuman;
I call it death-in-life and life-in-death.

What this stanza represents is already unclear, though it certainly refers back to the last poem of *The Tower*, 'All Souls' Night', which is also the epilogue to *A Vision*, as 'Byzantium' as a whole refers to the first poem in that volume, 'Sailing to Byzantium'. The last stanza of 'All Souls' Night' might assure us that the unwinding of the winding path by 'Hades' bobbin' alludes to a purgatorial act of reliving one's life after death, a theme which runs throughout *The Winding Stair*. Such a reading, however, still does not resolve the meaning of the image in the larger context of the poem. I can offer no resolution to that problem and make no apology for leaving the question in suspension in order to turn to the other, rhetorical obscurities which the stanza equally exemplifies. The first is a syntactical ambiguity which would not have great significance except that the same grammatical form is found, to similar effect, in the following stanza. In the line 'Before me floats an image, man or shade,' one hesitates momentarily before deciding whether 'image, man or shade' is a list of equivalent and alternative substantives, or one substantive, 'image', qualified uncertainly by one or other of two further substantives in apposition, 'man or shade'. Certainly, this ambiguity is rapidly resolved by the following line and, a point I will return to, would cause no trouble in a *performance* of the poem. Nonetheless, this moment of hesitation belongs with a pattern of similar ambiguities in this and other poems that I would term 'redundant', being unable to assign any thematic function to them individually beyond the refractory resonances which, collectively, they set in motion.

Of more crucial importance to any interpretation of this stanza is the reading of the lines:

A mouth that has no moisture and no breath
Breathless mouths may summon.

These produce a syntactical ambiguity which is resolutely irreducible, since it is impossible to decide whether the subject of this sentence is 'A mouth' which may summon 'Breathless mouths' or 'Breathless mouths' which may summon 'A mouth'. To decide one way or another would make considerable difference to one's understanding of the cultic – or political – direction of the image: is it, for example, the mouth that gathers and organizes the assembly, Nuremberg-like, or the many mouths which invoke, as at the festival of the Supreme Being, the one mouth? Final choice is detained by the undecidability of the syntax producing one of those effects of vertiginous reversibility which, as we shall see further, produce a radical destabilization of meaning in *The Winding Stair*.

At this juncture, I want to insist on the purely rhetorical nature of such cruxes and on their absolute irreducibility for interpretation. Any decision made at the syntactic level must be informed by an interpretative choice whose arbitrariness is signalled by its very decision to decide between grammatically absolutely equivalent possibilities. No appeal to external evidence can assist the reader, since whatever evidence is adduced will always be inflected or limited by the necessity of an exclusive grammatical decision. Other such moments occur in later stanzas. In the fourth,

> Where blood-begotten spirits come
> And all complexities of fury leave,

may be read to assert that the spirits, in coming, depart from complexity, where 'spirits' is the subject of both 'come' and 'leave', or that as the 'spirits come', so 'complexities of fury leave', where spirits and complexities would each be subjects in their own right, crossing one another's path, so to speak, in departure and arrival. In the final stanza, the lines 'Those images that yet/Fresh images beget' leaves it similarly uncertain whether it is the 'Fresh images' or 'Those images' that do the begetting, and, further, uncertain whether 'That dolphin-torn, that gong-tormented sea' is a fresh image which is begotten, one of 'those images' out of which 'fresh images' are begotten, or, as is quite possible, an image of images in apposition to all that has gone before which summarizes paratactically the interchange of uncertain and complex images begotten upon the sea alternately by the fleshly and mobile dolphins and the austere, formal gong. In every case, the grammatical decision makes a real difference to how one conceives Yeats's depiction of the relation between, for example, form and matter in the creative process: whether, for instance, the process of forming is final or is constantly threatened by the very material it needs to overcome. In every case, that decision is strictly speaking impossible, insofar as every decision must ignore and exclude syntactically equally valid but semantically incompatible readings.[8]

This crux is, of course, entirely apposite to a poem which is apparently concerned with, among other things, the generation and mastery of images and which is tormented by the question of control. Are the 'smithies' who 'break the flood' aloof masters taming its fury from above or, like breakwaters, immersed in and potentially eroded by what breaks over them? As I have suggested, the impossibility of resolving the syntactic cruxes of the poem satisfactorily is met by an equally inescapable impossibility of *not* resolving them in any and every reading, and especially in a reading which performs the poem aloud. Yeats, a poet for whom performance was always a crucial preoccupation of poetic creation, was doubtless highly aware of this, and it is scarcely accidental if what are from every perspective the obscurest lines of the poem seem to evoke, as if in response to their very obscurity, a set of performative speech acts which are exceptionally common in the later Yeats.[9]

> I hail the superhuman;
> I call it death-in-life and life-in-death.

Not that this invocation and this naming resolves anything for us: the very reversibility of identification that was our syntactical problem persists, as does the problem of defining its cultic or political valency. But, in the face of the irreducible refractoriness of language, the purely formal intervention of a performative speech act may appear to reaffirm the authority of the poet, who might otherwise seem swamped by the energies of his own material. Such emphasis on acts of voicing tends to assert vigorously the continuing (self-) presence of the poet precisely where one might have most cause to question the unity of his intentions.

Indeed, the recourse to performatives at this juncture only compounds our problems of understanding, since it is by individual authorial fiat that allegorical significance is assigned to the image of the mouth here. Personal arrogation of the power of naming – 'I hail', 'I call it ... ' – prevents any easy assumption that the allegory is rooted in a generally recognizable body of traditional correspondences. The allegorical image, or, in other, more Yeatsian terms, the 'emblem', equally intervenes to prevent a reading of the poem in relation to that tradition of symbolism wherein an organic continuity inheres between the particular symbol and the universal totality which it represents, difficult as it may be at times to recompose the universal from the particulars.[10] Thus, while it may be reassuring to be referred to the mosaic pavement of the Byzantine forum for the origins of 'the Emperor's pavement', or to mystical traditions for the dolphins and the 'flames begotten of flame', this knowledge helps us little in understanding the poem. The meaning of the image emerges, rather, in a quite radical, even arrogant, detachment of the sign from any referent in the real, its significance being looked for rather in the overall syntax of its possibly shifting and certainly cumulative relationship to other, similarly dislocated signs.[11]

What is asserted of the quasi-mythical Byzantium is perhaps even more true of the apparently more naturalistic poems in *The Winding Stair*. To take one instance, the opening stanza of 'Coole and Bally-lee, 1931' appears on first reading to be a quite referential descrip-tion of the path of the river between two locations, and it is only the stanza's final line which disturbs that assumption:

> Under my window-ledge the waters race,
> Otters below and moor-hens on the top,
> Run for a mile undimmed in Heaven's face
> Then darkening through 'dark' Raftery's 'cellar' drop,
> Run underground, rise in a rocky place
> In Coole demesne, and there to finish up
> Spread to a lake and drop into a hole.
> What's water but the generated soul?

That final interpretation of the whole scenario forces one to a re-reading, noting the careful distribution of elements above and below, the allegorical significance of the descent of the waters, the cryptic network of significance invoked by the allusion to the blind Gaelic poet Raftery, and, if one attend either to the Ordnance Survey or to the editor's notes, the quite arrogant indifference to the actual land-scape: Ballylee's river does not emerge as a lake in Coole Park.[12] It is a mark of the success of Yeats's arrogation of landscape to allegory that it takes us so long to recognize, if we do at all, that the proper response to the question 'What's water but the generated soul?' might simply be 'Many things.' The triumph of rhetoric is for a rhet-orical question to become an unquestioned fiat, coercing landscape and reader alike into complicity with allegory. Yeats's writing here is far from the consolatory tradition in recent Irish poetry which seeks to maintain symbolic continuity between place and poetic intention, however much that tradition may seem to take its permission from his will.[13]

Yeats is rather more our contemporary here, recognizing before its time that principle of contemporary advertising which knows that for a reader to be confronted openly with hype is not for that reader to be any less sold on the product. 'Coole and Ballylee, 1931' is a truly hyperbolic performance, the line of its argument casting far beyond any apparently natural setting.[14] The arrogance of the performance is such that it virtually blinds the recipient to the visualization which its rhetorical flourish dares:

> And in a copse of beeches there I stood,
> For Nature's pulled her tragic buskin on
> And all the rant's a mirror to my mood.

If the naturalistic description up to the first line here cited provokes visualization and the attempt to compose a naturally symbolic land-scape, the improbable image of Nature in buskins in conjunction with a ranting assertion of correspondence between that hyperbolic landscape and the subjective mood seem virulently to parody that attempt. The pathetic fallacy here so knowingly asserted is under-written by an unapologetically flaunted tense shift which accentuates the performative power of an imagination deliberately eschewing or-ganic correspondence in favour of the setting of 'another emblem there'.[15]

For the sudden appearance of the swan here in the moment of its vanishing mimes the process by which a minimal reference to a real representation ('actual shells of Rosses' level shore') subtends the curve of allegorical hyperbole. The assuredness of the rhetoric per-mits what is in fact metaphoric drift to appear as merely an extension of natural correspondence, whereas, in the following lines, 'morning' is dragged in purely in service of the extended *allegory* to which alone it can be referred:

> And, like the soul, it sails into the sight
> And in the morning's gone, no man knows why.

In the very arrogance which constitutes their grace, such gratuitous acts of the allegorical imagination are precisely what the swan itself allegorizes – the wilful if beautiful appropriation of theological acts of grace in order to redeem simultaneously knowledge and ignorance:

> And is so lovely that it sets to right
> What knowledge or its lack had set awry,
> So arrogantly pure, a child might think
> It can be murdered with a spot of ink.

Only the mind in which ignorance is still the condition of innocence would think to appeal now to organic purity against the artifice of *written* allegory. The purity of the image is rather the reappropriation of grace by arrogation, is realized in, not sullied by, artificiality.[16]

It is thus, of course, that this apparently robust process of allegorization rejoins with the melancholy traditionally associated with allegory.[17] For precisely as the emblem arises in the vanishing of its real referent, so the aristocratic house of Coole Park, with its redeemingly artificial 'ceremonies of innocence', is to be celebrated only in the moment of its demise. This is neither accurate prophecy nor uncanny insight on Yeats's part, but at most a transformation of what both he and Lady Gregory knew to be imminent, the destruction of Coole Park, into the basis of a poetics. As in 'Coole Park, 1929', it is on the exposed 'foundations of a house' that the poet 'takes his stand', the poetic act being the foundation of a tradition in its demise. One is reminded of Yeats's remark that Burns represents the end, not the beginning, of a tradition, a remark which is reflected in his own position in the 'We were the last romantics' of the final stanza.

This act of settlement is nonetheless poised carefully and shrewdly against the image of the nomad:

> Where fashion or mere fantasy decrees
> Man shifts about – all that great glory spent –
> Like some poor Arab tribesman and his tent.

What looks here like mere deprecation by contrast is more complex: nomadism, normally taken to *precede* the foundation of settled civilizations, is here taken to come in their wake – 'all that great glory spent' – and one might reflect that the very emblems through which the foundations of the house are celebrated are fashioned deliberately by the arbitrary decree of Yeats's mere fantasy. Decree is the very process by which foundation is established poetically in the moment of its actual demise. The poem's achieved design is to forge a moment of foundation out of the explicit failure to produce the epic which would ensure the foundation or renewal of a tradition:

> But all is changed, that high horse riderless,
> Though mounted in that saddle Homer rode
> Where the swan drifts upon a darkening flood.

The conjunction of an appeal to the Homeric epic tradition (clearly assimilated here to 'what poets name/The book of the people') with the assertion of the faltering or aborting of that tradition induces another of those moments of syntactic instability which we have seen to produce redundant ambiguities. The inversion which defers Homer to the end of the line makes the past participle 'mounted' refer logically to the 'high horse riderless'. In this case, we need to read the lines to mean that even though this horse, the Pegasus of heroic legend, is still mounted in the same saddle as that in which Homer rode, it is riderless here at Coole Park 'where the swan drifts upon a darkening flood'. Alternatively, we read the lines to mean that the high horse is now riderless despite the fact that Homer once rode it here where the swan now drifts. It would be easy to contend that the first of these readings strains against the natural grain of the lines, were it not for the paradox that the more natural reading, the second, places a much greater strain on the imagination, forcing the entirely hyperbolic claim that Homer actually rode at Coole Park. The most conventional reading of the syntax produces the highest degree of poetic arrogation while the equally logical, though less conventional, reading produces a more unexceptionable assertion. As Yeats reminds us, he is here on his 'high horse' rhetorically, performing a linguistic *tour de force* whose instability plays paradoxically for a reinforcement of his control.

To try to summarize and clarify what is occurring here demands holding both sides of a paradox simultaneously in mind. The poem is about a founding, but about one which is poetically brought into being only in the moment of its demise. It asserts the value of settlement and tradition, but in a language and imagery which are deliberately and even hyperbolically detached from any organically mimetic relationship to their supposed setting. It asserts correspondence between the mind and its natural 'mirror' (already a strong inversion of the more conventional reflection of nature in the mind) while at the same time radically denaturalizing its natural imagery. It is as though it is precisely in his radical dislocation that the poet, unlike his 'poor Arab tribesman' perhaps, finds the sources of his power, with the result that even, if not most intensely, the very destabilization of his language becomes the index of his strength.

Deft allusion to a poem other than Homer's in these last lines indicates both the reasons for that dislocation and the necessity for the process of recuperation in which Yeats is engaged. That the poem is his own coheres with the act of self-begetting which he is here setting in motion, becoming his own tradition. I refer to the allusion to 'Easter 1916' in 'But all is changed', which takes up the earlier poem's celebrated refrain: 'All changed, changed utterly'. At the very moment where Yeats in 'Coole and Ballylee, 1931' seeks to retrieve a poetic tradition from its demise, he dares reference to the poem in his canon which most thoroughly explores the poet's marginalization or redundancy. For where 'Coole and Ballylee' writes out the failure to maintain epic continuity between the tradition of one family and that of the people, 'Easter 1916' concerns the foundation of a nation by the transformation of individuals into symbols. What disturbs Yeats here, though, is that this transformation takes place not through the intermediary of poetry but in consequence of violence itself. The passive voice of 'All changed, changed utterly' betrays the secondariness of poetic reflection to a process of transformation which has already completed itself, impersonally, as it were.

Simultaneously, change appears in two other domains, that of the poet's function *vis-à-vis* the national struggle and that of reflection upon the symbol. Yeats, as is well known, devoted three decades of his life to a cultural nationalism whose object was to forge a sense of national identity in Irish subjects such that their own personal identity would be fulfilled only in the creation of the nation. For the Irish tradition of cultural nationalism, literature has always had a primary productive role, both in providing the national institutions that stood in for the political institutions yet to be, and in forming citizens in anticipation of the founding of the state of which they were to be the citizens. Within this tradition, the literary artist represents the nation in the fullest possible sense, not only depicting its life-forms, but simultaneously speaking in its name and being its exemplary prefiguration. This tradition clearly demands of the artist a total ethical and cultural identification with the nation. The national artist not only deploys symbols, but is a symbol, participating organically in what he represents, that is, the spiritual identity of the nation-yet-to-be.[18] It is this function which seems to be erased by the Easter Rising of 1916, the poet losing his projective or prefigurative role to one which is merely commemorative:

> our part
> To murmur name upon name,
> As a mother names her child
> When sleep at last has come
> On limbs that had run wild.

Not only is it surprising to find Yeats adopting a collective pronoun and figuring it in a maternal image, but the act itself is clearly a redundant one: the obsessive repetition of the child's name after it is asleep no longer serves as a lullaby, but only asserts one's own anxious continuity with it in its virtual absence. It is one of Yeats's earliest reflections upon the obsessive rituals of repetition by which nation states assure the legitimacy of their foundations and maintain their equilibrium.

I shall return to this point, as also to the question of gender which this image raises. I want first, however, to examine further the function of the symbol for nationalism and Yeats's implicit reflection upon that here, since, though in different terms, I would concur with Samuel Hynes in finding 'Easter 1916' to mark a certain rupture in Yeats's poetics. Where Hynes traces a greater awareness of evil, I would concentrate rather on Yeats's intense questioning of the status of the symbol and on the legitimacy of the artistic act.[19] These two are not entirely separable. In a famous letter to Lady Gregory, written shortly after the Easter Rising, Yeats mentions how a couple of years earlier Maud Gonne had told him of her dream in which she saw Dublin in flames and in the grip of armed struggle. Yeats remarked to her then that if this dream were prophetic, it was so in a purely symbolic sense.[20] We can read here Yeats's own anxiety as to the appropriation of symbols by militant nationalism, an anxiety which concerns his own possible displacement. That displacement would, of course, be perfectly logical. When Patrick Pearse refers to the national martyrs as 'burning symbols', his terms are as much aesthetic as religious. Just as the poet represents the nation he prefigures, so the martyr in his death identifies utterly with the nation to which he appeals. The acts of militant nationalism are always more significant as symbols than as pragmatic deeds. Both nationalist poetry and nationalist violence have the same end: to organize the incoherent desires of the population towards the goal of popular unity, which is the essential prerequisite of an effective political struggle for national liberation. The narrative of symbolism is one which progressively leads its subjects on by way of symbols which are consubstantial with the nation which they represent. There is thus a very real sense in which those martyrs, whose self-sacrifice in the name of Ireland asserts their utter identity with the nation, displace or substitute for the poet's symbolic deployment of the lore and landscape of the country. Both intend, as Yeats put it in speaking of his early decision to turn to Gaelic matter, to 'deepen the political passion of the nation that all, artist and poet, craftsman and day-labourer would accept a common design'.[21]

What is crucial to the design in both cases is the organic continuity between the symbol and what it represents. The national martyr is a member of the inchoate people of which he seeks to make a unified nation; Kathleen Ni Houlihan or Knocknarea are elements of the tradition which has yet to be fulfilled as a poetic unity. Similarly the narrative of desire invoked here is always implicitly one of return, the ultimate return of the desiring subject to identity with itself, a desire therefore which is perpetually deferred and in turn perpetually invoked until symbol, subject and nation come to form a single totality. It is the narrative of that desire which Yeats figures in relation to *The Wanderings of Oisin* as the ceaseless pursuit of the hornless deer by a hound with one red ear: 'the desire of the man, which is for the woman, and the desire of the woman which is for the desire of the man', as Yeats elsewhere glosses it. The dissymmetry keeps open the pursuit in a perpetual deferral which could find closure only in death, but it is the promise of ultimate reconciliation that provides the motive force for a desire that *in its process* is as politically formative as it is erotically compulsive.[22]

The paradox of 'Easter 1916' is that the achievement of such politically symbolic status, the transformation of lout or clown into martyr that brings about the foundation of the nation, is seen to produce not reconciliation but a troubled tension. The tension subsists metaphorically between the symbolic 'stone' and the continuing 'living stream' that it troubles; the question posed is the relation between the singular moment in which a nation is founded or constituted and the future history of the citizens it brings into being. Yeats represents that relationship as simultaneously one of trouble and of anxious, obsessive rememoration. For though the stone, like any symbol, continues to reside 'in the midst of all', its finality as gravestone on which the names of the national martyrs are inscribed would appear to be at odds with the opening of a future history which its function as foundation-stone implies. Its double status obliges a continual recurrence to and questioning of the moment of foundation it represents, with the result that the formerly unificatory function of the symbol is irrevocably ruptured.

Yeats's questions are therefore not so rhetorically disabling to the claims of the men of 1916 as they first appear, being tonally genuinely ambivalent: 'Was it *needless* death after all?' or 'Was it needless death(,) after all?' and 'What if *excess of love*/Bewildered them till they died?' or 'What if excess of love/Bewildered them till they died?' That second question as I have last stressed it, one whose form is notoriously exploited in 'Meditations in Time of Civil War' as the index of transhuman indifference, here also implies an answer which tends violently to annul all questioning: the historical fiat of the founding of a nation is finally indifferent either to the motives or to the legitimacy or necessity of the act performed. The founding of any nation state is necessarily an act of violence irrupting as an absolute discontinuity in the course of history, an utter transformation by way of a singularly transformative utterance, and its legitimacy is established not in itself but in the subsequent rememoration it invokes.

The logic of this acknowledgment is deeply antagonistic to the symbolist tradition that informed cultural nationalism and gave, however disingenuously, an ethical structure to militant nationalism. This is not, of course, to express a preference, ethical or otherwise, for one version of nationalism over another. Cultural nationalism, in Ireland as elsewhere, continues to legitimate a state ultimately founded and maintained by a violence whose explicitness alone varies, while militant nationalism continues to appeal to an organic model of representation to justify its symbolic acts of violence. An appeal to ethics is beside the point where it is precisely this organic model of representation which is to be questioned, common as it is to both versions of nationalism, and fundamental to any ethical judgment of a political act or system. For when Pearse, in the name of the people of Ireland, declares Ireland's independence, he does so in a purely performative act that simultaneously constitutes that people and his own status as its representative. This act spells the passage from a symbolic nationalism that seeks to develop the nation in continuity with what it conceives as its original, self-identical essence, to an 'allegorical state' whose relationship to that which it represents is always by appeal to an arbitrary act of constitution.[23]

In the repeated acts of commemoration required by the allegorical state to revalidate the legitimacy of its representative function, we may find equally the rationale for that most striking but little-interrogated phrase, 'A terrible beauty is born'. It is a phrase which imperiously collapses two fundamental and distinct aesthetic categories, the sublime and the beautiful. Commemoration ensures the reproduction of a social form by way of the reinvocation of the moment of terror that founded it. In traditional aesthetics, those two categories are systematically distinguished in all their elements: the sublime is referred to the masculine domain of production and transcendence evoked in response to the terror of death and the potential dissolution of the self; the beautiful, on the other hand, is relegated to the feminine sphere of reproduction, both literally and in the sense of the harmonious reproduction of social forms. Both cultural and militant nationalism appeal to a version of the sublime, seeking to transcend death even in death by identifying with the greater life of the nation they are producing.[24] The actual foundation of the nation spells the end of this horizon of transcendence, as it spells an end to the developmental desire of cultural nationalism, absorbing terror into the heretofore feminine sphere of rememorative reproduction. Hence the necessary slippage in 'Easter 1916' from the militant (and therefore tasteless) Countess Markievicz to the mother 'murmuring name upon name', terror of dissolution being relegated to a sphere in which, in a certain sense, it in any case originated, that of reproduction.[25]

A sacrifice that thus leads to no further transcendence is one that seeks to establish itself outside historical time, to lodge in the unchanging space of a rupture in history. The foundation of the nation puts an end to the epic of its historical destiny in a performative act that abolishes history at the same time as it allows the epic to be fulfilled. The abolition of history, however, abolishes equally any principle by which the antinomies that organize the categories of nationalist thought – as indeed of all forms of bourgeois thought – can be synthesized, if only proleptically, by development towards reconciliation. The temporal space that opens in place of abolished historical time threatens to be filled by the merely formal antagonism between antinomial categories: the private interest and the public will, the human and the natural, the individual and the state, and so forth. What actually intervenes to contain this threat is the displacement of history into cultural education: culture becomes a sphere of reproduction – or recreation – rather than production, repetitively mediating the interpellation of individual subjects into citizens by way of a canon of works formally identical in their 'designs'.

Yet the undeniable fact that, perhaps more than any other modern poet, with the possible exception of T.S. Eliot, Yeats's work has been absorbed into the institutions of cultural education can be explained only in terms of the enormous interpretative effort of humanization and naturalization brought to bear on it, particularly the later work. Against this recuperative tradition, I would argue that Yeats's reaction to the rupture that 'Easter 1916' represents, within his own œuvre as in history itself, is at once relentlessly extreme and profoundly unsettling in political terms. For, far from seeking to offer aesthetic reconciliation, he writes out to its logical extremes the lesson of an act that threatened to displace him both as a poet whose cultural work becomes redundant and as one of the 'colonizers who refuse'.[26] This writing *in extremis* proceeds on four levels, distinct but interrelated: a refusal of a symbolism founded in an organic model of natural representation in favour of an allegorical mode; a wresting from the very condition of dislocation of a language use which depends for its authority on authorial fiat alone, being anti-mimetic and performative; the radical deployment of antinomies which, if posited in pure formality, often gain an extraordinary degree of semantic instability by the inorganic arrangements through which their elements produce meaning; a sustained reflection on the political significance of violence and death as the condition of any act of foundation.

III

Antinomy provides the structural principle of *The Winding Stair* at every level, though this involves neither bald opposition nor developmental synthesis, however much the title of the volume might seem to imply this latter. Certainly antinomy involves the principle that by 1933 is fundamental to Yeats's thought, namely, self-realization through opposition, and entails a transformation of his earlier, developmental notion of symbolism. The two principles are identical both for self-development and for the formation of national identity. The passage quoted above from *The Autobiography* on the need to 'deepen the political passion of the nation' is followed by this account of a later conviction:

Nations, races, and individual men are unified by an image, or bundle of related images, symbolical or evocative of a state of mind, which is of all states of mind not impossible, the most difficult to that man, race, or nation; because only the greatest obstacle that can be contemplated without despair rouses the will to full intensity. (*The Autobiography*, pp. 119–20)

The self-realization through opposition that Yeats here envisages is radically counter to the developmental organization of desire through organic symbols. It is also radically anti-historical, the time required being the purely formal and reversible, gyring time of transformation rather than the irreversible temporality of history.

These principles inform 'A Dialogue of Self and Soul', which furnishes the volume *The Winding Stair* with its title, determining the antithetical images through which each seeks its realization. On the one hand, the Soul, seeking fixity beyond thought and process, must establish as its emblem the winding stair, an image of process and movement, within the tower, which, though from one perspective an image of stability, is depicted as broken and crumbling. The instability of the image's valence is compacted if we recall that in the Tarot the tower is the card not of permanence but of imminent change. Rhetorically, the images are 'set' not mimetically but performatively:

> I *summon* to the winding ancient stair;
> *Set* all your mind upon the steep ascent,
> Upon the broken, crumbling battlement,
> Upon the breathless starlit air,
> Upon the star that marks the hidden pole;
> *Fix* every wandering thought upon
> That quarter where all thought is done (my italics)

Performative presentation reduces what could be taken as purely mimetically represented – the stair, the battlement, the starlit air – to equivalence with the purely emblematical – wandering thought, the hidden pole – both being subordinated to a rhetorical question that, as in the first stanza of 'Coole and Ballylee', is really an assertion of identity: 'Who can distinguish darkness from the soul?'

This assertion on the soul's part is met by the Self's retort, a descriptive image of the sword, which, as a counter-image, is fittingly 'still'. This word, repeated four times in a single stanza, accentuates the unchanging nature of the blade, whose curve, like the moon with which it is associated in 'The Tower', gives form to the emblems of change which entwine it:

> The consecrated blade upon my knees
> Is Sato's ancient blade, still as it was,
> Still razor-keen, still like a looking-glass
> Unspotted by the centuries;
> That flowering, silken, old embroidery, torn
> From some court-lady's dress and round
> The wooden scabbard bound and wound,
> Can, tattered, still protect, faded adorn.

I accentuate the formative rather than the *potentially* destructive nature of the sword in order to point up the formality of the representation of change in this poem as, indeed, throughout *The Winding Stair*. For Yeats is not so much interested here in historical time as in a pre-established form of transformation, imaged in the moon of 'Blood and the Moon', through which all things return into their opposites without ever overcoming the antinomies that determine their cycles – or gyres – of change. Or rather, if an end is postulated, it is the *same* end for both Self and Soul, the end of all dialogue in death. As Yeats put it in 'Pages from a Diary in 1930':

I am always, in all I do, driven to a moment which is the realisation of myself as unique and free, or to a moment which is the surrender to God of all that I am ... Could those two impulses, one as much a part of the truth as the other, be reconciled, or if one or the other could prevail, all life would cease. (*Explorations*, p. 305)

Evidently the condition of self-realization for the Soul entails the end of antinomy at the cost of thought itself:

> Such fullness in that quarter overflows
> And falls into the basin of the mind
> That man is stricken deaf and dumb and blind,
> For intellect no longer knows
> *Is* from the *Ought*, or *Knower* from the *Known* –
> That is to say, ascends to Heaven;
> Only the dead can be forgiven;
> But when I think of that my tongue's a stone.

It is perhaps less evident, but for all that no less true, that the end of the Self is identical with that of the Soul. Where the Soul ascends the winding stair towards 'ancestral night', Self in the second section descends that stair which is the ascent, or evolution, of the 'finished' man, repeating it 'again/And yet again' until the bitterness of life's ditches is purged and perfected:

> I am content to follow to its source
> Every event in action or in thought;
> Measure the lot; forgive myself the lot!
> When such as I cast out remorse

So great a sweetness flows into the breast
We must laugh and we must sing,
We are blest by everything,
Everything we look upon is blest.

This concluding stanza is not only a celebration of perfectly achieved repetition, but itself repeats the Soul's final stanza with its imagery of overflowing. And if, according to the Soul, the condition of forgiveness is death – 'Only the dead can be forgiven' – so too the destiny of the Self that forgives itself is a state of reciprocal blessedness achieved by laying itself to rest.

This is one reading of the act of 'casting out remorse' and, by way of conclusion, I shall consider further this complex term of Yeats's lexicon. Before doing so, however, I want to indicate how the complex structuring of the whole volume *The Winding Stair* time and again militates against closure, not in any organic mode of openness but through vigorous, at times even deliberately parodic counter-utterance. The two poems which bracket 'A Dialogue of Self and Soul', 'Death' and 'Blood and the Moon', may seem to suggest that such masterful utterance as 'A Dialogue' deploys is at once the condition of transforming the state of death into a moment of founding, and what troubles all foundation. For if, as 'Death' has it, 'Man has created death', it is no less true that death has created man, recurrent anticipation of death, or 'dread', being what defines man in opposition to the animal. Reading in the light of this poem, we are forcibly reminded that the entry of both Soul and Self into the reconciliation of death is in neither case achieved by any organic process, but precisely by acts of willed self-assertion that achieve only a momentary and tense equilibrium.

The contradiction involved here is taken up in the opening section of 'Blood and the Moon', which almost parodically takes up the conclusion of 'A Dialogue of Self and Soul': 'Blessed be this place,/ More blessed still this tower'. The passive, reciprocal blessing that concludes 'A Dialogue' returns here as wilful utterance, destroying that delicately posed equilibrium in the very act of enunciation. In the return to 'source' which follows, utterance conjoins with power and mastery as the condition of all foundations, 'A bloody, arrogant power' establishing itself in the image of the tower or establishing the tower in its image:

A bloody, arrogant power
Rose out of the race

Uttering, mastering it,
Rose like these walls from these
Storm-beaten cottages

But what the tower now signifies is radically unstable, as is the subject of any performative enunciation, always excluded from what its enunciation constitutes. On the one hand, the tower represents mastery itself, dominating the landscape and the cottages with which it is consubstantial. On the other hand, like the tower struck by lightning in the Tarot pack, it is 'half-dead at the top', caught in a moment of transition between life and death, though which will govern the direction of its transformation is uncertain. For this emblem is established 'in mockery', is antithetical, and one is reminded that the origin of the Fool card in the Tarot is the Egyptian god of writing, who was harried initially, not by a dog but by an ape that reversed and troubled all that the god wrote.[27] Like the 'stone' of 'Easter 1916', the tower becomes a duplicit emblem, it being unclear whether it is set up here in mockery of the arrogant power that, as 'Meditations in Time of Civil War' relates, dwindled, 'Forgetting and forgot', or in mockery of contemporary Ireland. The repetition of the phrase 'In mockery' allows the emblem to point in both directions at once, as well as back to the previous poem, such that the very power of the emblem becomes simultaneously an allegory for the instability of all foundation. By the final stanza, all that subsists is the eternal oscillation between wisdom and power, imaged in the relentless gyring of the lunar cycles, which make a mockery even of mockery itself:

Is every modern nation like the tower,
Half-dead at the top? No matter what I said,
For wisdom is the property of the dead,
A something incompatible with life; and power,
Like everything that has the stain of blood,
A property of the living; but no stain
Can come upon the visage of the moon
When it has looked in glory from a cloud.

Something desolate and empty stirs in the faintly Wordsworthian cadences of those concluding lines. These poems offer no hope of retrieving the reciprocal dance of man and nature that survives now only as the 'malicious dream' tormenting the speakers of the later poem 'The Crazed Moon'. The emblematical power of Yeats's rhetoric is wrested throughout from the ruin of that Romantic tradition in arbitrary declarations of self-creation. We may trace the reasons for this despairing exultation in the poet's own loss of any sense of organic connection with the nation that was founded by Easter 1916, or with his marginalization as a poet of cultural nationalism. If both dislocations find a kind of triumphant expression in the poetic declarations of an alternative Anglo-Irish tradition, the knowingly fictive, performative nature of that act is finally a mockery of any act of foundation claiming representative status. A tradition that finds expression only in its demise is the antithetical image of a state founded in the demise of its founders. Both are perpetuated only in the recurrent act of self-creation, which must constantly locate the foundations of social forms in violence and death rather than continuing organic life.

The terror of these poems lies in the relentlessness with which they discover death at the heart of culture and at the base of the state. Though their exultation in violent acts of the will points the way towards a fascist politics, it draws that political solution from a desperation by no means capable of offering the consolatory myths of belonging on which fascism relies for its legitimation. If, as Walter Benjamin put it, fascism is the 'aestheticization of politics', Yeats's writings are profoundly antagonistic to the representational aesthetics in which fascism finds its legitimation, deriving, for example, the power of the leader from his organic symbolic relation to the race.[28] But to recognize this is equally to realize the futility of any condemnation of Yeats's politics in the name of representative democracy, for it is to the same symbolic aesthetic that democratic states appeal for their own legitimation. And, on the contrary, the very stridency of both Yeats's poetry and his politics stems from the clarity of his recognition of the bankruptcy of the aesthetic or poetic foundations of the state.

No more than the faintest gleam of an alternative can be traced, and then, not unpredictably, in precisely what Yeats's aesthetics can only with difficulty accommodate and are always, obsessively, tempted to expunge: remorse and the erotic pleasure of women. The latter is celebrated triumphantly in the Crazy Jane poems of 'Words for Music, Perhaps' and in 'A Woman Young and Old', but it is as if that theme is incompatible with the mortal theme of The Winding Stair and must be relegated to a separate sequence. Remorse, a term with peculiarly complex resonances in Yeats's idiosyncratic usage, is in 'A Dialogue' that which must be cast out for the Self to be reconciled to itself. In 'Vacillation' it is the name given by the heart to that 'brand, or flaming breath' which 'Comes to destroy/All those antinomies/Of day and night' and which, in turn, the body calls death. What seems from one perspective to prevent reconciliation in another destroys antinomy. We need, I believe, to understand remorse as that emotion which, beyond the predetermined gyres of Yeatsian time, chooses to assert that things might have been otherwise. It is an appeal to the history of the possible, of what might have been. In the end, it is only such a history that opens the possibility of change, brushing the retrospectively inevitable history of what is against its tidy grain.[29] The loose ends produced by such a history are incompatible with the formal drive of Yeats's poetic, as indeed they are equally with any representative aesthetic, asserting the irruption of a content that is in excess of any form and inassimilable to narrative time.

It is in this respect that we can begin to understand how remorse associates with the erotic pleasure of women, surprising as the conjunction may seem. For if the tradition of aesthetics has always located the effect of verisimilitude in the domain of the *probable*, to the explicit rejection of the *possible*, we can trace the relationship of that aesthetic not only to the ideological verisimilitude of dominant social forces, i.e. to those narratives which alone can 'seem true' for any historical moment, but equally to the verisimilar structure of patriarchy. For, famously, patriarchy never seeks to derive the truth claims of its lines of descent (or ascent) from any final biological certainty as to the identity of the male child, but rather from the legal fiction established by the performative ceremonies of marriage. Thus an appeal to a probability supported by legislative performance excludes the subversive possibilities of another performance, that of woman's possibly unbounded pursuit of pleasure.[30]

Yeats's own sense of remorse is constantly associated with the erotic, with

> that most fecund ditch of all,
> The folly that man does
> Or must suffer, if he woos
> A proud woman not kindred of his soul.
> ('A Dialogue of Self and Soul')

At one point, late in his career, erotic pleasure and remorse conjoin in an unexpected constellation that, even then, can be represented only through a negative judgment. I refer to that extraordinary speech in *Purgatory* where the old man, contemplating the repetition by his parent's ghosts of the moment of his conception, is suddenly struck by the thought that the remorse for the destruction of a genealogical line that motivates this living back is indissociable from the reliving of the pleasure of the act:

> But there's a problem: she must live
> Through everything in exact detail,
> Driven to it by remorse, and yet
> Can she renew the sexual act
> And find no pleasure in it, and if not,
> If pleasure and remorse must both be there,
> Which is the greater?

The mother's pleasure represents a complete excess here: an excess beyond her identity as mother, beyond the end of conception and beyond that chain of determinate consequences that motivates both her remorse and her son's desire to put an end to history by murdering his own son. It is an irreducible remainder that cannot be subordinated to form or identity and therefore eludes the process of reproduction. As a play with one's supplementarity to the racial exigencies of reproduction, with what Freud terms 'the victory of the race over the individual',[31] erotic pleasure is the exact inverse of the 'terrible beauty' by which the foundation of the state ensures its commemorative celebration as the means to its continuation. Bizarre conjunction as it may seem, remorse, taken as the negative affect of the history of the possible, and feminine pleasure pose together the question as to what our aesthetic states cannot contain. Like Antigone, whose song closes *The Winding Stair and Other Poems*, they keep open the question as to the legitimacy of the state that is founded in the dour determinations of death.

A full consideration of the antagonism between certain feminisms and the nationalism of the state would require at least another essay, and once again the aporia of a male writer's texts lead us to the threshold of other questions than can be posed within their terms. In the essays that follow, I explore further the question of the history of the possible in terms of two cultural formations, popular song and agrarian movements, that are occluded by the dominant narratives of statist nationalism. Though space does not allow it here, one could show that the strands of radical feminism which intersected in the early twentieth century with militant socialist nationalism and with which, to different degrees, Maud Gonne and Constance Markievicz were identified, drew on subordinate popular traditions in a way that was deeply antithetical to the logic of the state formation. Indeed, to the state, in act as in principle, both women came to be strongly opposed. Behind Yeats's figure of the shrill and tasteless woman politician, condensed out of these two actual women, lies a significantly different material politics that brings out the aesthetic and theoretical unease that has been so much in evidence here.

NOTES

References to Yeats's works in the following editions are given in the text:
   The Autobiography (New York: Macmillan 1953)
   Collected Plays (London: Macmillan 1980)
   Essays and Introductions (London: Macmillan 1960)
   Explorations (New York: Collier 1973)
   The Poems of W.B. Yeats, new ed., Richard J. Finneran (ed.) (New York: Macmillan 1983)
   A Vision (New York: Collier 1966)

1. Gustave Flaubert, Sentimental Education, Robert Baldick (trans.) (Harmondsworth 1981), p. 181.
2. See 'Study of the First Scene of Shakespeare's "Coriolanus"' in John Willet (ed. and trans.), Brecht on Theatre: The Development of an Aesthetic (London 1964), p. 255.
3. The most forceful argument for Yeats's fatal engagement in and, literally, fatal influence on Irish nationalism is Conor Cruise O'Brien's still controversial essay, 'Passion and Cunning: An Essay on the Politics of W.B Yeats', in Norman Jeffares and K.G.W. Cross (eds.), In Excited Reverie: A Centenary Tribute to W.B. Yeats, 1865–1939 (London 1965). For more nuanced arguments concerning Yeats's part in and ambivalences towards the Irish national and anti-colonial struggle, see Seamus Deane, 'Yeats and the Idea of Revolution', in Celtic Revivals: Essays in Modern Irish Literature, 1880–1980 (London 1985), pp. 38–50, and Edward Said's 'Yeats and Decolonization', Field Day Pamphlet, no. 15 (Lawrence Hill 1988); repr. in Seamus Deane (ed. and intro.), Nationalism, Colonialism and Literature (Minneapolis 1990).
4. It is again Conor Cruise O'Brien's 'Passion and Cunning' which provides the strongest argument for the fascist implications of Yeats's poetry, especially pp. 244–79. Deane, on the contrary, in 'Yeats and the Idea of Revolution', p. 49, argues that '[his] so-called fascism is, in fact, an almost pure specimen of the colonialist mentality'. The indispensable account of Yeats's politics, which is especially judicious in its evaluation, is Elizabeth Cullingford's Yeats, Ireland and Fascism (Dublin 1981). For Yeats's sources in philosophy and political philosophy, see Grattan Freyer, Yeats and the Anti-Democratic Tradition (Dublin 1981).
5. On administered society, see especially Max Horkheimer's Preface to Critical Theory, Selected Essays, M.J. O'Connell et al. (trans.) (New York 1982), pp. vii–viii. The concept governs such essays as Max Horkheimer and T.W. Adorno's 'The Culture Industry: Enlightenment as Mass Deception' in The Dialectic of

Enlightenment, John Cumming (trans.) (New York 1972), pp. 120–67, or Friedrich Pollock's 'State Capitalism: Its Possibilities and Limitations' in Andrew Arato and Eike Gebhardt (eds), *The Essential Frankfurt School Reader* (New York 1978), pp. 71–94.

6. As will be immediately evident, my arguments have been greatly informed by Paul de Man's extraordinary essay 'Image and Emblem in Yeats' in *The Rhetoric of Romanticism* (New York 1984), pp. 145–238. I have critiqued de Man's argument concerning the temporality of symbolism, which structures some of his assumptions about Yeats, in 'Kant's Examples', *Representations*, 28 (Autumn 1989), pp. 34–54.

7. See A. Norman Jeffares, *A Commentary on the Collected Poems of W.B. Yeats* (Stanford 1968), pp. 353–4.

8. Paul de Man, in his essay 'The Resistance to Theory', makes a not dissimilar point concerning the title of Keats's poem, *The Fall of Hyperion*. As he puts it here, 'Faced with the ineluctable necessity to come to a decision, no grammatical or logical analysis can help us out.' See 'The Resistance to Theory', *Theory and History of Literature*, vol. 33 (Minneapolis 1987), p. 16.

9. I have been unable to ascertain whether Eric Griffiths' paper, 'Yeats's Performance', delivered at the University of Cambridge in 1979, has been published. It contained a very astute reading of Yeats's poetry in terms of performatives and performance, but, in its criticism of Yeats's lack of ironic sensibility, fell short of realizing its own implications for an understanding of Yeats's politics.

10. I am indebted for these distinctions to Paul de Man's 'The Rhetoric of Temporality' in *Blindness and Insight: Essays in the Rhetoric of Contemporary Criticism* (London 1983), pp. 187–228, especially p. 207. The provisos on the temporality of symbolism that I make above (n. 6) apply equally to this essay.

11. For these referents, see Jeffares, *Commentary*, pp. 358–9. One hitherto overlooked referent for Yeats's dolphins may in fact be those which decorate one of the pillars in Agia Sophia. The ecclesiastical significance of these dolphins, which I noted in June 1989, is still obscure to me, but they may have suggested Yeats's emblem. I have found no mention of this motif in W.R. Holmes's *The Age of Justinian and Theodora*, 2 vols (London 1905–7), which Jeffares cites as Yeats's principal source of information on Santa Sophia and Byzantium. In 'Image and Emblem', p. 193, de Man remarks on the 'intricate network of emblems' through which an understanding of Yeats's poetry must be assembled.

12. For Richard J. Finneran's notes correcting Yeats's geography, see Finneran (ed.), *The Poems of W.B. Yeats* (New York 1983), p. 656. I draw in my discussion of this poem on several commentaries, especially: Paul de Man, 'Landscape in Wordsworth and Yeats', in *The Rhetoric of Romanticism*, pp. 133–43; Daniel A. Harris, *Yeats: Coole Park and Ballylee* (Baltimore 1974), chapter 8, especially pp. 231–44; Thomas Parkinson, *W.B Yeats and W.B Yeats: The Later Poetry*, 2 vols in one (Berkeley and Los Angeles 1971), pp. 142–6. I should note that I adhere to the title given in Finneran's edition though it differs from that of most other editions in omitting the 'Park' of Coole Park.

13. On some aspects of the consolatory 'poetics of identity' involved in much of the landscape poetry of contemporary Irish poets see '"Pap for the dispossessed"' above.

14. For my understanding of hyperbole here, I am greatly indebted to Lee Monk's

discussion of the rhetorical and mathematical complexities of the trope in 'Tittles and Asymptotes: The Hyperbolic Function of Chance in *Ulysses*', chapter 5 of 'Standard Deviations: Chance and the Modern Novel' (Ph.D Dissertation, University of California, Berkeley, 1988).

15. Parkinson in *W.B. Yeats, The Later Poetry*, p. 145, notes this instability of tense but attributes it merely to Yeats's 'great difficulty with this particular poem'.

16. The oxymoronic concept of 'the ceremony of innocence', which Yeats deploys as early as the 1921 volume *Michael Robartes and the Dancer*, in 'The Second Coming', is glossed in 'A Prayer for my Daughter', in the same volume: 'How but in custom and in ceremony/Are innocence and beauty born?' It is intrinsically related to the idea of an aristocratic appropriation of the theological concept of grace to social usages such that ceremonial graces become indices of theological 'innocence'. This usage Yeats may well have derived from Baldesar Castiglione's *Book of the Courtier*, which Joseph Hone records him as having read in Italy in 1907. See *W.B. Yeats, 1865–1939* (New York 1943), p. 233. Castiglione discusses the acquisition of grace in the First Book, *The Book of the Courtier*, George Bull (trans.) (Harmondsworth 1976), pp. 65–7. The possible etymological connection of 'ceremony' to 'cerement' compounds the close relation in all of Yeats's writing between foundation and mortality. It is perhaps worth noting, as an instance of the sprezzatura which Yeats constantly affects here, that his rhyme scheme enforces a momentary half-rhyme which is itself oxymoronic between 'sets to right' and 'set awry' in this stanza.

17. Walter Benjamin's *The Origin of German Tragic Drama* is the clearest exposition of the relation of allegory and melancholy: 'the only pleasure the melancholic permits himself, and it is a powerful one, is allegory', John Osborne (trans.) (London 1977), p. 185. Benjamin's discussion of the intimate linking of nature (as site of mortality) with history in the composition of allegory, as well as the intimate connection he discerns between allegory and mourning, are extraordinarily pertinent to Yeats's similar usages of an allegorical poetic, especially where Benjamin discusses the relation between ruin and allegory. Ruin in Yeats becomes, unlike poets in the Romantic tradition, the index of a work of foundation, as we have been seeing, through allegorization rather than a celebration of or lament for the organic processes of history. If de Man cites early work of Yeats as privileging the symbolic over the allegorical, it is sure that the later Yeats is much closer to Benjamin's thinking. See Benjamin, pp. 167, 232–5, 177–82 and 162. In 'The Rhetoric of Temporality', p. 207, de Man insists also on the connection between allegory and the painful recognition of the non-self as non-self.

18. Following de Man's distinction between symbol and allegory, in 'The Rhetoric of Temporality', one could argue that, whatever symbolic status they claim, the nationalist representatives of a nation yet to be only ever produce allegories of the nation since the allegorical mode will always imply a concept prior to what it represents. Hence perhaps Fredric Jameson's concept of 'national allegories' as the typical form of third-world writing has some pertinence as an engagement with one particular instance or moment of third-world literary traditions where they are concerned with the failure of the symbolic claims made generally for the representative status of new national cultural and political institutions. See Jameson, 'Third World Literature in the Era of Multi-National Capitalism', *Social Text*, 15 (Autumn 1986), p. 69. The problematics of founding a people-nation

produces, as Jacques Derrida has shown in the case of the American Declaration of Independence, intractable theoretical problems for representation itself, where representation is said to take place in the sense of a representation which participates in that which it represents, as should the founder in the people in whose name he speaks. In the absence of an external point of origin, can that which originates also represent that which it brings into being? See Derrida, 'Déclarations d'indépendance', in *Otobiographies* (Paris 1984), pp. 13–32. This aporia of foundation induces a situation akin to that described by Benjamin in *The Origin of German Tragic Drama* as fundamental to allegorical representation until limited by the transcendental intervention of redemption: 'so would the allegorical intention fall from emblem to emblem down into the dizziness of its bottomless depths ... ' (p. 232).

19. I refer to Samuel Hynes's lecture, 'Yeats's Wars', delivered at the Yeats International Summer School, 1988. In 'Image and Emblem', de Man insists on an earlier dating of this shift from symbol to emblem at around 1900 (pp. 162–5), but I wish to argue that insofar as the symbol functions as a means to a narrative organization of desire rather than a mode of mimetic representation, the later shift is both fuller and more significant.

20. For this account, see Edward Greenway Malins, W.B. *Yeats and the Easter Rising* (Dublin 1965), who quotes Yeats's letter:

> Maud Gonne reminds me that she saw the ruined houses about O'Connell St and the wounded and the dying lying around the streets, in the first days of the war. I perfectly remember the vision, and my making light of it by saying that if it was a vision at all it could only have a symbolized meaning.

21. *The Autobiography* (New York 1953), p. 119. It should be remembered that the section 'Four Years: 1887–1891' was published in 1922, making its reflection upon Yeats's early cultural nationalism all the more apposite to his revisionary reflections after 1916.

22. Yeats's gloss is in his notes to the volume *Crossways, The Rose, Collected Poems*, p. 591. According to Richard Finneran, Yeats is recalling a remark of Coleridge's from *Table Talk* (cf. *Collected Poems*, p. 602). De Man, in 'Image and Emblem', pp. 176–7, remarks on the place of death as the *fulfilment* of Yeats's poetic and on his nihilism as the product of 'the unresolved conflict between image and emblem'.

23. The phrase 'allegorical state' I derive from Marx's remarks in 'On the Jewish Question': the 'political man is simply abstract, artificial man, man as an allegorical, moral person'. Karl Marx, *Early Writings*, Rodney Livingstone and Gregor Benton (trans.) (New York 1975), p. 234.

24. Benedict Anderson, in *Imagined Communities* (London 1983), pp. 17–18, remarks on the constant concern of nationalism in general with death. His observation needs to be extended, however, through the consideration not so much of nationalism's affinities with religion *per se* as of the ethical structure of subjectivity which its invocation of the willingness to die for the people or nation supposes.

25. The division of spheres in Irish nationalism between the masculine sphere not only of action and of production but also of martyrdom, and the feminine sphere,

in which the national ethos as well as the sons of the nation are literally and figuratively reproduced, is especially marked from Young Ireland on. Though this tradition draws on figures derived from the Celtic tradition of the queen/goddess Ireland perpetuated in the form of Mother Ireland or Kathleen Ni Houlihan, its specific form is both modern and democratic, directed not towards a concept of sacred kingship but towards a concept of ethical citizenship. I have argued this more extensively in *Nationalism and Minor Literature* (Berkeley and Los Angeles 1987), chapter 6. Such a gendered division of spheres may in fact be characteristic of all forms of nationalism. Partha Chatterjee, in 'The Nationalist Resolution of the Woman Question' in Kum Kum Sangari and Sudesh Vaid (eds), *Recasting Women: Essays in Indian Colonial History* (New Brunswick, New Jersey 1990), traces very similar formations in nineteenth-century Indian nationalism. With regard to the sexual division of the sublime and the beautiful, the earliest and perhaps clearest source is Edmund Burke's *Philosophical Enquiry into the Origin of our Ideas of the Sublime and Beautiful* (1757). It should be noted, however, that though the sublime and the beautiful are both experiences which the male subject has, the beautiful is subtended only by the female, woman's body providing, so to speak, the contours of the beautiful. Interestingly, in Burke as in 'Easter 1916', a certain collapse of the beautiful is cast as precisely that which threatens, in the experience of desire, to dissolve and melt the resolution of male subjectivity. In a certain sense, the feminine threat to male subjectivity is the source of both the sublime and the beautiful, subtending both, as indeed the feminization of both nature and culture might suggest. See especially Burke, *The Sublime and the Beautiful*, Section 19, 'The Physical Cause of Love'.

26. On the 'colonizer who refuses', see Albert Memmi's *The Colonizer and the Colonized* (New York 1965), pp. 19–44. See also Deane, 'Yeats and the Idea of Revolution', pp. 48–9. In 'A General Introduction for my Work', Yeats remarks with distinct ambivalence about the possible redundance of his own cultural politics and its displacement by another mode of imaginary identification:

> Sometimes I am told in commendation, if the newspaper is Irish, in condemnation if English, that my movement perished under the firing squads of 1916; sometimes that those firing squads made our realistic movement possible. If that statement is true, and it is only so in part, for romance was everywhere receding, it is because in the imagination of Pearse and his fellow soldiers the Sacrifice of the Mass had found the Red Branch in the tapestry; they went out to die calling upon Cuchulain. (*Essays and Introductions*, p. 515)

27. I derive this and other information from Aleister Crowley's versions of the Tarot. The relation of this representation of Thoth and the Afro-American tradition of the signifying monkey is a matter for interesting historical and transcultural speculation. On the latter, see Henry Louis Gates, Jr, *The Signifying Monkey* (Oxford 1988).

28. Walter Benjamin's now celebrated remark on fascism rendering politics aesthetic is to be found in his essay 'The Work of Art in the Age of Mechanical Reproduction', *Illuminations*, Hannah Arendt (ed.), Harry Zohn (trans.) (London 1973), pp. 243–4.

29. Cf. Benjamin, 'Theses on the Philosophy of History', VII, where the historical

materialist 'regards it as his task to brush history against the grain' (*Illuminations*, p. 259).

30. The distinction between the probable and the possible is derived from Aristotle's *Poetics*, chapter 9, where what the poet tells is 'what is possible according to probability or necessity'. See Aristotle, *On the Art of Fiction, An English Translation of the Poetics*, 2nd impression (Cambridge 1959), p. 29. This distinction of 'un ordre nécessaire, par opposition à la diversité aléatoire des événements réels', cf. Aristotle, *La Poétique*, Roselyne Dupont-Roc and Jean Lallot (ed. and trans.) (Paris 1980), p. 221, is equally what founds the universal and 'philosophical' claims of poetry. The distinction recurs, *mutatis mutandi*, in the founding text of modern aesthetics, Immanuel Kant's *The Critique of Judgement*, where the universal validity of the aesthetic judgment is predicated on its abstraction from the contingent or actual judgments of individuals and its consequent elevation to the status of a judgment made 'as if' in the name of all mankind. The necessity or universality of the accord that it claims is founded accordingly on a probability rather than on the range of actual possible judgments. Equally demanded here is the subordination of individual pleasure (*das Angenehme*) in all its contingent variability to a pleasure which is always identical, being that of the identical subject of aesthetic judgment. See especially #40 of *The Critique of Judgement*, James Creed Meredith (trans.) (Oxford 1952), pp. 150–4. On the patriarchal law that derives the identity of the child from the nuptial ceremonies, see Frederick Engels, *The Origin of the Family, Private Property and the State*, Eleanor Burke Leacock (ed.) (New York 1972), p. 131, where he cites the Code Napoléon, Article 312: 'L'enfant conçu pendant le mariage a pour père le mari.' These conjunctions raise the purely speculative query as to the possible historical relation between the emergence of Western aesthetics and the suppression of a prior matriarchal culture, evidence for which has often been sought in the very tragedies on which Aristotle bases his poetics, and the related query as to whether, on either historical or ideological grounds, a 'verisimilar' aesthetic could ever serve insurgent cultural practices, whether feminist, minority or class based. These speculations are material for a whole other essay and project.

31. Sigmund Freud, 'Some Psychical Consequences of the Anatomical Distinction Between the Sexes', in *The Complete Psychological Works* (London 1958–68), xix, p. 257.

ADULTERATION AND THE NATION

Irish cultural nationalism has been preoccupied throughout its history with the possibility of producing a national genius who would at once speak for and forge a national identity. The national genius is to represent the nation in the double sense of depicting and embodying its spirit – or genius – as it is manifested in the changing forms of national life and history. The idea could be reformulated quite accurately in terms derived from Kantian aesthetics: the national genius is credited with 'exemplary originality'.[1] That is to say, the national genius not only presents examples to a people not yet fully formed by or conscious of their national identity, but does so by exemplifying in himself the individual's ideal continuity with the nation's spiritual origins. True originality derives from the faithful reproduction of one's origins. Thus far, Irish nationalism represents, as indeed does Kant, merely another variant on the Enlightenment and Romantic critical tradition for which the originality of genius is understood as the capacity to reproduce the historical or individual sources of creativity itself. The Irish nationalist merely insists on a different notion of what is to be formed in the encounter with genius: not so much the intermediate subject of taste as, directly, the political subject, the citizen-subject, itself.

Unlike Kant, however, the Irish nationalist is confronted with a peculiar dilemma, succinctly expressed by Young Ireland's most influential aesthetician, D.F. MacCarthy, as the great national poet's being 'either the creation or the creator of a great people'.[2] The expression points to an unavoidable aporia for the doubly representational aesthetics of nationalism, since the poet must either be created by the nation which it is his (always his) function to create, or create it by virtue of representing the nation he lacks. Neither a continuous national history, which could connect the individual to the national genius, nor even nature, on whose invocation in the form of *Naturgabe* the category of genius has traditionally been grounded, are easily

88

available to the Irish nationalist.[3] For the nationalism of a colonized people requires that its history be seen as a series of unnatural ruptures and discontinuities imposed by an alien power while its reconstruction must necessarily pass by way of deliberate artifice. Almost by definition, this anti-colonial nationalism lacks the basis for its representative claims and is forced to invent them.[4] In this respect, nationalism can be said to require an aesthetic politics quite as much as a political aesthetics.

Historically, this constitutive paradox of Irish nationalism has not been practically disabling, though in cultural terms it leaves the problem that Ireland's principal writers have almost all been remarkably recalcitrant to the nationalist project. I have discussed this more extensively elsewhere in relation to the extreme demand for identification with the nation that nationalism imposes upon the Irish writer.[5] Here, I wish to explore more fully how not only the anti-representational tendency in Irish literature but also the hybrid quality of popular forms constantly exceed the monologic desire of cultural nationalism, a desire which centres on the lack of an Irish epic. Both the popular and the literary forms map a colonial culture for which the forms of representational politics and aesthetics required by nationalism begin to seem entirely inadequate, obliging us to conceive of a cultural politics which must work outside the terms of representation. Incidentally, this colonial situation may also suggest the limits of the Bakhtinian formulations on which this analysis will in the first place be based.

I

At several points in *The Dialogic Imagination*, Mikhail Bakhtin isolates as a definitive characteristic of the novel its capacity to represent the heteroglossia internal to an apparently unified but nonetheless stratified national language.[6] Requiring the depiction of the conflictual, dialogic nature of social relations, this characteristic underlies the generic mobility and, at given historical moments, subversiveness of the novel, opposing it to the epic, as well as to other stabilized and 'monologic' genres. The epic belongs to a closed and completed world, and characteristically represents the unity of that world and the integration of its exemplary heroes (p. 35). Typically, the epic casts backwards to 'an absolute past of national beginnings and peak times' (p. 15), correlative to which is its stylistic closure: unlike the novel, the epic is a genre closed to development and therefore insusceptible to the representation of historical development (pp. 16–17). Intrinsic to Bakhtin's discussion of epic and novel is, accordingly, an historical periodization which derives the novel from the disintegration of the epic and its culture.[7] In the long term, the dialectic of the novel form leads to the disintegration of the myth of 'a unitary, canonic language, of a national myth bolstered by a yet-unshaken unity' (p. 370), and a concomitant displacement of the ideological by the human speaking subject.

Bakhtin, as that last citation serves to recall, posits the moment of unitary national culture in the past. The instance of a decolonizing nationalism, such as Ireland's throughout the nineteenth and early twentieth centuries, leads us to pose the question in slightly different terms. What if the epic of a nation has yet to be written and if the unity of the nation is desired as a prerequisite to the anti-colonial struggle? In such a case, exactly what seems to be required is the monologic form of the epic as a means to rather than a mere legitimating record of national unity, while the function of the epic may be seen not only as the unification of a culture but also, in a quite specific sense, as the production of a dialogic subversion of the colonizing power. For these purposes, which are integral to the politically mobilizing project of cultural nationalism, the *heteroglossic* mode of the novel could be seen as distinctly counter-productive. Precisely that which, according to Bakhtin, the novel is constantly adapted to represent, the multiplicity of contending social voices, is what Irish nationalism must, for entirely coherent political reasons, seek to supersede in the form of a unified national identity. For the cultural nationalists of the nineteenth and early twentieth centuries, believing 'that Irishmen were enslaved because they were divided',[8] the principal task of nationalism was to overcome the sectarian, class and ethnic divisions that split Ireland. The task of producing representations of a common identity was accordingly entrusted to literature, and to a literature whose very rationale was monologic insofar as it was intended to produce exactly the 'national myth' that Bakhtin envisages as having collapsed when the novel supplanted the epic.[9]

As I have argued elsewhere, the literary project of Irish nationalism, stemming from the Young Ireland movement of the 1840s, involves a quite sophisticated theory of generic development linked to a universal history of cultural developments. In this argument,

fully developed cultures such as England's can rely on a political constitution which expresses the underlying unity of their conflicting
social forces, whereas underdeveloped cultures such as Ireland's must
turn to literary institutions for the same unificatory effects. Due,
however, to the apparently fragmentary and strife-ridden course of
Irish history and to the divided society of its present, that literature
has yet to be created. If, 'rightly understood, the history of Ireland ...
had the unity and purpose of an epic poem', that epic had yet to be
written and could not be prematurely forged. Before it could be
written, the prior stages of literary development had to be passed
through, permitting, as if at accelerated tempo, the recomposition of
all those ballads and folk-songs on which it was believed such epics
as Homer's were founded.[10] Hence the enormous quantity of ballads
produced and collected in nineteenth-century Ireland was not
merely a question of propaganda but directly concerned the constitution of an idea of Irishness which could 'contain and represent the
races of Ireland'.[11]

But this project of presenting to the Irish a single 'spirit of the
nation' (to cite the title of one enormously popular collection) is
confronted with peculiar problems as soon as it turns to extant
ballads as examples of that spirit. Collectors of Irish ballads classify
them generally into three subdivisions: Gaelic or peasant songs,
street ballads, and literary or Anglo-Irish ballads.[12] To the latter class
we will return, since it is the problematic status of the first two that
most acutely confronts the cultural nationalist.

By the mid-nineteenth century, the study of Gaelic language and
culture had proceeded little beyond the scarcely systematic amassing
of materials, while distinctions between 'high' and 'low' literary productions remained relatively fluid and uncertain.[13] Collections were
recognized to be provisional and incomplete. Yet despite the objective grounds for the fragmentary corpus of Gaelic literature, nationalists who review it in order to distinguish and define Irish identity
time and again trace in that corpus a fragmentariness lodged in the
artefacts themselves. Thus when Davis remarks that 'There are great
gaps in Irish song to be filled up,' he refers not to the state of
research but to the nature of the object, a nature that is for him historical and absolutely not essential. The 'bulk of the songs', he
asserts, 'are very defective':

Most of those hitherto in use were composed during the last century, and therefore
their structure is irregular, their grief slavish and despairing, their joy reckless and

bombastic, their religion bitter and sectarian, their politics Jacobite and concealed by extravagant and tiresome allegory. Ignorance, disorder and every kind of oppression weakened and darkened the lyric genius of Ireland.[14]

The historical oppression of the Irish has contaminated both the structure and the content of the Gaelic poetry, so that if it appears gapped, that gapping is internal to it, consisting in its 'defective' or 'extravagant' deviation from the essential 'genius' of the Irish nation. There is something alien in the poetry, and the job of the popular editor is accordingly one of condensation: 'cut them so as exactly to suit the airs, preserve the local and broad historical allusions, but remove the clumsy ornaments and exaggerations' (pp. 225–6). The *perfection* of the defective native Irish poetic tradition requires a process of refinement which is, in principle at least, the antithesis of supplementation, involving instead the purging of extraneous materials and the unfolding of an obscured essence. Davis's formulation is characteristic of nationalist reception of Gaelic songs, which are similarly perceived by D.F. MacCarthy as 'snatches and fragments of old songs and ballads, which are chapters of a nation's autobiography'.[15] In every case, the fragmentary autobiography is to be completed in the formation of a national identity properly represented in a national literature imbued with its spirit rather than with the accidental traces and accretions of its colonial history. Consistent with this is an implicit rejection of the allegorical in favour of the symbolic: in quite traditional Romantic terms, the extravagance of allegory is eschewed while historical and local allusion is promoted as 'participating in that which it represents'.[16] The aesthetic of nationalism accords with its political ends, subordinated at every level to the demand for unity.

It is on the same grounds that the second class of street ballads is criticized by nationalists, but with more vehemence. Condemnation of the ballads, purchased widely by the already substantial portion of the people whose principal language was English, was virtually universal among Young Ireland critics, who argued for their supplanting by ballads imbued with the national spirit, such as those published in *The Spirit of the Nation* or in Duffy's and MacCarthy's collections of Irish ballads. Though their dismissals are fairly summary, one can decipher the basis for the antagonism. Most importantly, the ballads are urban: 'The mass of the street songs', remarks Duffy, 'make no pretence to being true to Ireland; but only to being true to the *purlieus* of Cork and Dublin.'[17] Nationalist antagonism to urban

Ireland, which continues by and large to structure the nation's ideo-logical self-representation, is by no means as simple and self-evident a phenomenon as its constancy has made it seem. It belongs to the constitutive contradiction of a modernizing ideology forced to seek its authenticating difference from the imperial culture on which it remains dependent by way of an appeal to a rural and Gaelic culture already in decay. Indeed, it is not to that culture in itself that appeal is made, but rather to a 'refinement' or 'translation' of its essence, traced among the fragmentary survivals of an already decimated past life. The antagonism to the urban is, accordingly, an antagonism to the inauthenticity legible in its cultural forms. Cork and Dublin, along with Belfast, represent in mid-nineteenth-century Ireland, as already for several centuries in the case of Dublin, sites of cultural hybridization as well as centres of imperial authority and capital domination. Garrison as well as industrial or port cities, they repre-sent concentrations of an English domination which penetrates every level of Irish social life. They are both nodes for the flows of English capital and imperial authority, and conduits for the contrary flows of a dislocated population, the points to which a dislocated rural population gravitates in search of employment or prior to emi-gration. The Pale area around Dublin had always seemed, to English eyes, under constant threat of contamination by Gaelic culture and by the transformation of old or new English into a settler population 'more Irish than the Irish'. But a rapid acceleration of the process of cultural hybridization, now more threatening to the nationalist than to the English, would appear to have taken place in the late eigh-teenth and early nineteenth centuries as an overdetermined set of effects of the English Industrial Revolution, the serial crises in Irish agriculture after the Napoleonic Wars and the gradual lifting of the Penal Laws in the decades preceding the Union of Great Britain and Ireland in 1801. Simultaneously, the Irish language was perceived to be in decline.[18]

Even a quite casual collection of eighteenth- and nineteenth-century street ballads like Colm Ó Lochlainn's *Irish Street Ballads* indicates the extent to which such works register, both thematically and stylistically, these processes as they are apprehended by the Irish population.[19] A very high incidence of the songs is devoted to migra-tion or emigration, to conscription or enlistment in the British army, as well as to the celebration of the 1798 uprising and a range of rebel heroes. Even the many love songs are coursed through more by laments for grinding poverty, imprisonment under English law, or the necessity of emigration or vagrancy than by complaints of fickleness and inconstancy, a characteristic considerably at odds with their frequent use, by colonizer and nationalist alike, to ground the stereotype of pure Irish sentimentality. At the stylistic level, the street ballads at moments provide an even more intimate register of the processes of cultural hybridization. They are, most often, adaptations of traditional airs to English words, enforcing frequently a distortion of standard English pronunciation or syntax to fit Gaelic musical and speech rhythms, a trait frequently celebrated in the more refined literary productions of translators and adapters like Moore, Ferguson and Callanan.[20] This primary hybridization is matched by varying degrees of incorporation of Irish-language fragments into the predominantly English texts of the ballads. Usually phonetically transcribed by writers illiterate in Irish, these fragments can be whole refrains, as in 'The Barrymore Tithe Victory' (1831), which keeps as part of its refrain the words of the Gaelic ballad 'A Dhruimfhionn Donn Dílis', whose tune it appropriates, but which it transcribes as 'A Drimon down deelish a heeda na moe' and turns to a celebration of the popular hero and political leader Daniel O'Connell. Others, by far the majority, seem little more than tags from the Gaelic, place-names or mythological and legendary figures, which from the dominant perspective would appear as recalcitrant recollections of a culture in transformation but still politically and culturally resistant. From another perspective, however, that of the balladeers and many in their audiences, such tags would resonate with familiar and quite complex allusions to allegorical and historical figures from Gaelic culture, adding a richer, if occluded, dimension to the ballads' reception. Thus the refrain of 'A New Song in Praise of Fergus O'Connor and Independence', celebrating the election of Chartist O'Connor as MP for Cork, runs 'So vote for brave Fergus and Sheela na Guira', the Gaelic tag being again the original ballad, 'Sighile Ní Ghadhra' from which the tune is borrowed. Even less political street ballads, such as the later 'Kerry Recruit', which relates the story of a young peasant enlisted for the Crimean War, used fragments of Irish as well as of Anglo-Irish dialect as a means of linguistically dramatizing the experience of dislocation and the role of such institutions as the army in the transformation of the colonized population:

> So I buttered my brogues and shook hands with my spade,
> And I went to the fair like a dashing young blade,

When up comes a sergeant and asks me to 'list,
'Arra, sergeant a grá, put the bob in my fist.'

'O! then here is the shilling, as we've got no more,
When you get to head-quarters you'll get half a score.'
'Arra, quit your kimeens,' ses I, 'sergeant, good-bye,
You'd not wish to be quartered, and neither would I.'[21]

This last example, though somewhat later than the Young Ireland writings instanced above, features a further element of the street ballads which drew nationalist criticism: their frequently burlesque tone. Precisely because of the heterogeneity of the ballads, whether taken as collections or as individual specimens, it would be impossible to establish a 'typical character' for the street ballads or to fix their tone. In 'The Kerry Recruit', for example, it becomes exceedingly difficult to specify the object of the mockery, the country gosthoon or the sergeant, peasant ignorance or British institutions. Tonal instability of this kind is common, as is a similarly vertiginous mixture of realism and burlesque, 'high language' and slang. Two further examples will suffice: one, 'Father Murphy', being an anonymous rebel ballad on the 1798 rebellion; the other, 'Billy's Downfall', attributed to the most celebrated of Dublin street balladeers, 'Zozimus' (Michael Moran), being a satirical commemoration of the blowing up of a unionist monument to William III on College Green in 1836:

The issue of it was a close engagement,
While on the soldiers we played warlike pranks;
Thro' sheepwalks, hedgerows and shady thickets,
There were mangled bodies and broken ranks,
The shuddering cavalry I can't forget them;
We raised the brushes on their helmets straight –
They turned about and they bid for Dublin,
As if they ran for a ten-pound plate.

By brave Coriolanus and wiggy McManus,
    By dirty King Shamus, that ran from the Boyne,
I never was willing dead men to be killing,
    Their scurry blood spilling, with traitors to join.
For true-heart allegiance, without much persuadience,
    Myself and all Paddies we're still at a call,
But to burke a poor king, 'tis a horrible thing,
    Granu's sons never heard it in Tara's old hall.[22]

As both indicate, the processes of hybridization registered in the street ballads go far beyond the integration of Gaelic into English-language forms. To the ambiguities resulting from the refusal to differentiate the burlesque from the serious corresponds a similar indifference to cultural registers. Military language can cohabit with that of the racecourse, or classical references give way to citations of ancient and modern history, folk heroes and contemporary slang. Much of the pleasure of the street ballad, as with so many 'popular' forms, derives from precisely this indifference to cultural hierarchies.[23] It may even be that the very adaptability of the ballad, as a kind of template transformable to fit any given locality or momentary reference, subserves not only the continual demand for the 'new song' as instant commodity, but also a more discrete function. Beyond the cultural resistance they articulate, such ballads as 'Father Murphy' in their very descriptions of combat conceivably acted to preserve and transmit not merely the historical memory of insurrections but also the repertoire of means to resist, the tactical knowledge of how and where to conduct armed struggle. For a rural audience, 'Father Murphy' may serve exactly the same function in terms of tactical knowledge as John Mitchel's regular military lessons in the *United Irishman* of 1848, themselves adapted from a British military handbook.[24]

Such speculations aside, the stylistic elements of the street ballads throw into greater relief the grounds for cultural nationalist criticisms of them. The cultural nationalism developed within the Young Ireland movement was quite strictly a *Romantic* nationalism and, like its unionist counterparts, derived much from English and German high Romanticism. But the forces that a poet like Wordsworth seeks to counteract, the spectacle of the city as a 'perpetual whirl/Of trivial objects, melted and reduced/To one identity, by differences/That have no law, no meaning, and no end',[25] are accentuated in the Irish case by the colonial encounter that both accelerates the processes of cultural disintegration and gives a specific political name, anglicization, to the phenomenon of 'reduction to identity'. What we have described, in the wider sphere of the Irish political economy as well as in that of the street ballads, as 'hybridization' is necessarily grasped by nationalists as the paradoxically simultaneous process of multiplication or disintegration and homogenization. The flooding of the market with English commodities both disintegrates what is retrospectively constructed as a unified Irish identity and absorbs its residues into the single field of the British industrial and imperial empire. And since the only means to resist this process, in the absence of autonomous national political institutions, appears to be the formation of nationalist subjects through literary institutions, the field of popular literature becomes peculiarly fraught. For if the ultimate desire of the nationalist must be for the state (in every sense of the word 'for'), that desire must in fact be not first of all for the state itself, as a body of specific institutions to be controlled, but for what the state in turn is held to represent, namely, the unity or reconciliation of the people. Hence the necessity for a cultural nationalism, not merely as a supplement to, but as a prerequisite for, a military nationalism, and hence the requirement that that nationalist culture be monologic in its modes of expression. The representation as a desired end of an homogeneous Irish nation is a necessary preliminary to the political struggle in any form.

Accordingly, the aesthetic choices that oppose the nationalists' literary recreations of Irish ballad poetry to both the street ballads and to the Gaelic songs are also at every level political choices. Their collections are designed to give law, meaning and end to a specific difference which would constitute an Ireland independent of England and in opposition to the heterogeneous image of Irish social life and culture borne in the street ballad or in extant translations of Gaelic poetry. A national poetry must speak with one voice and, unlike those street ballads in which it is often difficult to tell if the hero is subject or object of the burlesque, must represent the Irish people as the agent of its own history, of a history which has 'the unity and purpose of an epic poem'. This demands a 'translational' aesthetic, in the sense that what must be constantly carried over is the essential spirit rather than the superficial forms of Irish poetry in each language.[26]

As Denis Florence MacCarthy puts it in his *Book of Irish Ballads*:

This peculiar character of our poetry is, however, not easily imparted. An Irish word or an Irish phrase, even appositely introduced, will not be sufficient; it must pervade the entire poem, and must be seen and felt in the construction, the sentiment, and the expression.[27]

In the examples cited above, 'Sheela na Guira' or the 'Granu's sons' are juxtaposed in contiguity to Fergus O'Connor or Coriolanus, achieving an expansion – and complication – of referential range without requiring the subordination of the elements to one another. MacCarthy's aesthetic programme, on the contrary, requires the subordination of the Gaelic element as a representative instance consubstantial with the homogeneous totality of Irish identity. In keeping with an antagonism to the allegorical tendency of Gaelic poetry and the street ballads in favour of a generally symbolist aesthetic, nationalist writing must perform a transfer from the metonymic axis of contiguity to that of metaphor. Where the metonymic disposition of popular forms lends itself to the indiscriminate citation of insubordinate cultural elements, the fundamentally narrative structure of metaphoric language seeks to reorganize such cultural elements as representative moments in a continuous epic of the nation's self-formation.[28]

MacCarthy himself provides us with an exemplary instance in his ballad 'The Pillar Towers of Ireland', which, though by no means the most celebrated of Young Ireland productions, almost self-consciously enacts the appropriation of historical Irish elements to a seamless representation of Irish destiny. The pillar towers become symbols of the continuing spirit of Ireland, both its products and its organizing representatives, giving shape and relationship to the several races which have passed through or settled the land in the course of its history:

> Around these walls have wandered the Briton and the Dane –
> The captives of Armorica, the cavaliers of Spain –
> Phoenician and Milesian, and the plundering Norman Peers –
> And the swordsmen of brave Brian, and the chiefs of later years![29]

A persistent and resistant element of the Irish landscape, the round or pillar tower stands as itself a metaphor for the metaphoric process by which an initial perception of difference can be brought over time into a superior recognition of identity:

> There may it stand for ever, while this symbol doth impart
> To the mind one glorious vision, or one proud throb to the heart;
> While the breast needeth rest may these grey old temples last,
> Bright prophets of the future, as preachers of the past!
> (Book of Irish Ballads, p. 128)

It is not necessary to be aware of the continuing exploitation of the round tower by the Irish Tourist Board and other such institutions to sense how rapidly this representation of an authentic Irish identity veers towards kitsch. Indeed, the constant gravitation of cultural nationalism towards kitsch is a virtually inevitable consequence of its aesthetic programme, if not, indeed, to some extent a mark of its success. The commodification of style and the mechanical reproduction of standardized forms of affect that define kitsch have their close counterpart in cultural nationalism.[30] Here, the incessant injunction to produce representative ballads which will reproduce Gaelic styles known to the producers only by way of representations is directed towards the homogenization of a political rather than an economic sphere. It similarly requires, nonetheless, the production of novelties which are always interchangeable, a condition partly of the journalistic sphere in which most nationalist ballads first appeared, and the immediate evocation of an affect which is the sign of identification with the nation. Congruent in most respects with Romantic aesthetics generally, the subordination of the nationalist ballad to a conscious political end denies it the auratic distance usually held, if often erroneously, to guarantee the critical moment of the modern artwork.

Ironically, what is properly, in Brechtian terms, an *epic* distance belongs more frequently to the street ballad than to the nationalist ballads intended to replace them. Self-consciously produced as commodities, and with the ephemeral aptness to momentary need or desire that is the property of the commodity, the street ballads often achieve an effect akin to montage in which the contours of an heterogeneous and hybridized culture can become apparent without necessarily losing political force. Indeed, a large part of the pleasure of the street ballad is political and lies in its use of 'extravagant allegories': what it exploits is precisely the unevenness of knowledge that characterizes the colonized society. The variegated texture of colonized society permits an exploitation by the colonized of those elements that are unfamiliar to the colonizer, and therefore appear encoded, like the Gaelic tags cited above, as a means of at once disguising and communicating subversion, as message to the colonized and as uncertainty to the colonizer. The very inauthenticity of the colonized culture enables an unpredictable process of masking. Where the colonizer, whose proper slogan should be that 'Ignorance is Power', seeks to reduce the colonized to a surveyable surface whose meaning is always the same, and where the nationalist responds with an ideal of the total translucence of national spirit in the people, the hybridized culture of the colonized offers only surfaces pitted or mined with uncertainty, depths and shallows whose contours vary depending on the 'familiarity' of each observer. On this surface, demarcations of the borderline between damage and creative strategies for resistance are hard to fix. As we shall see, neither the damage nor the resistance lend themselves easily to assimilation.

Captured in the contradiction between its modernizing effects and its conservative appeal, nationalist culture on the other hand is drawn into a process of stylization, the representation of a style, which constantly returns it to an inauthenticity akin to, though not identical with, that of the street ballad it seeks to supplant. This effect of stylization is probably inseparable from the fundamental dislocation which colonization effects in any culture and which is the necessary prior condition for the emergence of any specifically *nationalist* resistance. In proceeding, it is necessary only to insist again that the dislocation of the colonized culture should not be thought of in terms of a loss of a prior and recoverable authenticity. Rather, authenticity must be seen as the projective desire of a nationalism programmatically concerned with the homogenization of the people as a national political entity.

II

Unsurprisingly, given the virtually aporetic status of its contradictions, the terms of mid-nineteenth-century nationalist cultural discussions are reproduced half a century later in the Irish Literary Revival. James Joyce presents them prominently in *Ulysses* as a prelude to Stephen Dedalus's development of his own conception of genius out of Saxon Shakespeare:

— Our young Irish bards, John Eglinton censured, have yet to create a figure which the world will set beside Saxon Shakespeare's Hamlet though I admire him, as old Ben did, on this side idolatry.

...

Mr Best came forward, amiable, towards his colleague.

— Haines is gone, he said.

— Is he?

— I was showing him Jubainville's book. He's quite enthusiastic, don't you know, about Hyde's *Love Songs of Connacht.* I couldn't bring him in to hear the discussion. He's gone to Gill's to buy it.

> Bound thee forth, my booklet, quick
> To greet the callous public,
> Writ, I ween, 'twas not my wish
> In lean unlovely English.

— The peatsmoke is going to his head, John Eglinton opined.

...

— People do not know how dangerous lovesongs can be, the auric egg of Russell

100

warned occultly. The movements which work revolutions in the world are born out of the dreams and visions in a peasant's heart on the hillside. For them the earth is not an exploitable ground but the living mother. The rarefied air of the academy and the arena produce the sixshilling novel, the musichall song. France produces the finest flower of corruption in Mallarmé but the desirable life is revealed only to the poor of heart, the life of Homer's Phaeacians.[31]

It is not merely that Joyce alludes here, in compressed fashion, to the principal concerns that continue to play through Irish cultural nationalism: the desire for the masterwork; the opposition between the spirit of peasant song, 'racy of the soil', and the hybrid 'flowers of corruption'; the turn to Homer as the figure representing the unification of the work of genius with the 'genius of place'. Furthermore, he indicates the complexity of the cultural transactions that take place in the thoroughly hybridized culture of 'West Britain', where Irishmen discourse on English, German and Greek culture while an Englishman, Haines, studies the Celtic element in literature and Hyde regrets the necessity that forces him to exemplify a Gaelic metre in lean, unlovely English.

Joyce's evocation of Hyde at this juncture allows us to grasp both the extent to which turn-of-the-century cultural nationalism recapitulates its earlier forms and the extent to which its terms had become at once more sophisticated and more problematic. Douglas Hyde, founder-president of the Gaelic League, was a principal advocate of the Irish-language revival, a scholar, poet-translator and folklorist. His most famous single essay, 'The Necessity for De-Anglicising Ireland' (1892), resumes Young Ireland's attacks on the penetration of Ireland by English culture as well as capital, and on the consequent emergence of an entirely 'anomalous position' for the Irish race, 'imitating England and yet apparently hating it'.[32] In large part, this essay presents a dismal catalogue of hybridization which ranges through place and family names to musical forms and clothing. Its conclusion, that a de-anglicization of Ireland is the necessary prelude to and guarantee of eventual Irish autonomy, is prescriptive for efforts like Hyde's own laborious collection and translation of Irish folk-songs and poetry. In these, as he had already argued in his essay 'Gaelic Folk Songs' (1890), the Irish genius was properly to be deciphered:

We shall find that, though in their origin and diffusion they are purely local, yet in their essence they are wholly national, and, perhaps, more purely redolent of the race and soil than any of the real *literary* productions of the last few centuries.[33]

When it comes to deciphering that essence, nonetheless, Hyde is confronted with the dilemma that led to Young Ireland's translational aesthetic: there remain 'great gaps in Irish song'. For Hyde, however, as a scholar whose intimacy with the Gaelic material was far greater than Davis's or MacCarthy's, the question as to whether the 'gapped' nature of Irish folk-song was of its essence or an accident based upon the contingent, historical determinants of an oral culture, remains correspondingly more difficult to resolve. After giving a number of instances from Gaelic love songs, he pauses to remark on the necessity to cite examples in order to represent the nature of these songs in general. The ensuing reflections lead him to an unusually complex rendering of the 'nature' of the Gaelic spirit, leaving him unable to decide between the historical and the essential:

It may appear strange, however, that I have only given stray verses instead of translating entire songs. But the fact is that the inconsequentness of these songs, as I have taken them down from the lips of the peasantry, is startling.

Many adjectives have been applied by many writers to the Gaelic genius, but to my mind nothing about it is so noticeable as its inconsequentness, if I may use such a word – a peculiarity which, as far as I know, no one has yet noticed. The thought of the Irish peasant takes the most surprising and capricious leaps. Its movement is like the career of his own goblin, the Pooka; it clears the most formidable obstacles at a bound and carries across astonishing distances in a moment. The folk-song is the very incarnation of this spirit. It is nearly impossible to find three verses in which there is anything like an ordinary sequence of thought. They are full up of charms that the mind must leap, elipses [sic] that it must fill up, and detours of movement which only the most vivid imagination can make straight. This is the reason why I have found no popular ballads amongst the peasantry, for to tell a story in verse requires an orderly, progressive, and somewhat slow sequence of ideas, and this is the very faculty which the Gael has not got – his mind is too quick and passionate ...

But even this characteristic of Gaelic thought is insufficient to account for the perfectly extraordinary inconsequentness and abruptness of the folk-songs, as I have found them, I imagine that the cause of this peculiarity is not to be ascribed wholly to the authors of the songs, but also in great part to the medium which the songs passed through before they came to us – that medium, of course, being the various generations of local singers who have perpetuated them. These singers often forgot, as was natural, the real words of the song, and then they invented others, but more frequently they borrowed verses from any other piece that came into their head, provided it could be sung to the same tune, and hence the songs as we have them now are a curious mixture indeed. What between the 'unsequacious' mind of the original makers, the alterations made by generations of singers who forgot the words, and the extraneous verses borrowed from completely different productions, two out of three of the folk-songs which I have collected, resemble those children's toys of paper where when you pull a string you get a different pair of legs or a different head, joined to a different body. The most beautiful sentiments will be followed by the most grotesque bathos,

and the tenderest and most exquisite verses will end in the absurdest nonsense. This
has been done by the singers who have transmitted them. (pp. 113–14)

The folk-songs appear here as at once the representation of an
essence, the Gaelic spirit, and the products of the specific and contingent conditions of their transmission. But if we take these representations as those of an essence, then the essence itself makes it
impossible to define any essential character of the race, since a character, to have any identity at all, must be consistent, as Young
Ireland and their followers in the Literary Revival consistently
argued. On the other hand, the historical argument in its turn, recognizing the sheer contingency that has conditioned the forms and
peculiarities of the folk-songs, would make it impossible to derive a
national character from them.

Despite his momentary hesitation at this acknowledgment of the
overdetermined grounds for the 'great gaps in Irish song', Hyde
rapidly recuperates the Irish identity by offering, after citing a thoroughly adulterated verse, 'one specimen of a comparatively perfect
folk-song which has not been interfered with' (p. 115). The song,
'Mo bhrón ar an bhfarraige' ('Oh, my grief on the sea!'), which concludes with the lines,

> And my love came behind me –
> He came from the south –
> With his breast to my bosom,
> His mouth to my mouth,

appears as a perfect because consistent expression of 'genuine
passion', lacking any of the marks, 'the alliteration, adjectives, asso-
nance, and tricks of the professional poet' (p. 117). Hyde's 'restoration' of the essential folk-song requires, in other words, not only its
purification from hybridization internal to the culture or resulting
from external influence, but even the representation of the work of
the Gaelic bards as a deviation from the true passion of the people.
Irish folk culture is transformed into an ahistorical ground on which
the defining difference of 'Irishness' can be established over against
the homogenizing/hybridizing influence of 'Anglicization'. Ironically,
the values by which the genuine item is identified and canonized
themselves derive, perhaps by way of earlier translators, like the
unionist Samuel Ferguson, from the 'common language' of British
Romanticism.

It is more than probable that Joyce knew Hyde's essays, and
certain that he knew this particular song, if only from the slightly

revised version in *The Love Songs of Connacht*, since it appears transformed early in *Ulysses*. It reappears, however, not in the context of 'genuine passion', but in the course of Stephen's 'morose delectation' on Sandymount Strand as his thoughts shift back and forth between the cockle picker's woman passing him and the memory of his dead mother:

She trudges, schlepps, trains, drags, trascines her load. A tide westering, moondrawn, in her wake. Tides, myriadislanded, within her, blood not mine, *oinopa ponton*, a wine-dark sea. Behold the handmaid of the moon. In sleep the wet sign calls her hour, bids her rise. Bridebed, childbed, bed of death, ghostcandled. *Omnis caro ad te veniet.* He comes pale vampire, through storm his eyes, his bat sails bloodying the sea, mouth to her mouth's kiss. (*Ulysses*, p. 40)

The verses emerging here recur somewhat later, in the 'Aeolus' section, in a form closer to that given by Hyde:

> On swift sail flaming
> From storm and south
> He comes, pale vampire,
> Mouth to my mouth. (*Ulysses*, p. 109)

We may read in the gradual transformation of the folk-song a representation at several levels of the processes of hybridization as they construct the individual consciousness. Many of the elements of that hybridization are superficially evident: the chain of foreign, or rather 'anglicized', words used to describe the cockle picker's woman, the phrases from Homer and from the Latin of Catholic ritual, or the parody of biblical invocations. The *effect* of hybridization, however, needs more careful analysis, both at the formal literary level and at that of the representation of an individual subjectivity which it entails. The most familiar stylistic term in Joyce criticism used to describe the representation of subjective interiority is 'stream of consciousness', which implies a certain consistency within the representation as well as a relative transparency and evenness among the elements. As such, the term is largely inadequate, even in the earlier sections of the novel, to describe the staccato or interrupted rhythms, the varying accessibility of the allusions, whether to different readers or to the represented subject (Stephen or Bloom), or to the several levels of implicit 'consciousness' that these stylistic effects constitute.

Equally inadequate would be any description of these effects as instances of 'assimilation' or 'appropriation', terms employed by Bakhtin in his description of the normative dialogical formation of the subject:

As a living, socio-ideological concrete thing, as heteroglot opinion, language, for the individual consciousness, lies on the borderline between oneself and the other. The word in language is half someone else's. It becomes 'one's own' only when the speaker populates it with his own intention, his own accent, when he appropriates the word, adapting it to his own semantic and expressive intention. (p. 293) ... One's own discourse is gradually and slowly wrought out of others' words that have been acknowledged and assimilated, and the boundaries between the two are at first scarcely perceptible. (p. 345n)

Despite the difficulties he recognizes as afflicting these processes, Bakhtin is clearly operating here with an at least residually Kantian subject, one existent as potential prior to any engagement with word or object, and, perhaps more importantly, on its way to conformity with those maxims of enlightenment that for Kant define the autonomous subject: independence, consistency, and formal, universal identity.[34]

It is, of course, towards the production of such a subject, capable, for example, of assimilating the alien English language to Irish identity or the equally alien Gaelic language to the English 'mother-tongue', that Irish nationalism is directed. What it constantly diagnoses, however, is a subject-people always the *object* of imperfect assimilation to either culture, in a state, that is, of continuing *dependence*. It is for this reason that Joyce's 'citational' aesthetic in *Ulysses* cuts so strongly against both Bakhtin's description of the subjective processes which the novel typifies, and the translational aesthetic of Irish nationalism. One could, indeed, argue that Bakhtin's assimilation is itself a version of a generally translational aesthetic for which the subject is formed in a continual appropriation of the alien to itself, just as translation, as opposed, for example, to interpretation or paraphrase, is seen as essentially a recreation of the foreign text in one's own language.[35] Joyce's, or Stephen's, version of this love song of Connacht rather insists on its heterogeneity in the course of an essentially 'inconsequential' meditation or miscegenates it with an entirely different – but no less 'Irish' – tradition of Gothic vampire tales.[36]

Accordingly, where the principal organizing metaphor of Irish nationalism is that of a proper paternity, of restoring the lineage of the fathers in order to repossess the motherland, Joyce's procedures are dictated by adulteration. Joyce's personal obsession with adultery is well documented and it is a commonplace that the plot of *Ulysses* itself turns around Molly Bloom's adulterous relationship with Blazes

Boylan.[37] That the figure of the nineteenth-century leader of the Home Rule party, Charles Stewart Parnell, recurs from Joyce's earliest works as a victim of betrayal consequent on his adulterous relationship with Kitty O'Shea underlines the extent to which adultery is also an historical and political issue for Irish nationalism. The common tracing of the first Anglo-Norman conquest of Ireland in 1169 to the adulterous relationship between Diarmaid MacMurchadha, King of Leinster, and Dearbhghiolla, the High King's wife, establishes adulteration as a popular myth of origins for Irish nationalist sentiment. As the Citizen puts it, in the 'Cyclops' chapter of *Ulysses*: 'The adultress and her paramour brought the Saxon robbers here ... A dishonoured wife ... that's what's the cause of all our misfortunes' (*Ulysses*, p. 266).

For the nationalist citizen, the identity of the race is adulterated by 'la belle infidèle' and, as in the old expression, the restoration of that identity by translation (*traditore*) is haunted by the anxiety of a betrayal (*traduttore*). This chapter, that in *Ulysses* in which issues of nationalist politics and culture are played out most intensely and in which the various elements of Irish culture are most thoroughly deployed, circulates not only thematically but also stylistically around adulteration as the constitutive anxiety of nationalism. For while the citizen is militant against the hybridization of Irish culture, the chapter itself dramatizes adulteration as the condition of colonial Ireland at virtually every level. Barney Kiernan's pub is at the heart of Dublin, but also located in Little Britain Street, in the vicinity of the Linenhall, the law courts and the Barracks, and across the river from Dublin Castle, the centre of British administration. Most of the characters who pass through the bar (already a parodic form of the legal bar, both being sites of censure and debate) are connected in one or other way with these institutions, while the legal cases cited continually associate the influence of British institutions with economic dependency in the form of debt, and that in turn with the stereotype of financial and cultural instability, the Jew.[38] The slippage among institutional, cultural, racial and political elements is a function of a stylistic hybridization that refuses to offer any normative mode of representation from which other modes can be said to deviate.

These features of the 'Cyclops' chapter have been noted in different ways by many commentators. What needs to be stressed, however, is that by and large the mingling of stylistic elements is rendered by critics in terms which reduce the process of hybridization to the juxtaposition of a set of equivalent representational modes, a reduction which, even where it refuses to posit the register of colloquial speech as an 'original' of which all other modes are 'translations', implies the essential coherence or integrity of each mode in itself. To do so is to leave fundamentally unchallenged the principle of equivalence on which the translational aesthetic is based. This is the case even in one of the most astute accounts of the chapter. After rewriting a passage from 'Cyclops' in what is effectively parallel text, Colin MacCabe comments:

> Ignoring for the moment that part of the second text which has no parallel in the first, what is important in this passage is not the truth or falsity of what is being said, but how the same event articulated in two different discourses produces different representations (different truths). Behind 'an elder of noble gait and countenance' and 'that bloody old pantaloon Denis Breen in his bath slippers' we can discern no definite object. Rather each object can only be identified in a discourse which already exists and that identification is dependent on the possible distinctions available in the discourse.[39]

MacCabe's description of Joyce's procedures at this juncture is comparable to Bakhtin's general description of the novel as a genre:

> The novel can be defined as a diversity of social speech types (sometimes even diversity of languages) and a diversity of individual voices, artistically organized. The internal stratification of any single national language into social dialects, characteristic group behaviour, professional jargons, generic languages, languages of generations and age groups, tendentious languages, languages of the authorities, of various circles and of passing fashions, languages that serve the specific sociopolitical purposes of the day, even of the hour (each day has its own slogan, its own vocabulary, its own emphases) – this internal stratification present in any given language at any given moment of its historical existence is the indispensable prerequisite for the novel as a genre. (pp. 262–3)

Adequate so far as they go, neither description is capable of grasping the internal heterogeneities, the adulteration of discourses as Joyce constructs them in 'Cyclops' and throughout *Ulysses*. This process of adulteration ranges from a phenomenon of colloquial Irish speech to which Oscar Wilde gave the name of 'malapropism' to the ceaseless interpenetration of different discourses. Malapropism varies from casual misspeaking, sometimes intentional, sometimes based on mishearings of an improperly mastered English ('Don't cast your nasturtiums on my character' [p. 263]), to deliberate and creative polemical wordplay (as in English 'syphilisation').[40] As a larger stylistic principle, the adulteration of interpenetrating discourses is unremitting, blending, among other things, pastiches of biblical/liturgical, medieval, epic (based in large part on Standish O'Grady's already highly stylized versions of old Irish heroic cycles), legal, scientific and journalistic modes. Frequently, the legal and journalistic discourses at once contain and disseminate adulteration, representing as institutional formations material sites for the clash of heterogeneous languages and interests. The following example instantiates the possible modulations among different registers:

And whereas on the sixteenth day of the month of the oxeyed goddess and in the third week after the feastday of the Holy and Undivided Trinity, the daughter of the skies, the virgin moon being then in her first quarter, it came to pass that those learned judges repaired them to the halls of law. There master Courtenay, sitting in his own chamber, gave his rede and master Justice Andrew, sitting without a jury in probate court, weighed well and pondered the claim of the first chargeant upon the property in the matter of the will propounded and final testamentary disposition *in re* the real and personal estate of the late lamented Jacob Halliday, vintner, deceased, versus Livingstone, an infant, of unsound mind, and another. And to the solemn court of Green street there came sir Frederick the Falconer. And he sat him there about the hour of five o'clock to administer the law of the brehons at the commission for all that and those parts to be holden in and for the county of the city of Dublin. And there sat with him the high sinhedrim of the twelve tribes of Iar, for every tribe one man, of the tribe of Patrick and of the tribe of Hugh and of the tribe of Owen and of the tribe of Conn and of the tribe of Oscar and of the tribe of Fergus and of the tribe of Finn and of the tribe of Dermot and of the tribe of Cormac and of the tribe of Kevin and of the tribe of Caolte and of the tribe of Ossian, there being in all twelve good men and true ... And straightway the minions of the law led forth from their donjon keep one whom the sleuthhounds of justice had apprehended in consequence of evidence received. (p. 265)

Categorization of this and similar passages as 'dialogic' would be limited insofar as what occurs here is not an opposition, conversational or polemical, between coherent 'voices', but their entire intercontamination. Indeed, precisely what is lacking or erased here is *voice*, which, as Bakhtin remarks, is a category fundamental 'in the realm of ethical and legal thought and discourse ... An independent, responsible and active discourse is *the* fundamental indicator of an ethical, legal and political human being' (pp. 349–50).

It is through the question of voice and its dismantling that we can begin to grasp the complex ramifications of Joyce's deployment of adulteration as both motif and stylistic principle in *Ulysses*. Where nationalism is devoted to the production, in stylistic terms, of a singular voice, and to the purification of the dialect of street ballads or Gaelic songs, it produces equally what we might envisage as a matrix of articulated concepts which provide the parameters of its political aesthetic or aesthetic politics. Thus this singular voice correlates with the formation of the Irish subject as autonomous citizen at one level and with a collective Irish identity at another. That analogical relation between the individual and the national moments is permitted by a concept of representation which requires a narrative movement between the exemplary instance and the totality that it prefigures. The identification of each representative individual with the nation constitutes the people which is to claim legitimate rights to independence as an 'original', that is, essential, entity. Consistent representation of that essence underwrites simultaneously the aesthetic originality, or autonomy, of the literary work that takes its place as an instance of the national culture. Such a self-sustaining and self-reinforcing matrix of concepts furnishes the ideological verisimilitude of cultural nationalism, permitting its apparent self-evidence.

Joyce's work, on the contrary, deliberately dismantles voice and verisimilitude in the same moment. Even if, as MacCabe has suggested, particular discourses attain dominance at given points in the text, the continual modulations that course through 'Cyclops', as indeed through the work as a whole, preclude any discursive mode from occupying a position from which the order of probability that structures mimetic verisimilitude could be stabilized. But even beyond this, the constantly parodic mode in which given discourses are replayed prevents their being understood as internally coherent, if rival, systems of verisimilitude. The double face of parody, at once dependent on and antagonistic to its models, constantly undercuts both the production of an autonomous voice and the stabilization of a discourse in its 'faithful' reproduction.[41] Adulteration as a stylistic principle institutes a multiplication of possibility in place of an order of probability and as such appears as the exact aesthetic correlative of adultery in the social sphere. For if adultery is forbidden under patriarchal law, it is precisely because of the potential multiplication of possibilities for identity that it implies as against the paternal fiction, which is based on no more than legal verisimilitude. If the spectre of adultery must be exorcized by nationalism, it is in turn because adulteration undermines the stable formation of legitimate and authentic identities. It is not difficult to trace here the basis for nationalism's consistent policing of female sexuality by the ideological and legal confinement of women to the domestic sphere.[42] Nor is there any need to rehearse here the anxieties that Bloom raises for the Citizen on racial as well as sexual grounds, or the extent to which the narrative as a whole occupies aesthetic, cultural and sexual terrains in a manner that continually runs counter to nationalist ideology.[43] What must be noted, however, is the extent to which its antirepresentational mode of writing clashes with nationalist orders of verisimilitude precisely by allowing the writing out of the effects of colonialism that nationalism seeks to eradicate socially and psychically. This is not merely a matter of the content of a representation but also inseparably an issue of stylistics. Thus, for instance, Bloom cannot be the exemplary hero of what might be an Irish epic, not only because of his status as 'neither fish nor fowl', to quote the Citizen, but because *Ulysses* as a whole refuses the narrative verisimilitude within which the formation of representative man could be conceived. The aesthetic formation of the exemplary citizen requires not alone the selection of an individual sociologically or statistically 'normative', but the representation of that individual's progress from unsubordinated contingency to socially significant integration with the totality. This requires in turn what Bakhtin describes as 'a combining of languages and styles into a higher unity', the novel's capacity to 'orchestrate all its themes' into a totality (p. 263). *Ulysses'* most radical movement is in its refusal to fulfil either of these demands and its correspondent refusal to subordinate itself to the socializing functions of identity formation.[44] It insists instead on a deliberate stylization of dependence and inauthenticity, a stylization of the hybrid status of the colonized subject as of the colonized culture, their internal adulteration and the strictly parodic modes that they produce in every sphere.

III

We will become, what, I fear, we are largely at present, a nation of imitators, the Japanese of Western Europe, lost to the power of native initiative and alive only to second-hand assimilation. (Douglas Hyde)

Everywhere in the mentality of the Irish people are flux and uncertainty. Our national consciousness may be described, in a native phrase, as a quaking sod. It gives no footing. It is not English, nor Irish, nor Anglo-Irish ... (Daniel Corkery)

[The *pachuco's*] dangerousness lies in his singularity. Everyone agrees in finding something hybrid about him, something disturbing and fascinating. He is surrounded by an aura of ambivalent notions: his singularity seems to be nourished by powers that are alternately evil and beneficent. (Octavio Paz)

ADULTERATION AND THE NATION

We Brazilians and other Latin-Americans constantly experience the artificial, inauthentic and imitative nature of our cultural life. An essential element in our critical thought since independence, it has been variously interpreted from romantic, naturalist, modernist, right-wing, left-wing, cosmopolitan and nationalist points of view, so we may suppose that the problem is enduring and deeply rooted. (Roberto Schwarz)

A European journalist, and moreover a leftist, asked me a few days ago, 'Does a Latin-American culture exist?' ... The question ... could also be expressed another way: 'Do you exist?' For to question our culture is to question our very existence, our human reality itself, and thus to be willing to take a stand in favor of our irremediable colonial condition, since it suggests that we would be but a distorted echo of what occurs elsewhere. (Roberto Fernandez Retamar)

The danger is in the neatness of identifications. (Samuel Beckett)

Riding on the train with another friend, I ramble on about the difficulty of finishing this book, feeling like I am being asked by all sides to be a 'representative' of the race, the sex, the sexuality – or at all costs to avoid that. (Cherrié Moraga)[45]

Since there is insufficient space for a more exhaustive account, the above citations must serve as indicators of a recurrent and problematic set of issues that course through numerous colonial situations, perhaps especially in those where an 'original' language has been displaced by that of the colonizing power.[46] This problematic can be described as a confrontation with a cultural hybridization which, unlike the process of assimilation described by Bakhtin and others, issues in *inauthenticity* rather than authentic identity. To describe this confrontation as problematic is to insist that the experience of inauthenticity intended here is not to be confused with that of the celebrated post-modern subject, though clearly the overlapping geographical and historical terrain of each ultimately requires that they be elaborated together. For the aesthetic freedom of the post-modern subject is the end-product of a global assimilation of subordinated cultures to the flows of multinational capital in the post-colonial world, and to fail to specify that subject is to ignore equally the powerful dissymmetry between the subject who tastes and the indifferent, that is, interchangeable objects of his/her nomadic experience.[47] It should be recalled that the experience of colonized cultures such as Ireland's, with differing but increasing degrees of intensity, is to be subjected to an uneven process of assimilation. What is produced, accordingly, is not a self-sustaining and autonomous organism capable of appropriating other cultures to itself, as imperial and post-modern cultures alike conceive themselves to be, but rather, at the individual and national-cultural level, a hybridization radically different from Bakhtin's in which antagonism mixes with dependence and autonomy is constantly undermined by the perceived influence of alien powers.

A complex web of specular judgments constructs this problematic. On the side of the colonizer, it is the inauthenticity of the colonized culture, its falling short of the concept of the human, that legitimates the colonial project. At the other end of the developmental spectrum, the hybridization of the colonized culture remains an index of its continuing inadequacy to this concept and of its perpetually 'imitative' status. The colonizer's gaze thus overlooks the recalcitrant sites of resistance that are at work in hybrid formations such as those we have been analysing. From the nationalist perspective, hybridity is no less devalued; the perceived inauthenticity of the colonized culture is recast as the contamination of an original essence, the recovery of which is the crucial prerequisite to the culture's healthy and normative development. The absence of an authentic culture is the death of the nation, its restoration its resurrection. In this sense, nationalist monologism is a dialogic inversion of imperial ideology, caught willy-nilly in the position of a parody, antagonistic but dependent.[48]

These remarks need to be qualified, however, by reiterated stress upon the dissymmetry of the specular relation. Nationalism is generated as an oppositional discourse by intellectuals who appear, by virtue of their formation in imperial state institutions, as in the first place subjected to rather than the subjects of assimilation. Their assimilation is, furthermore, inevitably an uneven process: by the very logic of assimilation, either the assimilated must entirely abandon their culture of origins, supposing it to have existed in anything like a pure form, or persist in a perpetually split consciousness, perceiving the original cultural elements as a residue resistant to the subject formed as a citizen of the empire. Simultaneously, the logic of assimilation resists its own ideal model: since the process is legitimated by the judgment of the essential inferiority of the colonized, its very rationale would be negated in the case of a perfect assimilation of colonized subjects without remainder. Therefore, it is at once the power and the weakness of assimilation as the cultural arm of hegemonic imperialism that a total integration of the colonized into the imperial state is necessarily foreclosed. Recognition of this inescapable relegation to hybrid status among 'native' intellectuals formed by the promise of an ever-withheld subjecthood is a principal impulse to nationalism at the same time as it determines the mono-logic mode of nationalist ideology.[49]

We should recall, however, that the desire for the nation is not merely to be formative of an authentic and integral subjecthood, but also the means to capture the state which is the nation's material representation. This fact has crucial theoretical and practical con-sequences. The formation of nationalist intellectuals takes place through both the repressive and the ideological state apparatuses of the empire, the army and police forces being as instrumental as the schools or recreationary spaces. This entails the space of the nation itself being constituted through these apparatuses which quite liter-ally map it and give it its unity in the form of the state. Accordingly, just as the state form survives the moment of independence, the for-mation of the citizen-subject through these apparatuses continues to be a founding requirement of the new nation state.[50] What is time and again remarked of the post-colonial world, that 'independent' states put in place institutions entirely analogous to those of the colonial states that dominated them, is not merely to be explained as a ploy by which the defeated empires continue their domination in renovated guise. For the state form is a requirement of anti-colonial nationalism as it was its condition. By the same token, post-colonial nationalism is actively engaged in the formation of citizen-subjects through those institutions and thereby on the analogy of the metro-politan subject. This is an instance of the 'modernizing' effect of the state as the ensemble of institutions which ensures the continuing integration of the post-colonial state in the networks of multina-tional capital. But it is no less an instance of the modernizing effect of nationalism itself.

The terrain of colonial hybridization here analysed in the Irish context but with specific counterparts virtually everywhere in the colonial world falls in a double and, for the new nation, contradic-tory sense under the shadow of the state. Even where its most imme-diate instruments seem to be economic or cultural forces remote from the purview of the state, hybridization is impelled and sustained by the intervention of the imperial state – by its commercial and criminal laws, its institutions, its language, its cultural displays. Against this process reacts a monologic nationalism which, though already marked by hybridization, seeks to counter it with its own authentic institutions. In the post-independence state, these very institutions continue to be the locus of a process of hybridization despite the separation out of a more or less reified sphere of 'national culture' whose functions, disconnected from oppositional struggle, become the formal and repetitive interpellation of national subjects and the residual demarcation of difference from the metropolitan power. In this respect also, the post-independence state reproduces the processes of metropolitan culture, the very formality of the 'difference' of the national culture ensuring that the interpellation of its citizens always takes the 'same form' as that of the metropolitan citizen.

Consequently, the apparatuses of the state remain crucial objects for a resistance which cannot easily be divided into theoretical and practical modes, not least because what determines both is an aesthetic narrative through which the theoretical is articulated upon the practical and vice versa. What begins as a Kantian precept finds specific material instantiation in post-colonial politics. For though the mode of formation of the citizen-subject may appear as a merely theoretical issue, the narrative of representation on which it depends for the principle by which individual and nation can be sutured determines equally the forms of schooling and of political institutions adopted. These in turn demarcate the limits of what can properly, in any given state, be termed a political practice. For, like any other social practice, politics is an effect of an ideological formation obedient to specific laws of verisimilitude. To have a voice in the sphere of the political, to be capable either of self-representation or of allowing oneself to be represented, depends on one's formation as a subject with a voice exactly in the Bakhtinian sense.

I have been arguing throughout that the processes of hybridization active in the Irish street ballads or in *Ulysses* are at every level recalcitrant to the aesthetic politics of nationalism and, as we can now see, to those of imperialism. Hybridization or adulteration resist identification both in the sense that they cannot be subordinated to a narrative of representation and in the sense that they play out the unevenness of knowledge which, against assimilation, foregrounds the political and cultural positioning of the audience or reader. To each recipient, different elements in the work will seem self-evident or estranging. That this argument does not involve a celebration of the irreducible singularity of the artistic work, which would merely be to take the detour of idealist aesthetics, is evident when one considers the extent to which *Ulysses* has been as much the object of refinement and assimilation in the academy as were the street ballads before. This is, after all, the function of cultural institutions, metropolitan or post-colonial, which seek to reappropriate hybridization to monology. By the same token, such works are continually reconstituted as objects in a persistent struggle over verisimilitude.

It is precisely their hybrid and hybridizing location that makes such works the possible objects of such contestations, contestations that can be conducted oppositionally only by reconnecting them with the political desire of the aesthetic from which they are continually being separated. The same could be said for the multiple locations that make up the terrain of a post-colonial culture: it is precisely their hybrid formation between the imperial and the national state that constitutes their political significance. If, as post-colonial intellectuals, we are constantly taunted – and haunted – by the potentially disabling question, 'Can the subaltern speak?', it is necessary to recall that to speak politically within present formations one must have a voice and that the burden of the question here cited is to deprive two subjects of voices: the subaltern, who cannot speak for herself, and the intellectual, who, by speaking for him or herself, is deprived of the voice that would speak for others. The post-colonial intellectual, by virtue of a cultural and political formation which is for the state, is inevitably formed away from the people that the state claims to constitute and represent and whose malformation is its *raison d'être*. What this entails, however, is not occasion for despair and self-negation but rather that the intellectual's own hybrid formation become the ground for a continuing critique of the narrative of representation that legitimates the state and the double disenfranchisement of subaltern and citizen alike. Within this project, the critique of nationalism is inseparable from the critique of post-colonial domination.[51]

NOTES

1. See Immanuel Kant, *The Critique of Judgement*, James Creed Meredith (trans.) (Oxford 1952), p. 181. I have discussed the ramifications of the concept of exemplarity for politics and pedagogy in 'Kant's Examples', *Representations*, 28 (Autumn 1989), pp. 34–54.
2. D.F MacCarthy, cited in Charles Gavan Duffy, *Four Years of Irish History, 1845–1849* (London 1883), p. 72.
3. On the concept of *Naturgabe* as grounding the economy of genius, see Jacques Derrida, 'Economimesis', Richard Klein (ed.), *Diacritics*, 11.2 (Summer 1981), pp. 10–11.

4. Jacques Derrida explores the logical paradoxes involved in the founding of the state in the name of the people in 'Déclarations d'indépendance' in *Otobiographies: l'enseignement de Nietzsche et la politique du nom propre* (Paris 1984), pp. 13–32. The consequences of these logical paradoxes are worked out later in Ireland's own declaration of independence in 1916, as I have tried to show in 'The Poetics of Politics' above.

5. See especially chapter 2 of my *Nationalism and Minor Literature* (Berkeley and Los Angeles 1987), and 'Writing in the Shit' above.

6. See Mikhail Bakhtin, *The Dialogic Imagination: Four Essays*, Michael Holquist (ed.), Caryl Emerson and Michael Holquist (trans.) (Austin 1981), pp. 67, 262–3, and *passim*.

7. To this extent, Bakhtin is still in accord with Erwin Rohde, whose history of the Greek novel he cites critically: both see the condition of emergence of the novel as being the collapse or disintegration of 'a unitary and totalizing national myth' (p. 65).

8. See Charles Gavan Duffy, *Young Ireland: A Fragment of Irish History, 1840–1850* (London 1880), p. 155.

9. As Thomas Flanagan has argued in his *The Irish Novelists, 1800–1850* (New York 1959), especially chapter 3, the problem for Irish novelists was precisely to overcome the polemical heteroglossia of 'race, creed and nationality' (p. 35). In a society in which identity is defined by opposition to others, the conventional form of the novel, which concentrates on individual development set over against social conventions, what Lukacs describes as 'second nature', is unavailable. I have discussed some of the crises of representation faced by Irish novelists and constitutional thinkers in the early nineteenth century in 'Violence and the Constitution of the Novel' below. The tendency of Bakhtin's analysis of the novel and its social determinants makes it impossible for him to grasp the normative socializing function of the novel and therefore to explore fully the implications of Hegel's remark, which he cites (p. 234), that 'the novel must educate man for life in bourgeois society'. Bakhtin's representation of the novel as a largely progressive and subversive genre stands in need of considerable correction by other theorists who have more fully grasped its ideological and socializing functions. See for example Franco Moretti, *The Way of the World: The Bildungsroman in European Culture* (London 1987) and D.A. Miller, *The Novel and the Police* (Berkeley/Los Angeles 1988), as well as Georg Lukacs, *The Theory of the Novel*, Anna Bostock (trans.) (Cambridge 1971).

10. See Lloyd, *Nationalism and Minor Literature*, chapter 2. Citation from Duffy, *Four Years*, p. 153.

11. See Thomas Osborne Davis, 'The Ballad Poetry of Ireland', in *Selections from his Prose and Poetry*, T.W. Rolleston (intro.) (Dublin n.d), p. 210.

12. It should be remarked that these classifications are constitutive more than analytic, inventing both demographic and aesthetic categories which, as this essay will suggest, subserve distinct political ends. All of them are, in different ways, highly problematic.

13. Daniel Corkery's *The Hidden Ireland: A Study of Gaelic Munster in the Eighteenth Century* (1924; Dublin 1967) is one of the first texts to decipher in Gaelic poetry of the eighteenth century the remnants of the traditions forged in a high or aristocratic tradition rather than the effusions of illiterate peasants.

14. Davis, 'The Songs of Ireland', *Prose and Poetry*, p. 225.

15. Denis Florence MacCarthy, *The Book of Irish Ballads*, new edition (Dublin 1869), p. 24.

16. Samuel Taylor Coleridge, 'The Statesman's Manual' (1816), in R.J. White (ed.), *Lay Sermons*, Bollingen Edition (Princeton 1972), p. 29. For the symbolist tradition in Irish nationalism's aesthetic politics, see 'The Poetics of Politics' above.

17. Charles Gavan Duffy (ed.), *The Ballad Poetry of Ireland* (Dublin 1845), p. xv.

18. On the anxiety concerning English miscegenation with the Gaels, see David Cairns and Shaun Richards, *Writing Ireland: Colonialism, Nationalism and Culture* (Manchester 1988), pp. 5–7. On the economic and social currents in nineteenth-century Ireland that affected the emergence of Irish cultural nationalism, see Lloyd, *Nationalism and Minor Literature*, chapter 2. The question of the decline of the Irish language is more vexed, since recent research gives us reason to doubt the inexorability and rapidity of the decline of the language. Akenson, *Irish Educational Experiment*, pp. 378–80, uses census data to corroborate the notion, current since at least Davis's 1843 essay, 'Our National Language', that the language was in use only in the western half of the country and among less than 50 per cent of the population. (See 'Writing in the Shit' above for the consequences of this view.) Yet it may be that such statistics reflect only the predominant language of literacy, and that for a far greater proportion of the population than was formerly acknowledged, oral proficiency in Irish went along with literacy in English. The ballads often seem to assume a considerable degree of passive competence in Irish, at the least, and certainly an awareness of Gaelic cultural referents. Kevin Whelan remarks:

> I would argue that in 1841 the absolute number speaking Irish was at an all-time high. Remember the population of Ireland in 1600 was ca. 1.5 million. By 1841, it was up to 8.5 million. 100% of 1.5 million is still 1.5 million, 50% of 8.5 million is 4.25 million. Thus, the decline model of 18th and 19th century Irish is misleading in absolute terms – and remember population was increasing rapidly in the west and south west – the Irish-speaking areas. The vitality and flexibility of pre-famine Gaelic-speaking culture has been severely underestimated. (Private correspondence)

See also Niall Ó Cíosáin, 'Printed Popular Literature in Irish 1750–1850: Presence and Absence' and Garrett FitzGerald, 'The Decline of the Irish Language 1771–1871' in Mary Daly and David Dickson (eds), *The Origins of Popular Literacy in Ireland: Language Change and Educational Development 1700–1920* (Dublin 1990), pp. 45–57 and 59–72 respectively, and Tom Dunne, 'Popular Ballads, Revolutionary Rhetoric and Politicisation', in David Dickson and Hugh Gough (eds), *Ireland and the French Revolution* (Dublin 1990), p. 142.

19. Colm Ó Lochlainn (ed.), *Irish Street Ballads*, (1939; revised ed., Dublin 1946).

20. See for example Robert Welch, *Irish Poetry from Moore to Yeats*, Irish Literary Studies, 5 (Gerrards Cross 1980), pp. 43–5, 71 and 131.

21. For 'The Barrymore Tithe Victory' and 'A New Song', see Georges-Denis Zimmermann, 'Irish Political Street Ballads and Rebel Songs, 1780–1900', doctoral thesis presented to University of Geneva (Geneva 1966), pp. 204–5 and 208–9; for 'The Kerry Recruit', see Ó Lochlainn, *Street Ballads*, pp. 2–3. I am grateful to

Brendán Ó Buachalla for alerting me to the wider significance of such allusions.

22. 'Father Murphy' in Ó Lochlainn, *Street Ballads*, pp. 54–5; 'Billy's Downfall' in Zimmermann, 'Irish Rebel Songs', pp. 220–1. Dunne, 'Popular Ballads', pp. 149–50, discusses six recorded versions of 'Father Murphy', and comments on the extent to which different versions may indicate either popular adaptations of bourgeois songs or, contrarily, bourgeois refinements of popular ballads.

23. An excellent account of the confusion of high and low in popular forms and of its pleasures is Peter Stallybrass and Allon White, *The Politics and Poetics of Transgression* (Ithaca, New York 1986). Zozimus's own defence at his trial for causing an obstruction in the Dublin streets is itself a magnificent example of the mixing of genres with exuberant disrespect for the canons:

> Your Worship, I love me counthry. She's dear to me heart, an' am I to be prevented from writin' songs in her honour, like Tommy Moore, Walter Scott an' Horace done for theirs, or from singin' them like the an-shent bards, on'y I haven't got me harp like them to accompany me aspirations! ... An' as a portion ov the poetic janius ov me country has descended upon me showlders, ragged an' wretched as the garmint that covers them, yet the cloth ov the prophet has not aroused more prophetic sintiments than I entertain, that me counthry shall *be* a free counthry! ... Homer sung the praises ov his counthry on the public highways; an' we are informed that dramatic performances wor performed in the streets, with nothing else for a stage but a dust cart. (Laughter.)

Quoted in the Dublin publican and antiquarian P.J. McCall's pamphlet, *In the Shadow of St Patrick's* (1893; Blackrock 1976), pp. 32–3, this account is clearly refracted through oral history. Yet even in its own parodic fashion, it stands as an interesting index of the unstable tone of the popular discourse on cultural politics, which reproduces serio-comically all the terms of nationalist aesthetics but with an indeterminacy of address calculated to pull the wool over the authorities' eyes.

24. See John Mitchel, 'Our War Department', *United Irishman*, I.ii (22 April 1848), p. 171.

25. See William Wordsworth, *The Prelude*, in *Poetical Works*, Thomas Hutchinson (ed.) (Oxford 1973), Book VII, p. 546, ll. 701–4.

26. I have developed these arguments in *Nationalism and Minor Literature*, chapters 2 and 3.

27. MacCarthy, *Irish Ballads*, p. 26.

28. Paul Ricoeur has noted the relation between the minimal element of metaphor and the maximal element of plot in Aristotle's *Poetics*, both narrating a coming to identity of disparate elements. See Paul Ricoeur, 'Metaphor and the Main Problem of Hermeneutics', *New Literary History*, 6, no. 1 (Autumn 1974), pp. 108–10. I have argued that the transfer from the metonymic to the metaphoric axis is the fundamental rhetorical structure of cultural assimilation and racist judgments in 'Race under Representation', *Oxford Literary Review*, 13 (Spring 1991), pp. 71–3. See also 'Violence and the Constitution of the Novel' below for further reflections on the political meaning of this distinction.

29. MacCarthy, *Irish Ballads*, p. 127. In his symbol-making, MacCarthy ignores recent discoveries by George Petrie, who showed that the round towers which are

so prominent a feature of Irish landscapes were of relatively recent Christian origin, thus dispelling numerous myths of origin which had gathered around them. See my *Nationalism and Minor Literature*, chapter 3.

30. On the proliferation of kitsch, nationalist and otherwise, see Kevin Rockett, 'Disguising Dependence: Separatism and Foreign Mass Culture', *Circa*, 49 (January/February 1990), pp. 20–5. Nationalist artefacts work precisely, and not without calculated political effect, as kitsch in the sense that Franco Moretti defines it: 'kitsch literally "domesticates" aesthetic experience. It brings it into the home, where most of everyday life takes place.' See *The Way of the World*, p. 36.

31. James Joyce, *Ulysses* (New York 1986), pp. 152–3.

32. Douglas Hyde, 'The Necessity for De-Anglicising Ireland' in Breandán Ó Conaire (ed.), *Language, Lore and Lyrics: Essays and Lectures* (Blackrock 1986), p. 154.

33. Douglas Hyde, 'Gaelic Folk Songs', in *Language, Lore and Lyrics*, p. 107.

34. In both *Anthropology from a Pragmatic Point of View*, pp. 96–7, and *The Critique of Judgement*, pp. 152–3, Kant describes the enlightened subject as adhering to three precepts: to think for oneself; to think consistently; and to think from the standpoint of all mankind. Though Bakhtin's formulation apparently abandons the final maxim, it is formally and therefore universally prescriptive in exactly the same manner as Kant's. Samuel Beckett's terse formulation, 'I'm in words, made of words, others' words,' is perhaps the most succinct deconstruction of both. See *The Unnamable* (London 1959), p. 390.

35. I have discussed the complexities, largely resistant to nationalist aesthetics, of the process of translation in chapter 4 of *Nationalism and Minor Literature*.

36. Robert Tracy, in his essay 'Loving You All Ways: Vamps, Vampires, Necrophiles and Necrofilles in Nineteenth Century Fiction', in Regina Barreca (ed.), *Sex and Death in Victorian Literature* (London 1990), pp. 32–59, gives an excellent account of the social and political background to the vampire tales of Irish writers like Sheridan Le Fanu and Bram Stoker, creator of Dracula. Alan Titley, *Dublin and Dubliners*, derives the name Dracula itself from the Gaelic Droch-Fhola, or bad blood, confirming its Irish origins. I am indebted to Kevin Whelan for this reference.

37. On Joyce's personal obsession with adultery and betrayal, see for example Richard Ellmann, *James Joyce* (Oxford 1959), pp. 255, 288–93. This obsession was written out not only in *Ulysses*, but also in 'The Dead', the last story of *Dubliners*, and *Exiles*, Joyce's only play.

38. On the question of the hybridization of Irish culture, the most useful study is Cheryl Herr's *Joyce's Anatomy of Culture* (Urbana/Chicago 1986), which analyses in detail the various institutions which compose and interact within colonial Ireland. As she remarks, 'The distortions of reality which one institution imposes on a semantic field operate endlessly in a culture composed of many competing institutions' (p. 14). The chapter pivots around Leopold Bloom's scapegoating as an alien Jew, and opens with the figure of the Jewish money-lender, Moses Herzog, whose name connects directly with the identically named Zionist leader. Since in this chapter Bloom is also given credit for Sinn Féin leader Arthur Griffith's adaptation of Hungarian nationalist strategies, it is clear that Joyce is deliberately playing up the paradox that lies at the heart of nationalism, namely, its

dependence on the dislocatory forces of modernization for its 'local' appeal. If Leopold Bloom be considered Everyman, that is, in Odysseus's own formulation to the Cyclops, 'Noman', then he is so only in the sense that he fulfils Karl Marx's prediction in 'On the Jewish Question', that the principle of exchange for which anti-Semitism castigates the Jew will be most fully realized in 'Christian' civil society. See especially the second essay in *Early Writings*, Rodney Livingstone and Gregor Benton (trans.) (New York 1975). Morton P. Leavitt, in 'A Hero for our Time: Leopold Bloom and the Myth of Ulysses', in Thomas F. Staley (ed.), *Fifty Years Ulysses* (Bloomington, Indiana 1974), p. 142, makes a representative claim for the notion that 'In the urban world in which we all live, no man could be more representative.' For J.H. Raleigh, 'he is modern, secular man, an international phenomenon produced in the Western world at large in fairly sizable numbers by the secular currents of the eighteenth, nineteenth and twentieth centuries, a type often both homeless in any specific locale and at home in any of the diverse middle-class worlds in the Europe and America of those centuries.' See 'Ulysses: Trinitarian and Catholic' in Robert D. Newman and Weldon Thornton (eds), *Joyce's Ulysses, The Larger Perspective* (Newark 1988), pp. 111–12.

39. See Colin MacCabe, *James Joyce and the Revolution of the Word* (London 1979), p. 92. See also Karen Lawrence, *The Odyssey of Style in Ulysses* (Princeton 1981), whose excellent analysis of the 'Cyclops' chapter recognizes its hybrid or uneven character stylistically (especially pp. 106–7), but confines its implications to a modernist problematic of style and to 'Joyce's skepticism about the ordering of experience in language *and* a personal desire to be above the constraints that writing usually imposes' (p. 119). The nature of this chapter has best been described, in terms that would be quite critical of MacCabe's rendering of it, by Eckhard Lobsien, *Der Alltag des Ulysses: Die Vermittlung von ästhetischer und lebensweltlicher Erfahrung* (Stuttgart 1978), p. 106: 'Die zunächst so selbstverständlich anmutende Perspektive des Ich-Erzählers zeigt sich alsbald ebenso verformt und von undurchschauten Spielregeln eingeschränkt wie die Interpolationen' ('The at first apparently self-evident perspective of the first person narrator reveals itself directly to be just as deformed and restricted by inscrutable rules as the interpolations'); and p. 110: 'Die verschiedenen, in sich geschlossenen Versionen von Alltagswelten werden derart in Interferenz gebracht, daß die Leseraktivität auf die Aufdeckung der geltenden Spielregeln und damit eine Desintegration des Textes abzielt' ('The various, self-enclosed versions of everyday worlds are thus brought into interference with one another so that the reader's activity aims at discovering the appropriate rules and thereby a disintegration of the text'). Lobsien emphasizes throughout the 'interference' that takes place at all discursive levels in 'Cyclops' and its effect of relativizing the 'Repräsentationsanspruch jeder einzelnen Sprachform' ('representational claims of every individual form of language') (p. 108). In the present essay, I seek to give back to that 'claim to representation' its full political purview.

40. Joyce's fascination with malapropism is evident from as early as the first story of *Dubliners*, 'The Sisters', in which Eliza speaks of the new carriages' 'rheumatic wheels', to *Finnegans Wake*, for which it might be held to be a stylistic principle. Unlike the pun, which generally is more likely to be 'forced', i.e. the product of an eager intention to subvert, malapropism (as the name nicely implies) evokes a

subject not entirely in control of the metonymic productivity of language. If puns condense, malapropisms displace. *Finnegans Wake* clearly plays on the borderline between the two, generating more displacements than an individual subject can master. The Citizen's pun on 'civilisation' and 'syphilisation' is especially interesting insofar as it invokes standard nationalist attacks on the corrupting effects of English civilization on a morally pure Irish culture in the form of a verbal corruption. The movements of displacement or dislocation that construct colonized society are grasped in the displaced language of the colonized. Both are at once indices of damage and impetuses to the dismantling of the appropriative autonomous speaking subject.

41. See Lloyd, *Nationalism and Minor Literature*, pp. 113–15, for a fuller discussion of the oscillation between antagonism and dependence in parody. An excellent study of the dynamics of parodic forms is Margaret A. Rose, *Parody/Metafiction: An Analysis of Parody as a Critical Mirror to the Writing and Reception of Fiction* (London 1979).

42. In first writing this essay for a publication on Chicano culture, I was forcibly reminded of the figure of La Malinche in Mexican/Chicano culture, who, as Cortez's mistress and interpreter, condenses with exceptional clarity the complex of racial betrayal, translation and adultery that Joyce equally seeks to mobilize in 'Cyclops'. On La Malinche, see Octavio Paz, 'The Sons of La Malinche' in *Labyrinths of Solitude* (New York 1961), pp. 65–88; Norma Alarcón, 'Chicana Feminist Literature: Re-vision through Malintzin/or Malintzin: Putting Flesh Back on the Object' in Cherrié Moraga and Gloria Anzaldua (eds), *This Bridge Called My Back: Writings by Radical Women of Color* (New York 1983), pp. 182–90; and Cherrié Moraga, 'A Long Line of Vendidas' in *Loving in the War Years: lo que nunca paso por sus labios* (Boston 1983), especially pp. 113–14 and 117. In his essay 'Myth and Comparative Cultural Nationalism: the Ideological Uses of Aztlan', in Rudolfo A. Anaya and Francisco Lomeli (eds), *Aztlan: Essays on the Chicano Homeland* (Albuquerque 1989), Genaro Padilla provides a valuable critical history of such recourses to mythic figures in Chicano cultural politics and indicates the similarities in political tendency and value of such tendencies across several cultural nationalisms, including Ireland's. In the Chicano as in the Irish context, what is politically decisive is the appropriative or malapropian displacing effect of the mythic gesture with regard to dominant culture.

43. Colin MacCabe explores all these issues in Joyce's writings throughout *James Joyce and the Revolution of the Word*. See also Bonnie Kime Scott, *Joyce and Feminism* (Bloomington, Indiana 1984), especially chapter 2, 'Mythical, Historical and Cultural Contexts for Women in Joyce', pp. 9–28; Dominic Manganiello, *Joyce's Politics* (London 1980); Hélène Cixous, *L'Exil de James Joyce ou l'art du remplacement* (Paris 1968), especially II.1, 'Le reseau des dépendances', is a valuable exploration of the linkages between family, church and nation, which perhaps surprisingly takes the father's rather than the mother's part.

44. On the socializing function of the novel, see especially Moretti, *The Way of the World*, pp. 15–16. Even where he lays claim to Irish identity ('I'm Irish; I was born here'), or where he seeks to define a nation ('The same people living in the same place'), Bloom appeals to the contingencies of merely contiguous relationships as opposed to the nationalist concern with a lineage of spirit and blood which must be kept pure. Bloom's insistence on contiguity underwrites his own

figuration as a locus of contamination or hybridization as against the assimilative principles of nationalist ideology.

45. See respectively: Hyde, 'The Necessity for De-Anglicising Ireland', p. 169; Daniel Corkery, *Synge and Anglo-Irish Literature* (Cork 1931), p. 14; Paz, 'The Pachuco and Other Extremes' in *Labyrinths of Solitude*, p. 16; Roberto Schwarz, 'Brazilian Culture: Nationalism by Elimination', *New Left Review*, 167 (January/February 1988), p. 77; Roberto Fernandez Retamar, 'Caliban' in *Caliban and Other Essays*, Edward Baker (trans.) (Minneapolis 1988), p. 3; Samuel Beckett, 'Dante ... Bruno. Vico ... Joyce' in Ruby Cohn (ed.), *Disjecta: Miscellaneous Writings and a Dramatic Fragment* (New York 1984), p. 19; Cherrié Moraga, *Loving in the War Years*, p. vi.

46. Retamar writes in 'Caliban' (p. 5) of the singularity of Latin American post-colonial culture in terms of its having always to pass through metropolitan languages, those of the colonizer. In this, as in many other respects, there are evidently close affinities between the Irish and the Latin American experience. But this appeal to specificity may in fact be spurious. As Ngugi Wa Thiong'o has pointed out, African literature has also by and large been written in the colonizer's languages despite the ubiquitous survival of African vernacular languages. See *Decolonising the Mind: The Politics of Language in African Literature* (London 1986), pp. 4–9. What this indicates, as I shall argue in what follows, is that the crucial issue is the space constituted for the citizen-subject in the post-colonial nation not only by the languages but also by the institutional and cultural forms bequeathed by the departing colonizer. As Thiong'o grasps, these are the sites and the subjects in which colonialism continues to reproduce itself.

47. See for example Jean-François Lyotard, *The Postmodern Condition: A Report on Knowledge*, Geoff Bennington and Brian Massumi (trans.) (Minneapolis 1984), p. 76:

> When power is that of capital and not that of a party, the 'transavant-gardist' or 'postmodern' (in Jenck's sense) solution proves to be better adapted than the antimodern solution. Eclecticism is the degree zero of contemporary general culture: one listens to reggae, watches a western, eats McDonald's food for lunch and local cuisine for dinner, wears Paris perfume in Tokyo and 'retro' clothes in Hong Kong; knowledge is a matter for T.V. games. It is easy to find a public for eclectic works ... But this realism of anything goes is in fact that of money; in the absence of aesthetic criteria, it remains possible and useful to assess the value of works of art according to the profits they yield. Such realism accommodates all tendencies, just as capitalism accommodates all 'needs', provided that the tendencies and needs have purchasing power. As for taste, there is no need to be delicate when one speculates or entertains oneself.

Perceptive as this critique is of a vulgar post-modernism's 'cosmopolitanism', we might note that the 'one' of 'general culture' is restored at a higher level only by the invocation of 'taste' and 'aesthetic criteria', that is, at the level of the cosmopolitan point of view of the Subject.

For an excellent critique of the confusion between post-colonial and post-modern forms, see KumKum Sangari, 'The Politics of the Possible', *Cultural Critique*, 7 (Autumn 1987), pp. 157–86. Both she and Julio Ramos, in his 'Uneven

Modernities: Literature and Politics in Latin America', forthcoming in *Boundary*, 2, have pointed out that many of the distinguishing characteristics of Latin American literature, which often appear as post-modern effects, can in fact better be derived from the uneven processes of modernization that have occurred there. This is not, of course, to suggest a single developmental model for all societies but, on the contrary, to suggest the radical variability of modes as well as rates of change. Given the contemporary allure of the 'nomadic subject' or of 'nomadic theory', it is perhaps cautionary to recall that the legitimating capacity of the imperial subject is his ability to be everywhere (and therefore nowhere) 'at home'. For some exploration of this notion as it structures imperialist and racist representations, see Satya Mohanty, 'Kipling's Children and the Colour Line', in *Race and Class*, special issue, 'Literature: Colonial Lines of Descent', 31, no. 1 (July/September 1989), especially pp. 36–8.

48. Early-twentieth-century nationalist appeals to Celticism are an excellent instance of this process, reversing the value but retaining the terms of stereotypes of the Celt first promulgated systematically by Samuel Ferguson and then extended by Matthew Arnold. I have discussed the formation of this stereotype in Ferguson's writings of the 1830s and Arnold's in the 1860s in 'Arnold, Ferguson, Schiller: Aesthetic Culture and the Politics of Aesthetics', *Cultural Critique*, 2 (Winter 1986), pp. 137–69.

49. Homi Bhabha has explored the hybrid status of the colonized subject in 'Of Mimicry and Man: The Ambivalence of Colonial Discourse', *October*, 28 (Spring 1984), pp. 125–33. On the foreclosure of the native intellectual's assimilation to the imperial state, see Benedict Anderson, *Imagined Communities* (London 1983), p. 105. I owe the distinction between the dominant and hegemonic phases of colonialism to Abdul JanMohamed's powerful essay, 'The Economy of Manichean Allegory: The Function of Racial Difference in Colonial Literature', in Henry Louis Gates, Jr (ed.), *'Race', Writing and Difference* (Chicago 1985), pp. 78–107. JanMohamed criticizes Bhabha in this essay for failing to respect the dissymmetry between the colonizing and colonized subject in the Manichean social relations of colonialism. I try to show here that the two positions are intervolved, insofar as any nationalist opposition to colonialism is first articulated through the transvaluation of forms furnished by the colonial power. The moment of dependence in the relationship in no way diminishes the force of the antagonism in the national struggle for independence, but it does determine the forms taken by the post-colonial state and the necessity for a continuing critique of nationalism as a mimicry of imperial forms. On these aspects of nationalism, see Partha Chatterjee's *Nationalism and the Colonial World, A Derivative Discourse?* (London 1986), especially chapters 1 and 2. With regard to the logic of assimilation and its perpetual production of residues, I am greatly indebted to Zita Nune's analysis of the formation of Brazilian national identity in literary modernism and anthropology of the 1920s and 1930s. Her work lucidly shows how the Manichean construction of otherness and the hybrid forms produced by colonialism are logically interdependent moments in the process of assimilation. It thus provides a means to repoliticizing Bhabha's understanding of 'hybridization', since that process is shown to be captured in the hierarchic movement of assimilation which necessarily produces a residue that resists. Hybridization must accordingly be seen as an unevenness of incorporation within a developmental

structure rather than an oscillation between or among identities. Nunes also demonstrates clearly the necessarily racist constructions implicit in cultural solutions to problems of national identity, thus introducing an invaluable corrective to concepts such as *mestizaje* which continue to be uncritically espoused even by thinkers such as Retamar. See Nunes, 'Os Males do Brasil: Antropofagia e Modernismo', Papeis Avulsos do CIEC (Rio de Janeiro), no. 22.

50. My terms here are indebted to Louis Althusser's essay 'Ideology and Ideological State Apparatuses (Notes towards an Investigation)' in *Lenin and Philosophy and Other Essays*, Ben Brewster (trans.) (New York 1971), pp. 127–86. Anderson, *Imagined Communities*, pp. 108–9, indicates the extent to which nationalist intellectuals are formed within the colonial state apparatus, a perception borne out in the case of Young Ireland by Jacqueline Hill's analysis of the social composition of the movement in 'The Intelligentsia and Irish Nationalism in the 1840s', *Studia Hibernica*, 20 (1980), pp. 73–109. See also Frantz Fanon's essays 'The Pitfalls of National Consciousness' and 'On National Culture' in *The Wretched of the Earth* (New York 1963), pp. 148–205 and 206–48 respectively. These essays analyse the dialectical process by which a bourgeois anti-colonial nationalism may give way to a popular nationalism in the post-independence state which is not subordinated to a fetishized 'national culture'. As such, they provide the ground for a critique of intellectual tendencies such as Irish revisionist history which criticize the anti-modernist and Manichean tendencies of nationalism only to valorize British imperialism as an essentially modernizing force.

51. I allude of course to Gayatri Chakravorty Spivak's seminal essay 'Can the Subaltern Speak?' in *Marxism and the Interpretation of Culture*, Cary Nelson and Lawrence Grossberg (eds) (Urbana and Chicago 1988), pp. 271–313. I make no attempt to paraphrase this essay here, wishing only to suggest that the opposition it establishes between *Darstellung* and *Vertreten* requires to be transformed dialectically through the concept of the state in which both are subsumed into a unity of being and of being capable of being represented. That the subaltern cannot speak in our voice is a problem only insofar as the post-colonial intellectual retains the nostalgia for the universal position occupied by the intellectual in the narrative of representation. Similarly, the inevitability of employing Western modes of knowledge is a critical condition of the intellectual's formation and inseparable from his/her occupation of a national space. The logical inverse of these propositions is that the contradictory existence of the post-colonial intellectual equally affects the coherence of Western modes of knowledge which are necessarily reformed and hybridized in other locations. The most interesting discussion of these issues is Homi Bhabha's 'The Commitment to Theory', *New Formations*, 5 (1988), pp. 5–24. In all this, as in the composition of this essay as a whole, I am indebted to conversations with Dipesh Chakrabarty.

VIOLENCE AND THE CONSTITUTION OF THE NOVEL

Violence upon the roads: violence of horses
                    W.B. Yeats, 'Nineteen Hundred and Nineteen'

I

With the possible exception of greenness, no quality has more frequently and repetitiously been attributed to Ireland than violence.
The last twenty-five years of our history have done little to diminish
either the regularity or the apparent self-evidence of the characterization: to cite A.T.Q. Stewart in *The Narrow Ground*, 'Violence
would appear to be endemic in Irish society, and this has been so as
far back as history is recorded.'[1] In such sweeping transhistorical
claims or in the slightly less noxious, because less authoritative, cari-
catures of the tabloid press, the notion of Irish violence scarcely proceeds beyond racial stereotyping. Within serious historiography, two
distinct understandings of violence can be broadly traced. For
nationalist historiography, the violence of Irish history is symptomatic of the unrelenting struggle of an Irish people forming itself in
sporadic but connected risings against British domination. The end
of this history of violence lies in the independent nation state. For
imperialist and, perhaps much the same thing, revisionist histories,
violence may or may not be an endemic quality of the Irish, but it is
what summons into being the emergence of a modern state apparatus
in Ireland: a national police force, administration and legal system,
education and even parliamentary democracy. Violence is understood as an atavistic and disruptive principle counter to the rationality of legal constitution as barbarity is to an emerging civility,
anarchy to culture. In one thing, both tendencies concur: the end of
violence is the legitimate state formation. By the same token, the
end of history is the emergence of the state. From such a perspective,

violence is radically counter-historical, even against narrative, always represented as an outburst, an 'outrage', spasmodic and without a legitimating teleology. Violence is always without the law. For, within nationalist history, what was violence becomes, in Walter Benjamin's terms, 'sanctioned' and thereby ceases to be violence insofar as bloodshed is subordinated to the founding of the state.[2] Nationalism itself requires the absorption or transformation of justifiable but nonetheless irrational acts of resistance into the self-legitimating form of a political struggle for the state.

In this respect, both modes of historiography conform, for all their differences, to what Antonio Gramsci, in the introductory section of his 'Notes on Italian History', defines as the hegemonic history of the ruling classes: 'The historical unity of the ruling classes is realised in the State, and their history is essentially the history of States and of groups of States.'[3] Against this dominant history, as is well known, Gramsci posed the history of 'subaltern classes', which, 'by definition, are not unified and cannot unite until they are able to become a "State"'. Gramsci's term gave a name to that movement of radical historians of the Indian subcontinent who, in reaction to imperial and nationalist traditions of historiography, have concentrated their researches on the history of workers' and peasants' movements and of other 'subaltern' groups.[4] Though this essay owes much to their example, I want to focus for a moment on Gramsci's own terms.

'Subaltern', one of the many euphemisms by which Gramsci sought to evade prison censorship, could possibly be translated accurately back into orthodox Marxist terms as 'proletarian'. Yet to read Gramsci in this fashion is to reduce the complexity of his legacy, whereas to read with his terms, even where they are imposed by circumstance, is often to read in the line of his potential, though occasionally, it may be, beyond his own limitations. The term 'subaltern' has accordingly been taken to apply to groups that do not conform to a classical Marxist definition of the proletariat: as above, and potentially in Ireland, to a range of peasant groups, or, elsewhere, to ethnic or sexual minorities, for example. Such an extension of the term clearly involves overstepping the limits of Gramsci's largely class-oriented thinking, multiplying the significant domains of possible counter-hegemonic practice. A more critical deployment of the term, however, detaches it equally from his understanding of proper historiographic method. For Gramsci clearly envisages subaltern history as one which is completed, unified, only at the moment when the subaltern group itself takes over or becomes a state:

> The history of subaltern social groups is necessarily fragmented and episodic. There undoubtedly does exist a tendency to (at least provisional stages of) unification in the historical activity of these groups, but this tendency is continually interrupted by the activity of the ruling groups; it can therefore only be demonstrated when an historical cycle is completed and this cycle culminates in a success. Subaltern groups are always subject to the activity of ruling groups, even when they rebel and rise up: only 'permanent' victory breaks their subordination, and that not immediately. (*Prison Notebooks*, pp. 54–5).

For Gramsci, the subaltern is the state in emergence, its history yet to be but inevitably to be unified. The 'episodic and fragmentary' nature of its history at any given moment is contingent upon its own fragmentary and emergent condition rather than an essential quality. Historical retrospection will endow its episodes with narrative unity from the perspective of the end of its history in the state. Yet we can read Gramsci's portrayal of the subaltern group's history against itself. If one defines the subaltern not as that which desires the state but as that which is subaltern because it resists or cannot be represented by or in the state formation, its 'episodic and fragmentary' history can be read as the sign of another *mode* of narrative, rather than an incomplete one, of another *principle* of organization, rather than one yet to be unified. Without the perspective of the state as that which governs history, subaltern history becomes something else. Of course, from the perspective of dominant history, the subaltern must be represented as violence. 'Must' in two senses: that which cannot be assimilated to the state can be understood only as outside of the law, disruptive and discontinuous, unavailable for narration; secondly, the history of the state requires a substrate which is counter to its laws of civility and which it represents as outrageous and violent, in order that the history of domination and criminalization appear as a legitimate process of civilization and the triumph of law. Subaltern groups can thus be thought of as having a double history: on the one hand, they play out their own discrete and complex formations and traditions; on the other, occluded by their difference from dominant narratives and forms and by those forms themselves, they are nonetheless 'intertwined with [the history] of civil society and thereby with the history of States and groups of States' (*Prison Notebooks*, p. 52). That intertwining, however, persists as an interface between the state form and what it cannot assimilate, transforming the residua of its historical processes into a limit on its unity and totality and, potentially at least, into sites for emergent and articulate resistance.

This essay covers one set of subaltern movements, the agrarian movements of eighteenth- and early-nineteenth-century Ireland, as they intertwine with increasingly dominant cultural and political narratives in the period before the Famine. My focus is on the crisis of representation that afflicted the Irish novel, and on received accounts of the reasons for that crisis as, generally, for the minor status of the Irish novel of the nineteenth century. But the issue is not merely literary, nor merely a matter of the accuracy or inaccuracy of any particular representation of Irish history, politics or culture. It concerns, rather, a problem of representation in general as a crucial element in the intersecting matrices of politics, aesthetics and historiography. For the repeated stereotyping of the Irish as violent permits the presumption of their incapacity for self-representation and underpins in turn the 'legality' of state violence in terms of both ends and means. Official history cannot address the possibility that both the persistence and the forms of violence in Irish history constitute not simply barbarous aberrations but a continuing contestation of a colonial civil society's modes of domination *and representation*. As we shall see, the very difficulty posed by various Irish forms of violence, reactive, tactical and strategic, for the grasp of legal and military power raises simultaneously a critical problem of narrative verisimilitude which cuts into literary and political spheres alike.

II

Accounts of the nineteenth-century Irish novel are troubled by the need to explain its perceived inadequacy in relation to British and continental models. There are examples of virtually every sub-genre from the historical to the domestic novel or the *Bildungsroman*, and no dearth of novels deserving of more extensive critical attention than they have to date received,[5] but against a double axis of comparison, scarcely a single nineteenth-century Irish novel seems to stand up. One axis is the enormous example of *Ulysses*, which can be seen as at once, to echo Victor Shklovsky's remark on *Tristram Shandy*, the most typical *Irish* novel in terms of its stylistic and narrative traits, and the novel most destructive of the novel tradition itself.[6] Against *Ulysses*, all other Irish novelistic production seems diminished. The other axis is that of the British, and occasionally, the European novel generally, strong traditions whose major achievements overshadow just as substantially as *Ulysses* the 'minor' tradition of Irish novel-writing. Yet the very classification of literary productions into the major and the minor begs analysis of the grounds of those concepts in relation to their political and cultural significance.[7] Accordingly, I shall attempt not a re-evaluation of the Irish novels in question, but an investigation of the terms of their evaluation. The configuration of the novel with other kinds of dominant social narrative may thus become clearer and the 'inadequacy' of the Irish novel in these terms may be read equally as symptomatic of the resistance of an anomalous Irish culture to modes of representation emerging into dominance. What I will show further is that the peculiarities of the Irish situation also call for a transformation of recently influential theories of the sociology and generic history of the novel – an effect of transformation which may even be typical for the impact of colonial situations on 'Western theory'.

The reasons usually given for the inadequacy of the nineteenth-century Irish novel can be classified as follows:

1. The general instability of Irish society, and in particular the constant outbreaks of rural violence, preclude the possibility of convincing resolutions in reconciliation or social integration that are characteristic of the English novel of the same period.
2. The absence of a strong and independent middle class, both as public and as matter of the novel, presents an obstacle to the development of the form along lines laid down by the normative history of the 'rise of the novel'.
3. The bilingual nature of Irish culture hampered the development of a stably transforming medium for literary production and therefore slowed the stylistic maturation of the genre.
4. In a related way, the predominance of an oral culture in Ireland, in the urban as well as the rural environment, produced alternative expectations of plot or narrative, hampering the development of forms of emplotment characteristic of the genre elsewhere.[8]

We can ignore for the moment the insistently binary form in which the characteristics of Irish culture detrimental to the novel are defined in terms of English conditions more evidently conducive to its rise and flourishing; we will return to the positivism of this opposition once the problematic nature of the assumptions involved has become clearer. Each of the above propositions is questionable insofar as it is held to furnish a rationale for the inadequacy of the Irish novel. To begin with, the novel is conventionally held to have reached its peaks in the nineteenth century not only in England but also in Russia and France. To speak of any of these nations as 'stable' is already to overlook the unprecedented demographic shifts taking place in the eighteenth and nineteenth centuries, the political and economic transformations, often violent in their own right, that underlay them, and the fact that the novel arises most frequently as the chosen mode of precisely those social groups who are registering those transformations most articulately. It would not, indeed, be impossible to argue that social instability is itself a *condition* of the novel in demanding access for those voices and narratives that had formerly been unrepresented and whose irruptions furnish the very dynamic of the genre.[9] However, it is important not to lose sight of the apparent explanatory power of this notion of a natural conjunction between stability and the novel form, precisely in order to interrogate more fully the formal assumptions of what has all the self-evidence of an ideological proposition.

A different set of criticisms can be directed at the problems of language and of the oral bias of Irish culture. From one perspective, bilinguality could be seen as a potentially rich version of the heteroglossia, to invoke Bakhtin's terminology, which is the fertile ground of the genre. Recent research indeed suggests that a large proportion of the Irish population in the first half of the nineteenth century was quite capable of manipulating both languages according to need and context so that the notion of linguistic deprivation of the native Irish requires nuancing to say the least.[10] It depends, amongst other things, on two precepts which are already loaded in the colonial situation, namely, that the only authentic language of expression, for individual or nation, is the mother tongue and that, correlatively, expression of whatever kind in a second language will inevitably be inauthentic, deracinated, lame. On such a basis, the hybridity of Irish English, until it is refined into a literary medium of expression with its own regularities, and the related interlingual shifts that early-nineteenth-century culture must have permitted and frequently witnessed, can be seen only as signs of cultural damage rather than as indices of versatility. The existence of forms such as the ballad in which shifts of register, language and cultural orientation can be positive assets under its characteristic conditions of reception points one towards the acknowledgment that the novel is, so to speak, an engaged social form often antagonistic to the survival of alternative genres. By this I mean that the novel must not merely be seen as a form which seeks passively to reflect, amongst other things, the linguistic habits of a given community, but that its development entails a regularization and hierarchization of sociolects such that its dominance relegates to marginality forms which depend on an instability of register or on the possibilities offered by linguistic instabilities. As a literary form, the novel is not simply the product and the reflection of certain social conditions but actively contributes to producing them as the very condition of its own reception. As oral forms, on the contrary, ballads and folk-tales strategically deploy the very conditions of instability that determine their production, reception and transmission as well as their materials and stylistic techniques. We may therefore need to rethink the relation of an oral culture to the novel less in terms of merely formal differences between modes of emplotment or characterization, for example, and more in terms of those formal differences as expressive of and participant in quite antagonistic social or cultural forms. The problem of the novel in this respect becomes, then, not just that where oral modes of narrative dominate, standard models for novelistic narrative are lacking, but that a real antagonism exists between the novel and the social forms it desires and the 'oral' culture it would displace.[11]

This leads us to the even more vexed question of the novel's relation to the middle classes. The problem I wish to isolate here is not with the variously articulated argument as to the connection between the rise of the novel and the growing size and hegemony of the middle classes in England, a connection which, however it is understood, seems fairly well established. Nor do I wish to claim that a very different class structure in Ireland produced very different conditions for the novel there, in terms of its matter as in terms of its dissemination and consumption. On the contrary, commentators on the emerging Irish novel are right to emphasize the peculiar economic condition of its being written principally for an English public in the absence of any large potential Irish market, and equally right to emphasize that early-nineteenth-century novelists in Ireland themselves tended to perceive its class structure as a problem (and to this point we will return).[12] That is to say, the Irish novelists of the first half of the nineteenth century and their critics by and large assume that Irish conditions *ought* to conform to English ones in order for the novel to thrive. They do not see in the anomalous condition of Ireland the potential for an alternative mode of narrative let alone an alternative set of social relations. Once again, however, the problem lies rather in the tendency of such arguments to consider the conditions of the novel as a question of what it represents rather than seeing it as one among many narrative formations concerned to produce and define social relations in the very process of representing them. The question becomes, then, one as to the significance of representations of the Irish class structure.

Class structure in nineteenth-century Ireland has been the object of considerable debate and redefinition ever since that century itself. The representation of Irish society as 'divided ... into two distinct bodies, without common interest, sympathy or connexion' has continued to have remarkable currency since Edmund Burke formulated it thus in his letter to Sir Hercules Langrishe of 1792.[13] This binary image of Ireland has also undergone considerable and often contradictory shifts of valence. It has been deployed, as by Burke, to portray a dangerous and destabilizing imbalance in the social formation and in this form has recurred as the still powerful image of a colonial Ireland divided abruptly between landlords and peasants. For many writers in the Literary Revival, on the contrary, the image of Ireland as divided between aristocracy and peasantry or folk was a figure for a harmonious, anti-modern social formation whose feudal structure preserved the authenticity of a still vital Gaelic culture. As is well known, this vision of Irish society had as its correlative a distaste for middle-class Ireland, expressed most stridently by Yeats, but figured equally in the distrust evinced by Synge, Russell, or Hyde for the effects of commercialization on Irish culture, effects that are grasped in nationalist terms as the inroads of anglicization. The contradiction is equally familiar, not only insofar as a group of largely middle-class writers turn against their class of origin and against the very class that had tended to sustain the political culture of nationalism, but moreover insofar as Irish nationalism itself both emerged as a middle-class ideology and was peculiarly concerned with the need to expand the middle class – 'the intelligence, the wealth, and the strong mind of the land'.[14] For Young Ireland, the apparent polarities of Irish society, divided between 'landlords who are rich in present income and past savings; and tenantry who are poor beyond comparison with any People, civilized or savage in the universe',[15] are a hindrance to the development and dissemination of nationalism rather than a means to preserving national culture. Only the most militant of the Young Irelanders, like John Mitchel, inspired at the height of the Famine by James Fintan Lalor's virtually apocalyptic articles on the social dissolution under way, were drawn to see Ireland's anomalous social constitution as an opportunity rather than an obstacle for nationalism.

Almost all accounts, however, tend to view the eighteenth century as a period of at least stable and in some versions even harmonious relations between a landlord class and its peasantry. Against this representation, which is really a representation of a mode of domination without sustained opposition, the progressive decline of ascendancy hegemony in the nineteenth century is registered as social dissolution. Clearly this is an idealized portrait of a century which began with the imposition of the Penal Laws and concluded with the 1798 uprising and which saw some of the most spectacularly organized campaigns by rural secret societies through the 1770s and 1780s. What I wish to argue here is neither the accuracy of this dualistic image of society for any period, nor, on the contrary, that the intrinsic instability of Irish society or its difference from English society made imported novel forms inapplicable,[16] but rather that a certain conjunction between demographic shifts, rural violence and social movements produces a crisis of representation for the novel precisely in terms of the ideological ends with which it seeks to intervene actively as a hegemonic force in an unstable society. This assumes that the representational structure of the novel as a genre has to be understood rather in terms of its socializing ends than of its mimetic function alone.

The realist novel has always been remarkable as a genre for its capacity to draw on an exceptionally wide range of social and cultural materials for its representations. Formally, however, it is distinguishable from related modes of narrative such as the picaresque or the romance in that its elements are not arranged contiguously or episodically but according to laws of integration or harmonization which are themselves 'socially symbolic acts', to borrow Fredric Jameson's term.[17] As both Hegel and, following him, Lukacs recognize, the most significant aspect of the integrations performed by the novel, that which makes it the 'epic' of the bourgeois era, lies in its narrations of the socialization of the individual.[18] This implies that the virtual law of the realist novel, which, rather than any putative adequacy of mimesis, makes it *realist*, the law that it should take as its object the representative individual, is not merely a matter of seizing on socially significant agents but far more importantly of repeatedly telling the tale of an individual's passage from singularity or particularity to social integration. The anomalous individual learns to be reconciled with society and its projects, whether, as mostly for men, through labour or, as mostly for women, through love and marriage. The verisimilitude of realism resides in its capacity to make such narratives of self-formation normative. If this account may seem to make the *Bildungsroman* too narrowly the type of realism, it must be emphasized that the individual narrative of self-formation is itself subsumed in the larger narrative of the civilizing process, the passage from savagery to civility, which is the master narrative of modernity and which informs equally the historical novel of the same period. Ethical identity is thus the end of the novel in a double sense. On the one hand, it narrates the passage of an individual or a people-nation from contingent particularity to universal value, their history becoming representative exactly insofar as it reproduces the general form of universal human history. On the other, it seeks to produce ethical identity as an intrinsic element of its aesthetic effect: the mechanisms of identification, or in nineteenth-century terms, 'sympathy', are crucial to the pedagogical claims of the novel as means to induce in the reader an ethical disposition. The process of reading ideally repeats the learning process undergone by the novel's protagonist. The production of ethical subjects, and not merely their figuration, is the end of the novel's 'narrative of representation'.[19]

There is no doubt that the Irish novelists of the 1830s and 1840s, realist and historical alike, were conscious of confronting a crisis of representation. The remarkable consensus among writers of the 1830s as to the intractable difficulties presented by Irish social realities to novelistic representation is a striking phenomenon in Irish cultural history. Despite their well-known political antagonism, and despite the differences in their perspectives on Irish history, Maria Edgeworth and Lady Morgan arrive at strikingly similar conclusions in the mid-1830s. Edgeworth writes to her brother in 1834:

It is impossible to draw Ireland as she now is in the book of fiction – realities are too strong, party passions too violent, to bear to see, or to care to look at their faces in a looking glass. The people would only break the glass and curse the fool who held the mirror up to nature – distorted nature in a fever.[20]

At the same time, in her Preface to *Dramatic Scenes from Real Life* (1833), Lady Morgan concludes that 'charming historical romances, which were not historical, whose material was taken from inventories; and whose events were coloured from the political creed of the author' had to give way to these more fragmentary scenes of rural disorder, injustice and provocation:

We are living in an era of transition. Changes moral and political are in progress. The frame of the constitution, the frame of society itself, are sustaining a shock, which occupies all minds, to avert or modify.

Under such conditions, 'there is no legitimate literature, as there is no legitimate drama'.[21]

Tom Dunne's recent essays have traced similar hesitations and problems in the Banims and in Griffin and, more importantly, indicate the extent to which this coming to crisis in the 1830s of various attempts to represent Ireland in the novel was long prepared for in the various exclusions and stereotypings of elements of Irish society which had already seemed inassimilable to fictional narratives.[22] Common to all these writers, whatever the significant differences in their political positions or advocacies, is an acceptance of the 'colonial settlement' by which the possibility of reconciliation or resolution in Ireland takes place within the historical frame of a movement from barbarity and lawlessness to civility or cultivation. The endeavour of the Irish novel of the period is to find the means to narrate such an historical movement at both the national and the individual levels, whether through novels of the private sphere, like Griffin's *The Collegians*, or novels with a larger historical framework, such as Banim's *The Boyne Water*, Edgeworth's *Ormond* or Morgan's *O'Donnel*. For reasons well indicated in an article from the *Nation* of 1846, Irish history is not easily susceptible of such resolutions, given the difficulty of locating a *common story* in a chronicle of conquest and dispossession:

The era to which Englishmen point as that in which their constitution was finally established in highest perfection, and once for all made the envy of surrounding nations, is precisely the day from whence Ireland's lowest debasement and bitterest sorrow must be dated. The 'Glorious Revolution' is to us an abomination; the 'Bill of Rights' a fraud, the 'privileges of Parliament', and the whole system of parliamentary government then set up for worship and obedience, a delusion and a cruel mockery.[23]

By the same token, the successive agrarian disturbances of the period between the mid-eighteenth century and the Famine, and in particular the Tithe Wars of the 1830s, must have seemed peculiarly inassimilable to a narrative of reconciliation to exactly the extent that they could be seen as struggles between the dispossessed and the settlers. In both cases, crucially, narrative problems are inextricably entwined with problems of the legitimacy of the state formation and its apparatuses.

A number of problems trouble such an account, however, despite the extent to which it begins properly to locate the problem of novelistic representation not in the domain of mere depiction but rather in the ends of narrative. To one problem we will return, namely the extent to which the depiction of agrarian disturbance in this period as anti-colonial is adequate, whatever its partial truth. For another problem insists more immediately, which can be encapsulated in the question as to why, in principle, manifestations of violence which could have been taken, and indeed often were, as indices of the lack of cultivation or civility of the native Irish, should in principle raise problems for representations which might equally have drawn on rural anarchy as the very ground for narratives of cultivation and reconciliation.[24] It is, after all, notably out of the recent and violent past of Scotland that Walter Scott, whose influence on Irish novelists is well documented, could forge novels of reconciliation, drawing on the crucial figure of the minor mediating character. Georg Lukacs has shown the importance of such characters to the narrative resolutions of Scott's novels, and there is no doubt that writers like Banim quite consciously sought to adopt this model in novels like *The Boyne Water*.[25]

To recall this is to begin to acknowledge the full importance of the Irish crisis of representation in the 1830s and its profounder relation to the linked problems of the depiction of violence and the absence of a middle class. More or less contemporaneously with Edgeworth and Morgan, and at the moment of his closest involvement with Caesar Otway's evangelical unionism, William Carleton expresses his own understanding of the crisis as follows. Remarking that 'there is scarcely such a thing in this unhappy country as a middle class', he continues:

This absence has split the kingdom into two divisions, constituting the extreme ends of society – the wealthy and the wretched. If this third class existed, Ireland would neither be so political nor so discontented as she is; but on the contrary, more remarkable for peace and industry. At present, the lower classes being too poor, are easily excited by those who offer them a better order of things than that which exists. The theorists step into the exercise of the legitimate influence which the landed proprietors have lost by their neglect. There is no middle class in this country who can turn round to them and say, 'Our circumstances are easy, we want nothing; carry your promises to the poor, for that which you hold forth to *their* hopes, *we* enjoy in reality.'[26]

Crucial to Carleton's complaint here is the manner in which it extends the apprehension of the crisis beyond questions of mimesis to questions of representation in a fuller sense in ways apparently unavailable to Edgeworth and Morgan. For what he laments is not merely the absence of a middle-class reading public, nor simply the absence of a middle class as the potential matter for realist narratives, but the absence of a middle class that would provide for representative or exemplary figures. To put it in other terms, Carleton perceives that any narrative of reconciliation will lack verisimilitude or ideological persuasiveness exactly insofar as it cannot appeal convincingly to an existent middle class as exemplary of the achievements of an Ireland beyond political, class and sectarian divisions.[27]

Though his comments were written at a moment when he was perhaps most identified with Tory unionism, it finds constant echoes not only in the writings of other unionists but also in the pages of Young Ireland's *Nation*. There is, in fact, remarkable agreement on all sides as to the lack of a middle class and the deleterious effects of that lack in early-nineteenth-century Ireland for unionist and nationalist projects alike. Only rarely is scepticism expressed concerning this assumption, as in a comment in the *Dublin University Magazine*'s review of Gustave de Beaumont's memoirs of his Irish tour:

The want of a middle class between the rich and the poor is frequently lamented in Ireland; but it is invariably overstated, although we believe never to such an extent as by M. De Beaumont ... Even M. De Beaumont must admit a pretty numerous middle class in Ireland, when he dwells so much upon the evils of the middle-men, whose numbers, however, he considerably exaggerates.[28]

The reviewer's scepticism is to some extent borne out by recent historical demography, which suggests that even as early as the mid-eighteenth century there existed a quite substantial middle class and even a quite substantial Catholic middle class of large farmers, especially graziers. The significant exception is in the professional sector, forbidden to Catholics under the Penal Laws. The Catholic Relief Act of 1793 gave statutory expression to a tendency towards relaxation of the Penal Laws that had already long been evident, and in the wake of the Union, and especially of Catholic Emancipation, a considerable increase in the size of that middle class takes place in all sectors, mercantile and professional as well as agricultural.[29] In Ulster, of course, a substantial Protestant rural middle class, in addition to a proto-industrial and mercantile middle class, had been long established, due in part to more equable rights of tenure in the province. The emergence of bourgeois nationalism in Ireland is itself to a great extent determined precisely by a desire to protect middle-class interests from the inroads of a more powerful British capitalism and from the effects of the series of economic crises in Britain generally after 1815 over which the Irish could exert no control.[30]

This apparent discrepancy between predominant perceptions in the nineteenth century and contemporary demography seems to suggest that the grounds for the contention that Ireland lacked a middle class, whatever significance is attributed to this, fall outside the sphere of simple statistics concerning numbers and classes. Beyond this lies a problem of classification, complicated in turn by an instability of social relations overdetermined by Ireland's colonial history. Traditional dualistic representations of colonial Irish society as being divided between peasants and landlords, Gaelic and Anglo-Irish, country and city, and so forth, have become increasingly complicated by recent research which indicates the necessity for a far more finely graded set of classifications, including landless labourers, cottiers, farmers, middle men and land-owners, and far greater regional specificity.[31] Within themselves, these classifications are generally marked by a certain instability, insofar as the peculiar vulnerability of the Irish rural social system to economic crises or crop failures, combined with a gradual move towards the rationalization of agriculture throughout the period, could lead to sudden shifts in status. As is well known, the general tendency during the century, and one aggravated by the Famine, was for larger holdings to displace smaller ones, to the disadvantage of the cottiers and labourers.[32]

This tendency, with all its local or regional variants, does not evenly correspond, however, with the emergence of a stabilizing and reconciled middle class, nor for a long time to that of a class with certain regularities of disposition or ideological solidarity. Analyses over the past decade of the dynamics of agrarian disturbances, of their ends and organization, are peculiarly suggestive in this respect and allow us to reconnect the question of 'the endemic violence of Irish society' to that of the problem of the middle classes. They also enable greater specificity as to the colonial dimension of Irish history and its effects, beyond the broad strokes of the 'Manichean allegory', which remains a crucial framework for understanding the fundamental dynamics of nineteenth-century Irish society.[33] Essential to the assumption of the stabilizing character of the middle classes, an assumption derived largely from English models of civil and political society, is the notion of ownership of property. The yeoman farmer is for this reason the presiding spirit of English political theory, liberal and conservative alike. In this respect, to begin with, the formation of the middle classes in colonial Ireland is profoundly anomalous, since the vast proportion of middling and even large farmers were land-holders, or tenants, rather than proprietors. The history of the land wars, from the agrarian disturbances of the eighteenth century to the Land League of the later nineteenth century, would seem to indicate that lack of proprietorship in land, for reasons directly determined by the nature and maintenance of colonial occupation, produced the anomalous situation that social and political, as well as economic, instability was at its greatest precisely in those areas of the country where the largest 'middle class' formations could be held to be emerging. Contrary to what one might expect, the highest incidence of agrarian disturbance from the mid-eighteenth century through to the Famine took place in neither the areas of greatest destitution and social polarity, Connacht, the north-west and west Munster, nor the areas of greatest sectarian polarization, in Ulster, but in the belt of rich agricultural land stretching from Wexford and Kilkenny through to north Cork, Tipperary and Limerick.[34] As one historian of pre-Famine agrarian rebellion has put it:

This can perhaps be partially explained by the supposition that peasants who lived slightly above the margin of complete poverty, and still had something to lose, were more prone to agrarian rebellion than those peasants in the extreme west and north-west who had much lower expectations.[35]

This explanation can certainly be supported by the correlation, noted by most historians, between the incidence of 'outrage' and cycles of economic depression. At the same time, however, it risks implying a straightforward antagonism between land-owners or their representatives and tenants, an impression which would obscure the complexity of the dynamics of agrarian rebellions and oversimplify the shifting social composition, aims and objects of the secret societies involved. For while in many instances agrarian rebellion certainly expressed such antagonism, and could seem to represent a certain community of interest among land-holders from cottiers to middling farmers, this was by no means always the case. For throughout the period antagonism could equally be expressed between the labouring poor, including small tenants who paid part of their rent in kind by labouring for larger farmers, and those 'middle men' who sublet their plots, usually at inflated rates of rent. In such cases, the social composition of the secret societies would be very different from those directed against landlords, and their ends would be most likely to concern the fixing of just rates of pay or rent. In other cases, and particularly where tithes were at issue, community of interest could bring together a remarkable range of social groups, even including landlords and labourers at each end of the scale. It is not possible, in other words, to understand the agrarian disturbances of the pre-Famine period simply through invoking anti-colonial antagonisms, although in the final instance colonial land-holding practices do furnish the frame for a very complex articulation of social relations.

This is of course to say that the agrarian movements of the period were not, or, as in some views, 'not yet', nationalist, in terms of both their relative regionalism and their immediate aims and modes of organization.[36] Contrary to nationalism, they do not posit a transcendent community of interest constituting the 'middle ground' of the nation or people, but find their legitimation in the immediately perceived needs of a material and contingent community whose composition is defined directly by those interests. Returning momentarily to the real or apparent antagonism between the secret societies and nationalist political organization, analyses of the social structure and practices of agrarian movements in Ireland virtually oblige us to rethink both the question of violence and that of the middle classes in relation to the novel.

The 'frequently lamented want of a middle class', conceived as the lack of a locus of stability, has to be rethought in terms of the historical existence of a middle class that was the site of maximum instability, whether in terms of its fluctuating economic situation or in terms of its political or social affiliations. Affiliated at one moment with land-owners, at another with the landless, the middle classes of rural Ireland are not simply difficult to categorize or quantify, but present a peculiarly contested social terrain.[37] Precisely the social class that for the English novel furnished representative figures through whom progressive reconciliation could be envisaged, in Ireland eludes such a representative function, appearing instead as a locus of unstable transitions, uncertain affiliations and social disequilibrium. Even in the wake of the Famine, where the consolidation of larger holdings might be expected to have stabilized the middle classes, their increasing politicization around Catholic nationalist ideology would have made them participants in a continuing and open-ended struggle rather than agents of reconciliation. But before the Famine, the consequences for the novel are quite clear. For aristocratically oriented writers like Edgeworth or Morgan, the old resolution that appealed to benevolent and improving landlordism becomes untenable precisely insofar as the growing social and political power of the middle classes undermines the influence formerly taken for granted by the landlords. At the same time, for them as much as for Carleton, Griffin or the Banims, the middle classes do not offer an alternative assurance of reconciliation or middle ground. Resolution becomes highly problematic in 'an era of transition' in which it has to be recognized that the novel is itself partisan rather than transcendental, 'coloured from the political creed of the author', as Morgan had it. To reread Edgeworth's comments from this perspective is to acknowledge that the incoherence of her metaphor is an index of the very precise strains felt by the novelist at this historical juncture. Try as she will to maintain the image of the novel as a passive or specular mirror held up to nature, it is the very people represented in that mirror who become the novel's antagonists as well as its objects.

III

Accordingly, for the novel quite as much as for historical narrative, we need to rethink the question of violence less as one of the depiction or rationalization of a given phenomenon whose very excessiveness is beyond mimesis than as raising a problem of representation itself, of a representation whose insufficiency must appear as an effect of violence. Certainly it is a striking fact that while traditional accounts of Irish history, historical as well as literary, constantly stress the endemic and excessive violence of the culture, the more detailed studies of agrarian disturbances tend to suggest that actual levels of violence were far lower than such representations imply. Thus, for example, in his important essay 'An End to Moral Economy', Tom Bartlett calculates that the virtually continual disturbances from 1760 to 1790 involved only fifty deaths, considerably fewer even than the 300 that resulted from the Gordon Riots of

1780. Other historians bear out this finding.[38] But Bartlett's article is important for other reasons, insofar as it offers ways to understand the significance of violence in Ireland beyond the usual stereotypes. In the first place, as his comparison of the deaths resulting from agrarian disturbances with those resulting from military intervention in the Gordon Riots suggests, a distinction between popular and state-sanctioned violence is crucial in order to understand why one society might be characterized as violent and another as orderly. He further points out, as do other historians, that the focus of 'violence' in Ireland differed from that in England, or indeed France, in being not food but land, 'and was thus, to English eyes, old-fashioned, if not archaic'.[39] Apart from stressing a crucial distinction between a colonial and a proto-class situation, Bartlett's comments raise here a question of verisimilitude and its regulation: what might be called the economy of Irish violence seems literally improbable or illegitimate to English observers. His own analysis, which focuses on a set of disturbances which were unusually violent at least in terms of death toll, marks a distinction between those inspired by issues of land and its occupation and those inspired by the direct and abstract interventions of the state, here in the form of enlistment. This distinction, which is perhaps only a little too neatly correlated to a definitive transition, crucially highlights a conflict of representations insofar as it is a state military formation on a national basis which comes in conflict with a prior system of 'moral economy' and inaugurates the gradual transformation of local outrages into a national and nationally policed phenomenon. Within the latter formation, *local* outrages inevitably appear as archaic, whatever their own internal principles or logic of action.

To highlight this distinction, which is linked also to a transition from the moral to the market economy (p. 62), is, however, equally to broach a criticism of the limited sense in which Bartlett uses the term 'moral economy' and to suggest its further potential. For Bartlett, the notion of the moral economy entails primarily relations of deference or 'that balance, that tacit understanding between governor and governed' (p. 42; and p. 62) which was disintegrating towards the end of the eighteenth century but which had underwritten what he sees as the relatively harmonious social relations of the preceding period. Even without questioning, as one would have to, the image of comparative harmony in eighteenth-century Ireland, it must be said that Bartlett's use of the notion of 'moral economy' somewhat reduces the complexity of the concept as introduced by E.P. Thompson in his seminal essay, 'The Moral Economy of the English Crowd in the Eighteenth Century'.[40] For though Thompson certainly defines the concept in relation to 'the paternalistic tradition of the authorities' (p. 79), and implies its articulation within an at least notional system of reciprocity, the burden of his argument is to show how precisely in moments of crisis for such a system the appeal to a moral economy hyperbolically displaces dominant morality. A popular definition of legitimate practices

was grounded in a consistent traditional view of social norms and obligations, of the proper economic functions of several parties within the community, which, taken together, can be said to constitute the moral economy of the poor.

While this moral economy cannot be described as 'political' in any advanced sense, nevertheless it cannot be described as unpolitical either, since it supposed definite, and passionately held, notions of the common weal – notions which, indeed, found some support in the paternalistic tradition of the authorities; notions which the people re-echoed so loudly in their turn that the authorities were, in some measure, the prisoners of the people. (p. 79)

Unlike Bartlett, Thompson deploys the term here to signal not the description of an existent state of harmonious social relations, but a concept which emerges at exactly the point at which the social antagonism underlying apparent reciprocity becomes clear. The concept of moral economy denotes not a common understanding but precisely a discrepancy between the expectations of the poor and those of the 'authorities', a discrepancy grasped critically and politically. Appeal is made to such a concept only at the moment of breakdown of the system to which it refers. One could argue then that, far from a state formation displacing a previously harmonious moral economy, a more or less conscious appeal to a ruptured moral economy and the state formation itself are mutually antagonistic responses to the breakdown of a previous mode of domination.

Something of this order appears to have been occurring in pre-Famine Ireland, disturbing in its anomalous way all kinds of dominant or emergent cultural and political formations from the novel to constitutional theory. Thus it is quite specifically both the historical division of Ireland into colonized and colonizer, a history substantially different from England's, as well as the anomalous class structure of contemporary Ireland that is seen by nationalists and unionists alike as preventing the satisfactory application of British constitutional theory to Ireland. In its stead, literature and historical research are seen as performing crucial intermediary roles as spaces for social reconciliation.[41] In this substitution of the literary for the constitutional, nonetheless, a certain form of narrative survives. That is to say, the evolutionary narrative of the British constitution, which marks its difference for Burke or Coleridge from the revolutionary, written constitutions of France or America, is to be reproduced in the cultural sphere. The evolution from barbarity to civility, formerly to have been assured by direct domination, will necessarily take place first through culture as a prelude to political resolutions. It is this new struggle for hegemony in the cultural sphere that makes the crisis of novelistic representation so significant. For both nationalists and unionists, the continuing agrarian disturbances had to be characterized as irrational 'outrages', as products of an anarchic and ill-organized population, in order for the narrative of development that both were trying to control to be maintained. Agrarian disturbance was to be read as a symptom of underdevelopment, and as instinctual and reactive, rather than in terms of its own rationality.[42] Similarly, it was safer to deny the existence of a middle class than to acknowledge the complex and shifting affiliations of the one which could be deciphered and which was still the object of hegemonic struggle.

This rather complicated argument can be summed up by saying that recent historical research shows that Ireland was neither endemically violent nor in a state of underdeveloped savagery; rather, the clash of representations in the struggle for hegemony demanded that certain acts of violence be seized on as symptomatic and generalized into a characterization of the people as a whole. This in turn required not only their apprehension as unrepresentable and quite strictly speaking chaotic but also their abstraction from the alternative system of representations, or moral economy, within which they made sense. Thus what at first might have seemed the paradox of an argument by which what was representative of the Irish appeared as unrepresentable dissolved when it was understood that in the longer narrative of representation these Irish who could not yet represent themselves had to learn to be represented through the intervention of political and cultural institutions. And these institutions demanded, in their turn, the dissolution of traditions or practices whose own modes of organization were inassimilable to them. Accordingly, I would suggest, what is unrepresentable in agrarian violence is not simply, if at all, the violence itself, but modes of organization which offer counter-possibilities to the social vision embedded in either constitutional or novelistic narratives. It is not only extra-legal acts of violence in themselves which are against representation, as they are finally against the state which sanctions and finds its legitimation in those systems of representation, but more significantly the modes of organization within which those acts find their rationale. To acknowledge the complexity and consistency of those organizations instead of characterizing them as instinctual or spasmodic would have been to call into question crucial emergent systems of representation in the political and the cultural domain, in that of the constitution of the political state as in that of the novel.

This argument involves extending somewhat the concept of moral economy beyond its deployment even by Thompson. We can thus grasp not only its value in apprehending the complex political consciousness and agency of the poor over a long history of resistance and transformation, as Thompson wishes, but also its potential 'signifying difference' from the theories of political organization which seek to contain or supplant it. That is to seek the radical moment in a largely conservative formation. For, as Thompson argues of the moral economy of the English poor in the eighteenth century, and as most historians have argued of the Irish agrarian movements, the ideologies involved are notably conservative both in their demands and in their ideas of social justice.[43] In common with so many resistance movements, as opposed to revolutionary ones, their demands seek the rectification rather than the radical transformation of social relations. But it is neither sufficient to condemn these movements as retrograde nor to understand them solely as reactions of the dominated to momentary excesses by the dominating classes, that is, as momentary ruptures in an otherwise harmonious system. For as I have argued in part above, the significance of movements in which moral economies are articulated lies not merely in what they advocate but in the fact that they emerge as organized social formations at a moment when economic and social transitions are in the process of dissolving an old order of domination. As successive attempts to suppress or contain agrarian movements show, the administration certainly acknowledged the very fact of their existence to be threatening even where their demands may not have been especially extravagant. Moreover, the nature of that response is equally revealing. For though the activities and membership of the secret societies were consistently acknowledged to be local, the threat that they represented was from the outset perceived to be to the state as a whole. However specific their demands, Dublin Castle would read in each a disavowal of a state-wide law and feared constantly an escalation to a national level.[44] Accordingly, by 1836, the response was to emerge in the form of a *national* police force, the Irish Constabulary, unprecedentedly centralized under a single Inspector General. The fact that this supplanted the former system of local magistrates and the county constabularies appointed by them underscores the fact that in a profound sense both the administration and the secret societies occupy the same new terrain, that made vacant in the demise of an older, ascendancy hegemony.[45]

Identical concerns, however, would not account for the antagonism of nationalists or members of the Catholic Association towards them, nor the crisis of representation they assist in producing. Nonetheless, the very organizational features of the agrarian movements that made them both extraordinarily rapidly disseminable and very difficult for the authorities to control make them equally inassimilable to bourgeois nationalism and to codes of novelistic verisimilitude. Tom Garvin has pointed to how 'regional agrarian societies such as the Defenders were organized from the bottom up' with the result that their 'local and cellular structure' made them virtually 'impermeable' to government interventions.[46] Perhaps even more suggestive is James S. Donnelly's account of the massive Rightboy campaign, which spread from Cork through to Wexford and to Clare between 1785 and 1788: it was organized not centrally but by the dissemination of a set of demands from village to village, each community in turn passing on the demands to several more.[47] Overwhelmingly, and even in the case of the almost national organization of the Ribbonmen before the Famine, the organization of the Secret Societies tended to be based on a principle of contiguity rather than on centralized organization and uniform identity. Their often condemned localism – which, as the instances just cited indicate, is greatly over-emphasized and ignores the geographical extent of rural organizations – and the specificity of their demands are part and parcel of an activism based on such a principle.

This rhetorical structure of agrarian movements allows us to focus on their significant difference to nationalism and to the state formation towards which nationalism generally tends. For if the organizational structure of the Whiteboys can be seen as occupying the metonymic axis of contiguity, nationalism and the state occupy the metaphoric axis, seeking to educe a moment of identity out of the disparate populations and individuals that constitute the people. Difference is subordinated to identity, as in any metaphorical construction, in a fundamentally ethical subsumption of the particular into the universal.[48] The antagonism of the nation state to the locality, often dissembled in a cultural fetishization of local traditions after their material conditions have been eroded, is thus more than a strategic necessity of anti-colonial struggle or of a pragmatic will to rationalize the administration of the territory as a totality. It must be understood rather in terms of the larger project of nationalism and of the state, which is to produce a population of citizens whose common ethical identity transcends their particular differences. In this project, the abstraction of national symbols representative of national identity (whether epics or images is immaterial) corresponds to the political necessity to produce the abstract citizen-subject as representative of the nation.[49] The incommensurability of such a metaphoric tendency with the metonymic organization of the secret societies is clear and might be best signalled by noting the difference between movements organized around figures at once apparently actual and allegorical, such as Molly Maguire or Terry Allt's mother, Shevane Meskill or Queen Sive ('a distressed, harmless old woman, blind of one eye, who still lives at the foot of a mountain in the neighbourhood') and the symbolic Kathleen Ni Houlihan in cultural nationalist representations. Though these manifestations are too often reduced to identity, a crucial difference of social dynamic distinguishes them. Whereas in the rhetoric of nineteenth-century nationalism, Kathleen operates as a symbol, literally calling upon good nationalists to subordinate their private interests into the greater will of the nation, Sive can be instantiated momentarily by any of the oppressed, transforming the individual into an allegory of collective distress.[50] The latter process requires a rhetoric of solidarity, but not necessarily of identification.

Nationalism has to be seen, accordingly, as demanding a radical transformation of consciousness, a transformation that one could summarize as requiring the transition from a moral economy to a political economy. This, as is well known, involves the work of nationalism with larger movements of rationalization and modernization concurrent with it in nineteenth-century Britain and Europe as well as with the projects of unionism and the British state in Ireland, whose congruency with nationalism I have been stressing throughout. As Thompson points out, the supersession of a long-standing tradition of moral economy in Britain is furthered and legitimated by the arguments of political economy itself as much as it is made inevitable by the economic and industrial revolution's transformation of social relations.[51] In the case of Ireland one could push this argument further, stressing the element of the political rather than the economic. There is already a congruence between nationalism and political economy insofar as the latter takes as its necessary unit of analysis the nation state (the wealth of nations) rather than either local or global movements of labour and capital. In Ireland, however, precisely because colonialism had held back the modernization of the economy, the economic consolidation of the nation and the emergence of a fully capitalist agricultural and industrial economy, political transformation is called on to precede an economic transformation that waits on independence. Where classical political economy, in its analysis of labour, accounts for a production of the abstract individual which is effectively taking place in an expanding capitalist economy, nationalism is in a sense required to form its abstract or representative individuals for the political sphere before corresponding economic developments have occurred. We can locate here both the grounds for the phenomenon, familiar enough now in other newly independent nations, of the instability of the state formation itself and the reason for the enormous importance of the cultural sphere to nationalism, in Ireland as elsewhere. Quite simply, culture is endowed with the task of forming citizens in the absence of the economic and political-institutional conditions for their emergence.

In this cultural economy, which seeks to supplant those moral economies that resist assimilation to nationalist or state projects alike, the novel, along with other literary forms, has a crucial role to play. To different political ends, writers like Edgeworth, Morgan, Griffin and the Banims, are involved in a labour which is directed towards reforming patterns of Irish socialization. As Tom Dunne has suggested, the novel for these writers in general, and not alone for Edgeworth, is, like a model estate, to be a 'moral school'.[52] For Lady Morgan, novels express precisely the ethical dimension of the political: 'They are expected, in their idlest trifling to possess a moral scope, and politics is but morals on a grander scale.'[53] But the project of the novel, to transform Ireland's social economy and to contribute to the production of ethical individuals within a reformed national political economy, confronted insuperable resistance in the form of agrarian moral economies. This resistance was not merely a function, as we have seen, of continual outbreaks of violence, but was more implicitly and profoundly located in the alternative mode of socialization represented by the underlying organizations.[54] Could the moral economies of the Irish poor have been successfully characterized as merely primitive and outmoded cultural forms, then they could have been easily enough incorporated into the novelistic frame. On the contrary, however, they occupy similar terrain to the novel, seeking to rearticulate the social formation through the gradual breakdown of ascendancy hegemony. But even in this, they are not easily classifiable, being at times nationalist in politics, at times politically indifferent; at times gaining middle-class adherence, at times antagonistic to the middle class; at times sectarian, at others not; at times merely local, at others of remarkable geographical range. And even if they were, as Garvin has argued, gradually incorporated into the nationalist struggle, this was not without, on the one hand, an extensive work of organizational recuperation on the part of nationalists and, on the other, the problematic survival of their differences in the multiple and often contradictory strands of militant Irish nationalism. Local violence indeed may even have accelerated the formation of national institutions in response, perhaps precisely because its representation as *local*, i.e. as opposed to national, is already necessarily structured by a metaphoric discourse that coincides with institutional forms. The discourse and the institutions emerge in the same time with an ever-reversible relationship of causality. For both, however, local violence is represented as a counter-principle and gains its significance in that representation. The modernity of the agrarian movement is a function of its structuring role in the emergence of the modern state form; simultaneously, its anti-modernity, represented retrospectively as such, and as archaism, is contemporaneous with that which represents itself unilaterally as the *modern* of multiple contemporary presents.[55] Though the novel has proved markedly less successful in incorporating the agrarian movements than nationalist politics, even at the level of narrative elements, it might be cogently argued that the multiplicity of modes of narrative that Irish fiction has developed in different genres is itself the index not simply of oral survivals, but of an as yet unreduced multiplicity of forms of socialization of which the agrarian movements are one significant instance.

A considerably larger research project would be desirable in order to specify more exactly the social conditions that define the difference of the Irish novel tradition from the British, or that perhaps connect it to the novel in other colonial settings. Part of that project would be to define more precisely the degree to which Ireland's colonial history overdetermines social developments which in some respects it shares with Britain and other European nations, providing a much more problematic field of resistances to cultural assimilation than could radical working-class movements in England or a much less normative and consistent code of middle-class values. By the same token, a history of popular reception of novels would be of value in indicating the extent to which the symbolic forms of the novel may have been reappropriated in popular culture, as indeed nationalist symbols may also have been, and refunctioned in ironic or allegorical fashion. What, for example, is the real difference between *The Collegians'* Eily O'Connor and the Colleen Bawn, whether in Boucicault's version or in her further refraction in popular culture? The disdain that tends to write off such popular reappropriations of high culture as sentimental kitsch may in fact be missing both the necessity of the mechanical reproduction of kitsch for high culture itself and the aesthetic and political potential of alternative emerging cultural forms.[56] Similar questions could be multiplied across the possible field of Irish cultural studies, but what is certain is that the tendency in literary criticism to understand the Irish novel and its conditions of emergence in binary terms, such that Irish society is read principally in terms of what it lacks *vis-à-vis* England or Europe, has seriously hampered the understanding of the phenomenon, even where the attempt has been made to revalue individual novels. What needs interrogation is both the specificity of Irish cultural and social forms and the active function of the novel in their transformation, not of its value as autonomous artefact but of the values which, as such, it represents and seeks to promote; it is to such work that I hope to have contributed here.

IV

As usual, the 'anomalous condition of Ireland' raises considerable problems for theoretical models developed under and for other circumstances. By way of conclusion, I wish to suggest some ways in which the problems posed here by the Irish novel demand a critical revision of the terms developed in two very different works which have had considerable influence lately on thinking about the sociology of narrative. The first of these is Mikhail Bakhtin's *The Dialogic Imagination*, which, along with his work on carnival, *Rabelais and his World*, had considerable influence on the understanding of cultural processes of rebellion, subversion and repression. The second, Benedict Anderson's *Imagined Communities*, persuasively connected the rise of nationalism to the more or less simultaneous emergence of the press and the novel. Very different as they are, these works are linked by a common meditation on the cultural forms of modernity and their relation to the nation state, though Bakhtin's emphasis is on the state as 'monologic' and repressive where Anderson focuses on nationalism principally in its oppositional and organizational moment. Both have been influential in a very extensive range of contexts, and the critique of them here, based on Irish materials, may well have implications beyond our immediate frame. At the same time, I am concerned here with the possibility of a positive critique; that is, rather than reject theory out of hand, as is the practice in some circles, on the sometimes correct grounds that it is merely a recuperative extension of Western thinking or of modes of domination, I am interested in how such theoretical models themselves are refracted and refunctioned in the very resistance of anomalous materials.[57]

In 'Adulteration and the Nation' I argued that Bakhtin's developmental schema, by which an initial epic culture that is monologic in nature is subsequently challenged and disrupted by the dialogic processes of the novel, cannot be applied to the Irish cultural situation of the mid-nineteenth century, where an emergent nationalist cultural politics confronts a society profoundly marked by what Bakhtin would term heteroglossia and seeks to produce monologic, epic forms in order to forge a dialogic resistance to British imperialism. It is not this limitation, a problem for Bakhtin's argument in the colonial situation generally, that I want to address here, but another, perhaps deeper flaw in Bakhtin's theory. The especial value of *The Dialogic Imagination* continues to lie not so much in its rather idealist generic history of the novel as it emerges from the epic as in its more descriptive account of the dialogic processes that inform the novel. These can be categorized in two ways. On the one hand there is the dialogic process by which the novel parodies, or 'novelizes', genres which are more fixed stylistically, such as epic, romance and lyric. The apparent generic instability of the novel, which has no given form, is a function of its parodic or dialogic relation to previous genres and an index of its relative freedom. On the other hand, beyond this formal dialogism, there is the dialogical nature of what is represented in the novel. Unlike epic or lyric, which establish for the national community and the individual subject respectively a proper, monologic mode of utterance, the novel is concerned to represent the multiple social languages (or sociolects) of a given linguistic community. The novelization of monologic genres corresponds accordingly to the inner disintegration of an officially monologic national culture into the competing and often incommensurable languages of class, sect, profession, gender or ethnicity, all of which are contained within a given community. It is this 'heteroglossic' reality which the novel represents.

The value of this account of the internal disintegration of the national culture to analysing Irish culture is prima facie quite evident, although by and large Bakhtin is remarkably inattentive to the extent to which social relations hierarchize and constrain the dialogic process. His account lacks, in other words, an analysis of the regulative effect of orders of verisimilitude which give to certain modes of discourse an effect of self-evidence while relegating others to virtual inaudibility. It is, however, this effect of 'improbability' which in any given field of social relations attaches to certain kinds of disenfranchised discourse that I have sought to describe in terms of the alternative narratives entailed in Irish agrarian movements. At a moment when dominant social forces are informed by symbolic narratives, the metonymic structure of the secret society can appear only as aberrant. This process of disenfranchisement can be taken quite literally: falling outside the forms in which the state or the nationalist movement that wills to seize it are organized, the alternative narrative is, strictly speaking, deprived of voice in the public sphere. As I have tried to suggest, the processes of symbolization or metaphorization are at the minimal level narrative in form, requiring implicitly a temporal structure through which the particular is subsumed into identity with the universal. The larger move of the realist novel recapitulates this micro-narrative, integrating the individual, or the local community, into the larger frame of national society. This entails, however, not only a movement of assimilation but also its necessary logical correlative, the negation or exclusion of what cannot be drawn into identity. One of the problems of the Irish novel, precisely insofar as it conforms to the symbolic mode of realism, is the sheer volume of inassimilable residue that it can neither properly contain nor entirely exclude.

The formation of the novel must be seen, accordingly, in terms of this double movement of assimilation and exclusion, in terms, that is, of its ends and of the careful regulation and hierarchization of sociolects that they require. But it is precisely this aspect of the novel to which Bakhtin gives little or no attention. His emphasis on the generically subversive and quasi-democratic aspects of the novel precludes any account of its normative ethical aims: in the celebration of the novel's discursive pluralism (which is one reason for his adoption by certain strains of liberal post-Marxism), Bakhtin forcibly ignores the social symbolism of narrative resolutions that give the form of the realist novel. At most he is able to allude to the manner in which authorial voice finally unifies the heteroglossia of novelistic discourse, but the connection between the idea of voice as a mode of ethico-political identity and the ethical ends of the novel seems to escape him at this level. Accordingly the social significance of novels in the British realist tradition or the German *Bildungsroman* cannot be adequately addressed. Nor, indeed, can the importance of the novel as an active force in processes of social transformation: like so much literary theory, even sociological, Bakhtin's account of the novel is finally tied to a merely mimetic notion of representation. As the example of the Irish novel has shown, such accounts are incapable of analysing the social dynamics within which the novel intervenes as one possible narrative form and from which its generic vicissitudes derive. In the colonial situation generally, the importance of the social significance of genres is irreducible insofar as Western forms are cultural interventions intended to prefigure and produce representative political subjectivity in contest with other possible narrative modes. Bakhtin accordingly not only reverses the logical order of literary formations in the colonial context but obscures both the relation of the novel to hegemony and the significance of deviations from metropolitan generic norms.

Anderson's *Imagined Communities* similarly is concerned with problems of exclusion and inclusion and with the constitution of both the novel and the nation out of disparate and dispersed materials. His argument, summarily, is that the rise of nationalisms is concurrent with that of print culture, and that the development of both the press and the novel entails a transformation of the image of social relations in order that an abstract community such as the nation can be imagined. Both the newspaper and the novel occupy what he terms, after Benjamin, 'homogeneous empty time', a time which is to be filled with events and social relations linked finally only by their identity as elements of national history. In this way, it becomes possible for citizens of the same nation to imagine their vital relation to one another (and, less emphatically, their enmity to foreigners) despite the fact that they will never have personal acquaintance with the vast majority of their fellow citizens.[58] Anderson's emphasis on the constructed nature of the nation is a valuable supplement to Bakhtin's work, as is his emphasis on the important role of the novel in the formation of national communities with a more or less homogeneous self-image.

Curiously, however, Anderson's emphasis on the formation of the imagined community against the imperial state seems to preclude his acknowledging that the dialogism of the novel is not confined to its production of an anti-*imperial* national culture but also involves, as again the Irish example makes evident, the subordination of alternative narratives within a multiply voiced national culture. For the novel not only gives voice to formerly voiceless national élites, but also disenfranchises other possible voices. As Renato Rosaldo has put it, the question remains as to 'Who isn't invited to the party?'[59] As with Bakhtin, the novel appears as finally merely mimetic, representing, in the sense of depicting, a more or less 'natural' national community, all of whose members occupy an undifferentiated space. What is erased is the more important sense of representation which points to the system of ethical and political terms by which participation in the national community as citizen is regulated. Like Bakhtin, Anderson omits the crucial regulative function of the novel that puts in place the developmental narrative through which the nation apes the empire and through which it orders internally a certain hierarchy of belonging, of identity with the nation. Far from being simply an intrinsically benign and democratic form, the novel enacts the violence that underlies the constitution of identity, diffusing it in the eliciting of identification.

In certain contexts, like that of colonial Ireland, that process of identification breaks down, not so much because truth is stronger than fiction, as Carleton claimed during the Famine,[60] but because no cultural space is offered for representations which are not already apparently partisan. (In this respect Edgeworth and Lady Morgan may have been sharper critical observers of their practice than Carleton.) At the moment of the nation's emergence, of the various attempts to gain hegemony over self-representation in every sphere, the novel, like other cultural forms, is engaged with unusual self-consciousness in the activity of social transformation. The necessary myth of the novel, its formal transcendence of or aesthetic disinterest in social conflicts, is unusually difficult to maintain. This is borne out in the little-noted fact that, quite apart from the articulate crisis of representation it underwent, and the general aesthetic dissatisfaction it produces in its critics, the nineteenth-century Irish novel produced not a single 'representative type' for Irish culture, with the dubious and in any case anomalous exceptions of the Colleen Bawn and Dracula. We are only just beginning to forge the theoretical terms in which the atypicality of the Irish novel can be analysed but, to borrow a line from Tom Dunne, it may be that we are approaching a 'less coherent but in many ways more interesting' theory of the novel.[61] The same may perhaps be said, in more general terms, of emerging theories of Ireland's putatively 'post-colonial' culture.

NOTES

1. A.T.Q. Stewart, *The Narrow Ground, The Roots of Conflict in Ulster*, new edition (London 1977; rev. 1989). This remarkable book, in cataloguing the violence of the Irish from Giraldus Cambrensis to Lord Denning, manages not to cite a single Gaelic source and scarcely a single nationalist one. Its notion of Irishness is very flexible, however, including from time to time both settlers and natives, leading one to conclude, against its ostensible argument, that the recurrence of certain patterns of violence must have more to do with the persistence of a colonial situation than with the consistency of an ethnic temperament.

2. Walter Benjamin, 'Critique of Violence', in Peter Demetz (ed.), Edmund Jephcott (trans.), *Reflections: Essays, Aphorisms, Autobiographical Writings* (New York 1978), p. 279.

3. Antonio Gramsci, *Selections from the Prison Notebooks*, Quintin Hoare and Geoffrey Nowell Smith (ed. and trans.) (New York 1971). Hereafter cited in the text with title and page numbers.

4. For a useful reader of their work, see Ranajit Guha and Gayatri Chakravorty Spivak (eds), *Selected Subaltern Studies* (Oxford 1988).

5. On the contrary, see James M. Cahalan, *The Irish Novel, A Critical History* (Dublin 1988), *passim* but especially pp. 304–8.

6. For Shklovsky's comments on the typicality of *Tristram Shandy*, see Lee T. Lemon and Marion J. Reis, *Russian Formalist Criticism: Four Essays* (Lincoln, Nebraska 1965), p. 37; Cahalan, *The Irish Novel* , pp. 127–8, makes similar claims for *Ulysses'* 'Irishness'. For some analysis of the way in which *Ulysses* problematizes strategically certain modes of narrative, political as well as aesthetic,

see 'Adulteration and the Nation' above.

7. See my *Nationalism and Minor Literature* (Berkeley and Los Angeles 1987), especially pp. 19–26. For reasons that this work may suggest, I find the term 'inadequacy' quite exact in describing the Irish novel of this period, insofar as it captures the sense of falling short of a model or norm projected ideally for the genre. This term accordingly preserves the relational nature of literary judgments.

8. Arguments of this nature can be found in all the standard works: Cahalan, *The Irish Novel*; Thomas Flanagan, *The Irish Novelists: 1800–1850* (New York 1959); John Cronin, *The Anglo-Irish Novel, Volume 1: The Nineteenth Century* (Belfast 1980).

9. This is in a sense the argument of Mikhail Bakhtin's *The Dialogic Imagination* (Austin 1981), despite its particular attention to generic definition and internal transformations. We will return to his work in relation to the Irish novel later. Less evidently, Georg Lukacs' *Theory of the Novel* emphasizes the determination of the genre by a breakdown of social stability, figured however in the 'problematic individual' in his alienated and complex relation to social convention. See *Theory of the Novel*, Anna Bostock (trans.) (Cambridge, Mass. 1971), pp. 78–83. On the conditions of the emergence of the novel, see Ian Watt's standard *Rise of the Novel: Studies in Defoe, Richardson and Fielding* (Berkeley and Los Angeles 1964); and Michael McKeon's brilliant revision of its terms in *The Origins of the English Novel, 1600–1740* (Baltimore 1987).

10. For further on the question of the Irish language, see note 18 to 'Adulteration and the Nation' above. Both Cronin, *The Anglo-Irish Novel*, pp. 9–11, and Cahalan, *The Irish Novel*, p. xxi, touch on the Irish linguistic situation, both on a more or less bilingual culture and on the hybrid forms of Irish English, as ambivalently providing a handicap and an opportunity, as against other commentators who see it only in terms of the handicap of an unmastered second language.

11. The fascination famously evinced by Edgeworth's *Castle Rackrent* with oral narrative form, like that shown by Griffin and other writers for the forms and often deliberate ambivalences of peasant speech, is almost always counterpointed by anxiety, an anxiety both as to the meaning of such speech in social terms (the fact that Edgeworth never repeated the formal experiment of her first novel and felt it was 'dictated' by her own tenant Langan is significant, as is Griffin's deep ambivalence towards lower-class Catholic culture) and as to its potential challenge to the forms of reconciliation posed by novelistic narrative itself. What novels seek to frame, as we shall see, as the uncultivated substratum of a social history ultimately reconciling in its tendency, reveals a dynamism antagonistic in form as in significance to that framing. Tom Dunne's various essays on these novelists are particularly suggestive with regard to the anxiety of the colonial mind in this regard. See especially '"A gentleman's estate should be a moral school": Edgeworthstown in Fact and Fiction, 1760–1840' in Raymond Gillespie and Gerard Moran (eds), *Longford: Essays in County History* (Dublin 1991), pp. 95–121; and 'Murder as Metaphor: Griffin's Portrayal of Ireland in the Year of Catholic Emancipation' in Oliver MacDonagh and W.F. Mandle (eds), *Ireland and Irish-Australia: Studies in Cultural and Political History* (London 1986), pp. 64–80. For further on ballad forms and their social implications, see 'Adulteration and the Nation' above.

12. See Flanagan, *The Irish Novelists*, pp. 178, 317, and Cahalan, *The Irish Novel*, p. 7.

13. Edmund Burke, 'Letter to Sir Hercules Langrishe ... On the Subject of the Roman Catholics', *Works*, 6 *Volumes* (London 1887), vol. 3, p. 511.
14. Anon., 'The Middle Classes', *Nation*, 25 January 1845, p. 249.
15. Anon., 'The Rents – The Question of the Day', *Nation*, 29 October 1842, p. 40.
16. Unlike Flanagan, who seems to accept this model, see *Irish Novelists*, pp. 35 and 180.
17. For this understanding of aesthetic forms, but especially of the novel, see Fredric Jameson, *The Political Unconscious: Narrative as a Socially Symbolic Act* (Ithaca 1981).
18. On Hegel's understanding of the novel as 'educating man for life in bourgeois society', see Bakhtin, *The Dialogic Imagination*, p. 234. Franco Moretti in *The Way of the World: The Bildungsroman in European Culture* (London 1987), pp. 15–21, discusses the genre as reconciling the contradictory demands of socialization and individuation. Georg Lukacs' *The Theory of the Novel* is a thoroughgoing critique of the Hegelian idea of the 'bourgeois epic' in underscoring the role of the 'problematic individual' and the virtual impossibility of reconciliation, see especially pp. 78–83.
19. I have developed this notion more fully in 'The Narrative of Representation: Culture, the State and the Canon' in Robert Bledsoe *et al.* (eds), *Rethinking Germanistik: Canon and Culture* (New York 1991), pp. 125–38.
20. Maria Edgeworth, letter to her brother, quoted by Timothy Webb, introduction to William Carleton, *The Black Prophet*, facsimile repr. of 1899 ed. (Shannon 1972), p. xiii.
21. Lady Morgan (Sydney Owenson), *Dramatic Scenes from Real Life*, 2 vols (London 1883), vol. 1, pp. iv–v.
22. See Dunne, 'Murder as Metaphor', *passim*, and 'The Insecure Voice: A Catholic Novelist in Support of Emancipation', in P. Bergeron and L. Cullen (eds), *Culture et pratiques politiques en France et en Irlande, XVIe–XVIIIe siècle*, Actes du colloque de Marseille, 1988 (Paris 1991), pp. 213–33. In 'Fiction as "the best history of nations": Lady Morgan's Irish Novels', in T. Dunne (ed.), *The Writer as Witness: Literature as Historical Evidence* (Cork 1987), pp. 137–8, Dunne discusses the differences between Lady Morgan's Whiggish understanding of history as a series of revolutions leading towards liberty *vis-à-vis* a Scottian notion of history as evolutionary and organic, a notion that equally informs Edgeworth's Irish novels and the Preface to *Castle Rackrent* in which the more sinister (for the Anglo-Irish) conclusions to that novel are defused. He also comments insightfully on the inability of the Banims and Griffin to represent the Anglo-Irish or to do more than stereotype the Irish peasantry in ways which reveal their anxiety with regard to the different dynamics and assumptions embedded in lower-class agitation. Lady Morgan is equally antagonistic to the Catholic Association, despite her support of its goals (pp. 141–2) for similar reasons, while Edgeworth's Irish fiction (which comes to an end after *Ormond* in 1817) is marked throughout by her experiences of displacement and threat in 1798. See Dunne, 'Edgeworthstown in Fact and Fiction', especially p. 105.
23. Anon., 'The British Constitution', *Nation*, 5 September 1846, p. 746.
24. Such narratives were, at a more abstract level of representation, certainly available: Samuel Ferguson's celebrated articles on James Hardiman's *Irish Minstrelsy* in the 1830s use the Gaelic material there presented to argue the possibility of

cultivating the native Irish towards loyalty to the union. For a discussion of this material, see Lloyd, *Nationalism and Minor Literature*, pp. 83–5.

25. See Georg Lukacs, 'Walter Scott and the Historical Novel' in E. San Juan (ed.), *Marxism and Human Liberation: Essays on History, Culture and Revolution* (New York 1973), pp. 150–5.

26. William Carleton, *Traits and Stories of the Irish Peasantry*, second series, 3 vols (Dublin 1833), II, pp. 448–9.

27. Carleton's argument thus suggests a crucial interdependence between the two categories of versimilitude, generic and referential, proposed by Tszetan Todorov in his brief but important essay, 'Introduction to Versimilitude', in *The Poetics of Prose*, Richard Howard (trans.) (Ithaca 1977), pp. 80–8, though it is important to recall that for Todorov, reference is to the doxa of public opinion (what is held to be the case) rather than any presupposed 'reality'. That Carleton's remarks come in the preface to his ethnographic *Traits and Stories* only emphasizes the generic problem, insofar as ethnographic narrative tends to cast its objects as alien rather than attempting to incorporate them into a larger narrative of assimilation. It is precisely in the attempt to make the transition from short stories based on the oral tradition to the novel form that Carleton is usually held to founder. This characterization of his literary development needs, however, to be considered outside its usual framework of aesthetic judgment in order for its full implications for Carleton's constantly provisional subject to become apparent.

28. Anon., 'Ireland, Social, Political and Religious', rev. of Gustave de Beaumont, *L'Irlande, sociale, politique et religieuse* (Paris 1839), *Dublin University Magazine*, 14, no. 79 (July 1839), p. 116.

29. See especially articles by Kevin Whelan: 'Catholic Mobilisation, 1750–1850', in Bergeron and Cullen, *Culture et pratiques politiques*, pp. 235–58; 'Catholics, Politicisation and the 1798 Rebellion', in Réamonn Ó Muiri (ed.), *Irish Church History Today* (forthcoming); and 'Mentalité and the Irish Catholic Middle Class: The example of Strong Farmers, 1700–1850', paper delivered to the ACIS conference, Madison, Wisconsin, April 1991. The Banim brothers and Griffin, as well as other Catholic Irish writers such as Callanan and Mangan, all come from these Catholic middle classes.

30. See *Nationalism and Minor Literature*, chapter 2. The sectarian aspect of the Irish conflict finds new ground and tones equally in this period, insofar as the rising middle class is perceived increasingly as a material threat by its Protestant counterpart; on this see Thomas Bartlett, 'Militarisation and Politicisation in Ireland', in Bergeron and Cullen, *Culture et pratique politiques*, pp. 125–36, and Whelan, 'Catholics, Politicisation and the 1798 Rebellion', pp. 70–2.

31. I am indebted to Kevin Whelan for allowing me to see his detailed manuscript on these issues, 'Settlement and Society in Eighteenth Century Ireland'. Bernard Escarbelt's paper, 'Un peuple de paysans: difficultés de terminologie dans l'étude de l'Irlande au début du XIXe siècle', delivered to the Conference of the SAES, Poitiers 1980, was a valuable critique of the cover-all usage of the term 'peasant' in sociological and fictional writings on Ireland and of its inadequacy to the actual diversity of the demography of the period.

32. For a full treatment of these transformations, see Samuel Clark, *Social Origins of the Irish Land War* (Princeton, NJ 1979).

33. On the 'Manichean' nature of social relations in the colonized society, see Fanon,

'Concerning Violence', in *The Wretched of the Earth*, pp. 41–3; Abdul JanMo-hamed has expanded the notion of the 'Manichean allegory' as a means to understanding the cultural dynamics of the colonial situation in 'The Economy of Manichean Allegory: The Function of Racial Difference in Colonialist Litera-ture', in Henry Louis Gates, Jr (ed.), *'Race', Writing and Difference* (Chicago 1986), pp. 70–106.

34. See James S. Donnelly, Jr, 'The Rightboy Movement 1785–8', *Studia Hibernica*, nos. 17 and 18 (1977–8), pp. 121–202, and 'The Whiteboy Movement, 1761–5', *Irish Historical Studies*, 31, no. 81 (March 1978), pp. 20–54. Also Kevin Whelan, 'Catholic Mobilisation, 1750–1850' in Bergeron and Cullen, *Culture et pratiques politiques*, and James W. O'Neill, 'A Look at Captain Rock: Agrarian Rebellion in Ireland 1815–1845', *Eire-Ireland*, 17, no. 1 (Autumn 1982), pp. 17–34.

35. O'Neill, 'Agrarian Rebellion', p. 28.

36. Thomas Garvin's *The Evolution of Irish Nationalist Politics* (Dublin 1981) is a valuable examination of links between the organizational structures of secret societies and those of later, more expressly nationalist movements, but tends to emphasize the localism of the interests of the societies in finally quite negative terms. M.R. Beames's article 'The Ribbon Societies: Lower Class Nationalism in Pre-Famine Ireland', *Past and Present*, 97 (1982), pp. 128–43, in many respects provides the rule-proving exception insofar as the membership of Ribbon Soci-eties seems to have brought together an urban proletariat with mobile labourers such as carmen, allowing the conditions for a strictly nationalist ideology to emerge.

37. In 'Can the Subaltern Speak', pp. 284–5, Gayatri Spivak comments on the insta-bility of a similar group of 'dominant indigenous groups at the regional and local levels' in Indian history, defined as a 'floating buffer zone' always differentially in relation to 'the "true" subalterns' and the élites. Her terms, which might be valu-ably deployed in the Irish context, are derived from Ranajit Guha.

38. Thomas Bartlett, 'An End to Moral Economy: The Irish Militia Disturbances of 1793', *Past and Present*, 99 (May 1983), p. 43. As Charles Townshend has pointed out, 'until the mid-nineteenth century, Irish disorder, while it may have appeared to English eyes different in nature, had scarcely been much different in scale from that endemic in the temple of civilization itself, the home of that ungovernable people'. See his *Political Violence in Ireland. Government and Resis-tance since 1848* (Oxford 1983), p. 2. For more on English society see John Brewer and John Styles (eds), *An Ungovernable People, The English and their Law in the Seventeenth and Eighteenth Centuries* (New Jersey 1980), pp. 13–14. Statisti-cally, it is also relatively easy to show that once the total amount of crime was separately categorized, as it was by the nineteenth-century authorities, into 'normal' and 'special or agrarian crime', the normal crime rate in Ireland was remarkably low. See Townshend, *Political Violence*, p. 6.

39. Thomas Bartlett, 'An End to Moral Economy', p. 41. Also see O'Neill, 'Agrarian Rebellion', p. 23.

40. See *Past and Present*, 50 (February 1971), pp. 76–136. The concept is adopted also by O'Neill, 'Agrarian Rebellion', p. 18.

41. See my *Nationalism and Minor Literature*, chapter 2.

42. Accordingly, what E.P. Thompson critiques as the 'spasmodic' theory of lower-class uprising in England, which deprives the labouring classes of all but reactive

political agency or consciousness ('Moral Economy', p. 76), gains an added dimension in the Irish context, where the representation of outrages as instinctual combines with a larger matrix of representation for which the Irish are, like all savages, dominated by impulses and needs. In this case, Thompson's comparison of his own analysis of moral economy to ethnographic accounts of Trobriand culture gains a rather complex and by no means merely analogical force.

43. Though Thompson is in many respects critical of E.J. Hobsbawm and others, he tends to concur that the 'moral economies' of the poor tended to be conservative or, to say the least, traditional in orientation (pp. 78–9). On this see also Joseph J. Lee, 'Patterns of Rural Unrest in Nineteenth Century Ireland: A Preliminary Survey', in L.M. Cullen and F. Furet (eds), *Ireland and France, 17th–20th Centuries, Towards a Comparative Study of Rural History* (Paris 1980), p. 226, and E.J. Hobsbawm, *Social Bandits and Primitive Rebels: Studies in Archaic Forms of Social Movement in the Nineteenth and Twentieth Centuries* (Glencoe, Ill. 1959), p. 5.

44. See Galen Broeker, *Rural Disorder and Police Reform in Ireland, 1812–1836* (London 1970), p. 18.

45. On the formation of the Irish Constabulary, see Broeker, *Rural Disorder*, pp. 23–9. He also points out (p. 57) that Peel had initially hoped to use the Magistrate system precisely to revitalize the 'natural leaders', but that by the mid-1830s this was seen as infeasible. Townshend perhaps unwittingly draws attention to the way in which agrarian outrages could appear virtually as an alternative system of law, not least because they operated most frequently through threat rather than deed:

> What the alarmist reactions of gentry and governments made plain about violence in Ireland is that the absolute level of 'crime' was considerably less important than the psychological construction placed upon each outbreak ... The threat of violence was always more common than its actual application, as any selection of statistics will indicate. The threat had its effect because of a fairly high expectation of retribution if it were ignored: in other words, it worked very much like what is ordinarily described as law. (*Political Violence*, pp. 8–9)

In what follows I shall be arguing that an alternative system of law presumes equally an alternative system of socialization.

46. Garvin, *Irish Nationalist Politics*, p. 27. Cf. also Broeker, *Rural Disorder*, p. 18.

47. Donnelly, 'The Rightboy Movement, pp. 127–37.

48. I have discussed the axis of metaphor/metonymy as a fundamental structuring principle of systems of culture in 'Race under Representation', *Oxford Literary Review*, special issue, 'Colonialism Now', 13 (Spring 1991), pp. 71–3. For an extensive discussion of this opposition see Roland Barthes, 'The Two Axes of Language' in *Elements of Sociology*, Annette Lavers and Colin Smith (trans.) (London 1967), pp. 58–62. I should note that my account of the realist novel throughout this essay is at odds with Roman Jakobson's seminal essay 'Two Aspects of Language and Two Types of Aphasia Disturbance', in *Selected Writings, Vol. 2: Word and Language* (Mouton: The Hague 1971), pp. 239–59, where metaphor and metonymy correspond respectively to poetry and the realist novel. In my view, clearly, the syntagmatic organization of the novel's narrative is paradigmatically dominated by the symbolic or metaphoric function of representation

whuch defines its socially symbolic function. Jakobson's contention might hold, of course, for what is conventionally understood as naturalism in the Lukacsian sense: see Lukacs, 'Realism in the Balance' in Fredric Jameson (ed.), *Aesthetics and Politics* (London 1977), pp. 36–45.

49. On the function of symbols within the organizational or politicizing logic of nationalism, see especially Breuilly, *Nationalism and the State*. Paul Thomas has analysed the formation of the citizen within the sphere of what Marx termed 'political emancipation' in 'Alien Politics: A Marxian Perspective on Citizenship and Democracy', in Terence Ball and James Farr (eds), *After Marx* (Cambridge 1984), pp. 124–40.

50. Donnelly, 'The Whiteboy Movement', pp. 27–9; Luke Gibbons, in 'Identity without a Centre: Irish Nationalism in a Colonial Frame', forthcoming in *Cultural Studies*, points out the frequent difficulty of determining when a popular figure, especially in ballads, should be considered actual or allegorical. Failure to make the necessary distinction between symbolic and metonymic (or ambivalent) usages of feminine figures in Irish popular culture has subserved historians' assumptions that all such figures can be seen as prototypes of the more famous Kathleen Ni Houlihan. Such assumptions overlook the crucial organizational difference that enters with the symbolic nationalist use of Kathleen and allows all too easily the view that all such manifestations are indices of atavistic mentality. In general, as Gibbons' article also implies, there is great need for more research on the gender ramifications of agrarian movements and their 'moral economies', both on the significance of female figures and the common practice of 'cross-dressing' and on participation by women in these movements. My analysis here has been informed by Ranajit Guha's seminal essay 'The Prose of Counter Insurgency', but where he emphasizes the transformation of the metonymic and often disjointed narratives of primary documents into secondary and tertiary retellings of events-as-history, which conform to the metaphoric axis, I hope to suggest that the two axes imply also two different modes of social organization. It is not just in historiography as it emerges in the colonizers' first signals of panic that the rural organization and its practices appear as metonymic, but in its actual structures, hard as these may be to read. The importance of this claim lies not merely in suggesting some reason for a consistent 'signifying difference' from nationalism and the state, but equally in suggesting that these movements are not spasmodic, but have a history and a rhetoric which are, at least in principle, decipherable. In this, if I interpret him correctly, I would differ from Homi Bhabha's reading of a peasant uprising at the moment of the Indian Mutiny in his brilliant essay 'In a Spirit of Calm Violence' (unpublished TS), one which seems to assert the radically performative and present dynamics of popular insurrection.

51. See Thompson, 'Moral Economy', pp. 89–90 and 129. Bartlett similarly argues that in Ireland in the 1790s, 'the precepts of "moral economy" were yielding to the forces of the "market economy"', 'An End to Moral Economy', p. 62.

52. See Dunne, 'Edgeworthstown in Fact and Fiction', *passim*.

53. Morgan, Preface to *O'Donnel*, quoted in Dunne, 'Lady Morgan's Irish Novels', p. 136.

54. Sir William Wilde, in his *Irish Popular Superstitions* (1853), suggests that Whiteboyism was closely related to other old customs like the Wrenboys, and that

'socialisation far outweighed any ideological principles': paraphrased in Thuente, 'Violence in Pre-Famine Ireland', p. 141. Though Thuente's article adduces some valuable materials, it is quite remarkable in identifying the position of the common Irish concerning violence with the moral and social views of middle-class writers who seek, anxiously, to represent them. With regard to the socializing function of the symbolic elements of agrarian movements, Michael Beames, *Peasants and Power, The Whiteboy Movements and their Control in Pre-Famine Ireland* (New York 1983), p. 33, suggests that they functioned to place agrarian violence on a par with other traditional but more celebratory practices.

55. This implies a limitation of E.J. Hobsbawm's seminal work on peasant and working-class movements in *Primitive Rebels*, which characterizes them as archaic survivals whose movements require organizational intervention from outside. See especially pp. 3–6.

56. See Gibbons, 'Identity without a Centre'. I have briefly discussed the tendency towards kitsch of nationalist cultural forms in 'Adulteration and the Nation' p. 98 above.

57. Dipesh Chakrabarty's 'Postcoloniality and the Artifice of History: Who Speaks of "Indian" Pasts?', *Representations*, 37 (Winter 1992), pp. 1–26, is a valuable and sustained consideration of the problematic interaction of Western method and its 'othered' objects.

58. Benedict Anderson, *Imagined Communities* (London 1983), p. 31.

59. See Renato Rosaldo, 'Re-imagining the Nation', forthcoming in Peter Hulme and Francis Barker (eds), *Colonial Discourse/Post-colonial Theory* (Manchester 1993). Luke Gibbons has critiqued Anderson's focus on the print cultural basis of nationalism in 'Identity without a Centre' as being inadequate to the importance of oral transmission even in contemporary Ireland.

60. Carleton, *The Black Prophet*, Timothy Webb intro., facsimile ed. of 1899 ed. (Shannon 1972), p. 8.

61. Dunne, 'Lady Morgan's Irish Fiction', p. 156.

BIBLIOGRAPHY

Adorno, Theodor, *Negative Dialectics*, E.B. Ashton (ed.) (New York: Seabury Press, 1973).
— and Horkheimer, Max, *The Dialectic of Enlightenment*, John Cumming (trans.) (New York 1972).
Akenson, D.H., *The Irish Educational Experiment: The National System of Education in Nineteenth Century Ireland* (London: Routledge, 1970).
Alarcón, Norma, 'Chicana Feminist Literature: Re-vision through Malintzin/or Malintzin: Putting Flesh Back on the Object', *This Bridge Called My Back: Writings by Radical Women of Color*, Cherrié Moraga and Gloria Anzaldua (eds) (New York: Kitchen Table, 1983), pp. 182–90.
Althusser, Louis, *Lenin and Philosophy and Other Essays*, Ben Brewster (trans.) (New York: Monthly Review Press, 1971).
Anderson, Benedict, *Imagined Communities, Reflections on the Origins and Spread of Nationalism* (London: Verso Press, 1983).
Arnold, Matthew, 'On the Study of Celtic Literature' and 'The Function of Criticism in the Present Time' in *Lectures and Essays in Criticism*, R.H. Super (ed.), *The Complete Prose Works*, vol. III (Ann Arbor: Michigan University Press, 1962).

Bakhtin, Mikhail, *The Dialogic Imagination: Four Essays*, Michael Holquist (ed.), Caryl Emerson and Michael Holquist (trans.) (Austin: University of Texas Press, 1981).
Bartlett, Thomas, 'An End to Moral Economy: The Irish Militia Disturbances of 1793', *Past and Present*, 99 (May 1983).
Beames, Michael R., *Peasants and Power: The Whiteboy Movements and their Control in Pre-Famine Ireland* (New York 1983).
Beckett, Samuel, *The Unnamable* (London: Calder, 1959).
—, *First Love and Other Stories* (New York: Grove Press, 1970).
—, *Disjecta: Miscellaneous Writings and a Dramatic Fragment*, Ruby Cohn (ed.) (New York: Grove Press, 1984).
Benjamin, Walter, *Reflections: Essays, Aphorisms, Autobiographical Writings*, Peter Demetz (ed.), Edmund Jephcott (trans.) (New York 1978).
—, *The Origin of German Tragic Drama*, John Osborne (trans.) (London 1977).
Benjamin, Walter, *Illuminations*, Hannah Arendt (ed.), Harry Zohn (trans.) (London 1973).
Bhabha, Homi K., 'Of Mimicry and Man: The Ambivalence of Colonial Discourse', *October*, 28 (1984), pp. 125–33.
—, 'The Commitment to Theory', *New Formations*, 5 (1988), pp. 5–24.
— (ed.), *Nation and Narration* (London: Routledge, 1990).
Boyce, George, *Nationalism in Ireland* (London: Croom Helm, 1982).

BIBLIOGRAPHY

Brecht, Bertolt, *Brecht on Theatre: The Development of an Aesthetic*, John Willett (ed. and trans.) (London: Methuen 1964).

Breuilly, John, *Nationalism and the State* (New York: St Martin's Press, 1982).

Brewer, John and Styles, John (eds), *An Ungovernable People, The English and their Law in the Seventeenth and Eighteenth Centuries* (New Jersey: Rutgers University Press, 1980).

Cairns, David and Richards, Shaun, *Writing Ireland: Colonialism, Nationalism and Culture* (Manchester: Manchester University Press, 1988).

Carlyle, Thomas, *Wilhelm Meister's Apprenticeship and Travels: Translated from the German of Goethe*, 3 vols (London: Chapman and Hall, 1888).

Chatterjee, Partha, *Nationalism in the Colonial World, A Derivative Discourse?* (London: Zed Books, 1986).

Cixous, Hélène, *L'Exil de James Joyce ou l'art du remplacement* (Paris: Grasset, 1968).

Clark, Samuel, *Social Origins of the Irish Land War* (Princeton, NJ: Princeton University Press, 1979).

Coleridge, Samuel Taylor, 'The Statesman's Manual' (1816), *Lay Sermons*, R.J. White (ed.), Bollingen edition (Princeton: Princeton University Press, 1972).

Corkery, Daniel, *Synge and Anglo-Irish Literature* (Cork: Cork University Press, 1931).

—, *The Hidden Ireland: A Study of Gaelic Munster in the Eighteenth Century* (1924; Dublin: M.H. Gill, 1967).

Cronin, John, *The Anglo-Irish Novel, Volume I: The Nineteenth Century* (Belfast: Appletree Press, 1980).

Daly, Mary and Dickson, David, *The Origins of Popular Literacy in Ireland: Language and Educational Development 1700–1920* (Dublin 1990).

Deane, Seamus, 'Unhappy and at Home', *The Crane Bag*, 1, no. 1 (1977).

—, 'Yeats and the Idea of Revolution', *Celtic Revivals: Essays in Modern Irish Literature, 1880–1980* (London: Faber and Faber, 1985), pp. 38–50.

Deleuze, Gilles and Guattari, Félix, *Anti-Oedipus* (New York: Viking Press, 1977).

—, *Kafka: pour une littérature mineure* (Paris: Minuit, 1975).

De Man, Paul, *Blindness and Insight: Essays in the Rhetoric of Contemporary Criticism* (London: Methuen, 1983).

—, *The Rhetoric of Romanticism* (New York: Columbia University Press, 1984).

Derrida, Jacques, *Otobiographies: l'enseignement de Nietzsche et la politique du nom propre* (Paris: Galilée, 1984).

—, 'Economimesis', Richard Klein (trans.), *Diacritics*, 11, no. 2 (Summer 1981).

Descombes, Vincent, *Le Même et l'Autre: quarante-cinq ans de philosophie française 1933–1978* (Paris: Minuit, 1979).

Donnelly, James S., Jr, 'The Whiteboy Movement, 1761–5', *Irish Historical Studies*, 21, no. 81 (March 1978).

—, 'The Rightboy Movement, 1785–8', *Studia Hibernica*, nos. 17 and 18 (1977–8).

Duffy, Charles Gavan, *Four Years of Irish History, 1845–1849* (London: Cassell, Petter, Galpin, 1883).

Dunne, Thomas (ed.), *The Writer as Witness: Literature as Historical Evidence* (Cork: Cork University Press, 1987).

Ellmann, Richard, *James Joyce* (Oxford: Oxford University Press, 1959).

Engels, Friedrich, *The Origins of the Family, Private Property and the State*, Eleanor Burke Leacock (ed.) (New York: International Publishers, 1972).

BIBLIOGRAPHY

Fanon, Frantz, *The Wretched of the Earth* (New York: Grove Press, 1963).

Flanagan, Thomas, *The Irish Novelists 1800–1850* (New York: Columbia University Press, 1959).

Freud, Sigmund, 'Some Psychical Consequences of the Anatomical Distinction between the Sexes', *The Complete Psychological Works*, xix (London: Hogarth Press, 1958–68).

Galbraith, John Kenneth, *The New Industrial State*, 2nd ed. (Harmondsworth: Penguin, 1974).

Garvin, Thomas, *The Evolution of Nationalist Politics* (Dublin: Gill and Macmillan, 1981).

Goethe, J.W., *Wilhelm Meisters Lehrjahre, Werke, 10: Romane und Erzahlungen II* (Berlin: Aufbau-Verlag, 1962).

Gramsci, Antonio, *Selections from the Prison Notebooks*, Quintin Hoare and Geoffrey Nowell Smith (ed. and trans.) (New York: International Publishers, 1971).

Haffenden, John, *Viewpoints* (London: Faber and Faber, 1981).

Hall, Stuart, 'Cultural Studies: Two Paradigms', *Media, Culture and Society*, 2 (1980), pp. 57–72.

—, 'Gramsci's Relevance for the Study of Race and Ethnicity', *Journal of Communications Inquiry*, 10 (1986), pp. 5–25.

Heaney, Seamus, *Death of a Naturalist* (London: Faber and Faber, 1966).

—, *Door into the Dark* (London: Faber and Faber, 1969).

—, *Wintering Out* (London: Faber and Faber, 1972).

—, *North* (London: Faber and Faber, 1975).

—, *Field Work* (London: Faber and Faber, 1979).

—, *Preoccupations* (London: Faber and Faber, 1980).

Herr, Cheryl, *Joyce's Anatomy of Culture* (Urbana/Chicago: University of Illinois Press, 1986).

Hill, Jacqueline, 'The Intelligentsia and Irish Nationalism in the 1840s', *Studia Hibernica*, 20 (1980), pp. 73–109.

Hyde, Douglas, *Language, Lore and Lyrics: Essays and Lectures*, Breandán Ó Conaire (ed.) (Blackrock: Irish Academic Press, 1986).

Jameson, Fredric, 'Third World Literature in the Era of Multi-National Capitalism', *Social Text*, 15 (Autumn 1986).

JanMohamed, Abdul, 'The Economy of Manichean Allegory: The Function of Racial Difference in Colonial Literature', *'Race', Writing and Difference*, Henry L. Gates Jr (ed.) (Chicago: Chicago University Press, 1985), pp. 78–107.

Joyce, James, *Ulysses* (New York: Random House, 1986).

—, *Dubliners* (Harmondsworth: Penguin 1956)

Kamenka, E. (ed.), *Nationalism: The Nature and Evolution of an Idea* (London: Edward Arnold, 1973).

Kant, Immanuel, *The Critique of Judgement*, James Creed Meredith (trans.) (Oxford: Clarendon Press, 1952).

—, *Anthropology from a Pragmatic Point of View*, Mary J. Gregor (trans.) (The Hague: Nijhoff, 1974).

Kearney, Richard, 'The IRA's Strategy of Failure', *The Crane Bag*, 4, no. 2 (1980–1).

Kedourie, Elie, *Nationalism* (London: Hutchinson Press, 1961).

BIBLIOGRAPHY

Kiberd, Declan, 'Writers in Quarantine? The Case for Irish Studies', *The Crane Bag*, 3, no. 1 (1979), pp. 346–50.

Kristeva, Julia, *Desire in Language, A Semiotic Approach to Literature and Art*, Leon S. Roudiez (ed.), Thomas Gora, Alice Jardine and Leon Roudiez (trans.) (New York: Columbia University Press, 1980).

Lloyd, David, *Nationalism and Minor Literature: James Clarence Mangan and the Emergence of Irish Cultural Nationalism* (Berkeley: University of California Press, 1987).

—, 'Arnold, Ferguson, Schiller: Aesthetic Culture and the Politics of Aesthetics', *Cultural Critique*, 2 (1985–6), pp. 137–69.

Lobsien, Eckhard, *Der Alltag des Ulysses: Die Vermittlung von Aesthetischer und Lebensweltlicher Erfahrung* (Stuttgart: J.B. Metzler, 1978).

Lowe, Lisa, *Critical Terrains: British and French Orientalisms* (Ithaca: Cornell University Press, 1991).

Lukacs, Georg, *The Theory of the Novel*, Anna Bostock (trans.) (Cambridge, Mass.: MIT Press, 1971).

Lyons, F.S.L., *Ireland Since the Famine* (London: Weidenfeld and Nicholson, 1971)

MacCabe, Colin, *James Joyce and the Revolution of the Word* (London: Macmillan, 1978).

MacCarthy, Denis Florence (ed.), *The Book of Irish Ballads* (Dublin: J. Duffy, 1846).

Mc Cormack, W.J., *The Battle of the Books: Two Decades of Irish Cultural Debate* (Mullingar: The Lilliput Press, 1986).

Manganiello, Dominic, *Joyce's Politics* (London: Routledge and Kegan Paul, 1980).

Marx, Karl, *Early Writings*, Lucio Colletti (intro.), Rodney Livingstone and Gregor Benton (eds) (New York: Vintage Press, 1975).

McKeon, Michael, *The Origins of the English Novel, 1600–1740* (Baltimore: Johns Hopkins University Press, 1987).

Memmi, Albert, *The Colonizer and the Colonized* (New York 1965).

Miller, D.A., *The Novel and the Police* (Berkeley: University of California Press, 1988).

Mohanty, Sattya, 'Kipling's Children and the Color Line' in *Race and Class*, 31.1 (1989).

Moraga, Cherrié, *Loving in the War Years: lo que nunca paso por sus labios* (Boston: South End Press, 1983).

— and Anzaldua, Gloria (eds), *This Bridge Called My Back: Writings by Radical Women of Color* (New York: Kitchen Table, 1983).

Moretti, Franco, *Signs Taken for Wonders: Essays in the Sociology of Literary Forms* (London: Verso, 1983).

—, *The Way of the World: The Bildungsroman in European Culture* (London: Verso Press, 1987).

Morrison, Blake, *Seamus Heaney* (London: Methuen, 1982).

Ngugi, Wa Thiong'o, *Decolonizing the Mind: The Politics of Language in African Literature* (London: James Currey, 1986), pp. 90–4.

Nunes, Zita, 'Os Males do Brasil: Antropofagia e Modernismo' (Rio de Janeiro: CIEC, 1990).

O'Brien, Conor Cruise, 'Passion and Cunning: An Essay on the Politics of W.B. Yeats', *In Excited Reverie: A Centenary Tribute to W.B. Yeats, 1865–1939*, Norman Jeffares and K.G.W. Cross (eds) (London: Macmillan, 1965).

BIBLIOGRAPHY

Ó Lochlainn, Colm (ed.), *Irish Street Ballads* (1939; rev. ed. Dublin: Three Candles, 1946).

O'Neill, James W., 'A Look at Captain Rock: Agrarian Rebellion in Ireland 1815–1845', *Eire-Ireland*, 17, no. 1 (Autumn 1982), pp. 17–34.

Parkinson, Thomas, *W.B. Yeats and W.B. Yeats: The Later Poetry*, 2 vols in one (Berkeley and Los Angeles: University of California Press, 1971).

Paz, Octavio, *Alternating Currents*, Helen R. Lane (trans.) (New York: Viking Press, 1973).

—, 'The Sons of La Malinche' in *Labyrinths of Solitude* (New York: Grove Press, 1961), pp. 65–88.

Regan, Colm, 'Latin American Dependency Theory and its Relevance to Ireland', *The Crane Bag*, 6, no. 2 (1982), pp. 15–20.

Retamar, Roberto Fernandez, *Caliban and Other Essays*, Edward Baker (trans.) (Minneapolis: Minnesota University Press, 1988).

Said, Edward, 'Yeats and Decolonization', *Field Day Pamphlet*, no. 15 (Lawrence Hill: Field Day, 1988).

Sangari, KumKum, 'The Politics of the Possible', *Cultural Critique*, 7 (1987), pp. 157–86.

Scott, Bonnie Kime, *Joyce and Feminism* (Bloomington: Indiana University Press, 1984).

Spivak, Gayatri Chakravorty, 'Can the Subaltern Speak?' in *Marxism and the Interpretation of Culture*, Cary Nelson and Lawrence Grossberg (eds) (Urbana and Chicago: University of Illinois Press, 1988), pp. 271–313.

— and Guha, Ranajit, *Selected Subaltern Studies* (Oxford: Oxford University Press, 1988).

Stallybrass, Peter and White, Allon, *The Politics and Poetics of Transgression* (Ithaca: Cornell University Press, 1986).

Stewart, A.T.Q., *The Narrow Ground, The Roots of Conflict in Ulster* (London: Faber and Faber, 1977; rev. ed. 1989).

Thuente, Mary Helen, 'Violence in Pre-Famine Ireland: The Testimony of Irish Folklore and Fiction', *Irish University Review*, 15, no. 2 (Autumn 1985).

Tiongson, Nicanor *et al.*, 'Ideology and Culture of the New Society', in *Synthesis, Before and Beyond February 1986*, The Edgar M. Jopson Memorial Lectures, Lilia Quindoza Santiago ed. (Manila: Interdisciplinary Forum of the University of Philippines, 1986), pp. 49–65.

Townshend, Charles, *Political Violence in Ireland, Government and Resistance since 1848* (Oxford: Clarendon Press, 1983).

Watt, Ian, *Rise of the Novel: Studies in Defoe, Richardson and Fielding* (Berkeley and Los Angeles: University of California Press, 1964).

Welch, Robert, *Irish Poetry from Moore to Yeats*, Irish Literary Studies 5 (Gerrards Cross: Colin Smythe, 1980).

Williams, Raymond, *Marxism and Literature* (Oxford: Oxford University Press, 1977).

Yeats, W.B., *The Autobiography* (New York: Macmillan Press, 1953).

—, *Essays and Introductions* (New York: Macmillan Press, 1960).

—, *A Vision* (New York: Collier, 1966).

BIBLIOGRAPHY

—, *Explorations* (New York: Collier, 1973).

—, *Collected Plays* (London: Macmillan Press, 1980).

—, *The Poems of W.B. Yeats*, Richard J. Finneran (ed.) (New York: Macmillan, 1983).

Zimmermann, Georges-Denis, 'Irish Political Street Ballads and Rebel Songs, 1780–1900' (Geneva: University of Geneva, 1966).

INDEX

INDEX

Fanon, Frantz, 7–8, 11n, 55, 58n
fascism, 59, 60, 79, 82n, 86n
'Father Murphy', 95, 96, 118n
'Feeling into Words' (Heaney), 39n
feminism, 81, 87n
Ferguson, Samuel, 94, 103, 123n, 157n
Fianna Fáil, 18
Field Work (Heaney), 4, 13, 33, 34–6, 38n, 39n, 40n
Fine Gael, 18
Finnegans Wake (Joyce), 120–1n
First Love (Beckett), 41, 42, 56, 56n; analysis of, 47–54
Flaubert, Gustave, 59, 82n
folk-songs, 5–6, 91, 101–4
folk-tales, 131
Frankfurt School, 60, 83n
Freud, Sigmund, 81, 87n

Gaelic culture, 23, 24, 71; and ballads, 91–100; commercialization of, 132; goddess traditions, 86n; and loss of language, 44–6
'Gaelic Folk Songs' (Hyde), 101, 119n
Gaelic League, 101
Garvin, Tom, 146, 149, 159n, 160n
gender; and agrarian agitation, 152, 161n; in Heaney, 20, 26, 31–3, 39n; in Joyce, 105–6, 109; and nationalism, 85–6n; in Yeats, 70, 73, 81–2
'General Introduction for my Work, A' (Yeats), 86n
Glanmore Sonnets (Heaney), 34–5
Glob, P.V., 27, 32
Goethe, J.W. von, 51, 57n
Gonne, Maud, 70, 81, 85n
Gordon Riots, 141–2
Gramsci, Antonio, 9, 11n, 38n; 'subaltern classes', 126–7, 155n, 159n
Great Famine, 128, 133, 135, 138–41, 143, 146, 154
Gregory, Lady, 67, 70
Griffin, Gerald, 135, 141, 148, 156n, 157n, 158n
Griffith, Arthur, 119n
Guha, Ranajit, 9, 155n, 159n, 161n

Hardiman, James, 157n
Heaney, Seamus, 3–4, 13–40 *passim*; on

cultural identity, 13, 20; and poetics of identity, 13–38
Hegel, Georg, 133, 157n
hegemony, 19, 30, 55, 112, 123n; concept of, 3, 7; counter-hegemony, 6, 126; cultural, 9, 145–6; decline of the ascendancy, 133, 146, 149; and the novel, 155; post-colonial negation of, 42
'Hercules and Antaeus' (Heaney), 38n
historiography, 125–6, 128, 161n
history; historicism, 10–11, 134; subaltern history, 127–8; violence within, 125–6
Homer, 67–9, 91, 101, 104, 106, 111, 118n
hybridization, 101, 120n, 123n; and literary revival, 94–6, 103–4, 114–15, 119n; result of colonization, 93, 101, 106, 112–13
Hyde, Douglas, 100–4, 110, 119n, 122n, 132
Hynes, Samuel, 70, 85n

identity; adulteration of, 89–116; in Beckett, 49–50; canonization, 8–9; ethical identity, 134, 147; formation of, 88, 110; in national literature, 44; and nationalism, 7–8, 14–17; Northern Ireland, 3–4; in the novel, 153; opposed to class difference, 55; poetics of, 13–37, 83n; politics of, 19; and racism, 124n
illiterate, culture of, 22–3
imperialism, 5, 23, 38, 56n, 93, 96, 111–15, 123n, 124n, 126; anti-imperialism, 154; attitude to violence, 125–6; critique of, 14–15; effects on nationalism, 37, 43, 45–7, 49, 54
insurrections; *see* agrarian disturbances
Irish Free State, 18; culture of, 43–4; Yeats and founding of, 60–82
Irish language, 16, 23–4, 93; assimilation, 91, 104–5, 110–12, 114, 118n, 120n, 123n; effects of loss of, 44–6; extent of use of, 117n; hybridization, 130, 156n; in street ballads, 93, 114
Irish Street Ballads (Ó Lochlainn), 93, 117

INDEX